The snowy flanks of Mount Fuji present a
spectacular backdrop to a flight of B-29s
forming for a raid on the Japanese homeland
in 1945. The highest peak in Japan at 12,389
feet, and less than 15 minutes flying time
from Tokyo, Mount Fuji became a regular
rendezvous point for American bombers.

BOMBERS OVER JAPAN

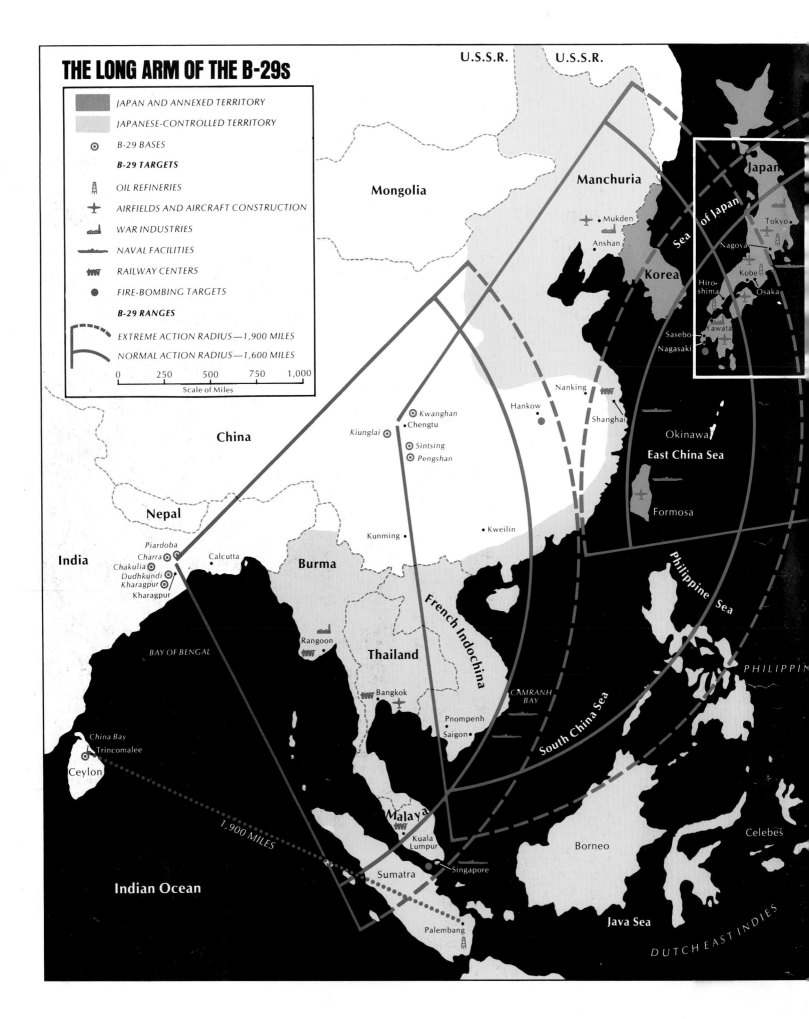

THE LONG ARM OF THE B-29s

JAPAN AND ANNEXED TERRITORY

JAPANESE-CONTROLLED TERRITORY

⊙ B-29 BASES

B-29 TARGETS

OIL REFINERIES

AIRFIELDS AND AIRCRAFT CONSTRUCTION

WAR INDUSTRIES

NAVAL FACILITIES

RAILWAY CENTERS

● FIRE-BOMBING TARGETS

B-29 RANGES

EXTREME ACTION RADIUS—1,900 MILES

NORMAL ACTION RADIUS—1,600 MILES

0   250   500   750   1,000
Scale of Miles

U.S.S.R.   U.S.S.R.

Mongolia

Manchuria

• Mukden

Anshan •

Korea

Sea of Japan

Japan

Tokyo

Nagoya

Kobe

Hiro-shima

Osaka

Sasebo-

Yawata

Nagasaki

China

Kwanghan ⊙

• Chengtu

Kiunglai ⊙

Sintsing ⊙

Pengshan ⊙

Nanking •

Hankow

Shanghai

Okinawa

East China Sea

Nepal

Kunming •

• Kweilin

Formosa

India

Piardoba

Charra ⊙

Chakulia ⊙

Dudhkundi ⊙

Kharagpur ⊙

Kharagpur

Calcutta •

Burma

Philippine Sea

BAY OF BENGAL

Rangoon

Thailand

French Indochina

PHILIPPIN

Bangkok

CAMRANH
BAY

Pnompenh •

Saigon •

South China Sea

China Bay

Trincomalee

Ceylon

1,900 MILES

Indian Ocean

Malaya

Kuala
Lumpur

• Singapore

Borneo

Celebes

Sumatra

Java Sea

Palembang •

DUTCH EAST INDIES

2

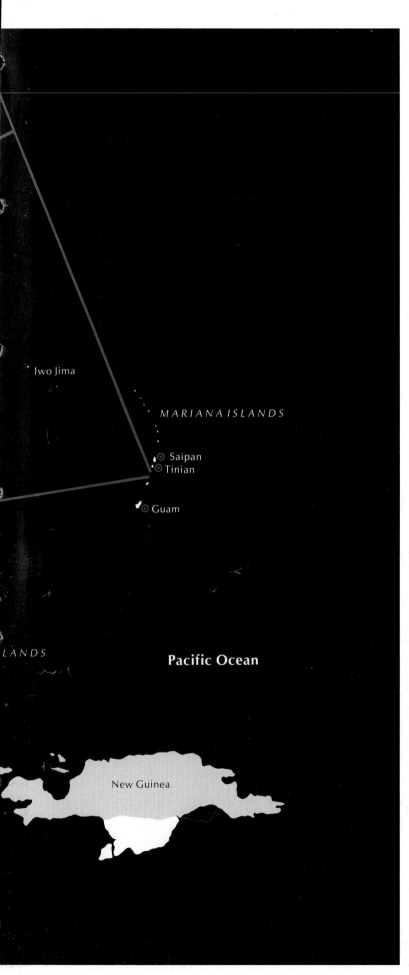

Late in the spring of 1944, U.S. B-29 Superfortresses began to fly missions from airfields in India and China, focusing on targets in Japanese-occupied Asia (one strike was launched from Ceylon against oil refineries in Palembang, Sumatra). Japan was then largely out of reach, protected by the vast bulwark of its Asian and Pacific conquests. Even the B-29, with a normal radius of 1,600 miles and a maximum radius of 1,900 miles, could barely reach Japan from advance bases in China. In October 1944, when bases became available in the Mariana Islands, the main thrust of B-29 operations shifted to the Pacific. From Saipan, Tinian and Guam, the U.S. Army Air Forces mounted increasingly heavy strikes—climaxed by massive fire-bombing raids (inset)—on the heart of Japan.

3

Other Publications:
PLANET EARTH
COLLECTOR'S LIBRARY OF THE CIVIL WAR
LIBRARY OF HEALTH
CLASSICS OF THE OLD WEST
THE EPIC OF FLIGHT
THE GOOD COOK
THE SEAFARERS
THE ENCYCLOPEDIA OF COLLECTIBLES
THE GREAT CITIES
HOME REPAIR AND IMPROVEMENT
THE WORLD'S WILD PLACES
THE TIME-LIFE LIBRARY OF BOATING
HUMAN BEHAVIOR
THE ART OF SEWING
THE OLD WEST
THE EMERGENCE OF MAN
THE AMERICAN WILDERNESS
THE TIME-LIFE ENCYCLOPEDIA OF GARDENING
LIFE LIBRARY OF PHOTOGRAPHY
THIS FABULOUS CENTURY
FOODS OF THE WORLD
TIME-LIFE LIBRARY OF AMERICA
TIME-LIFE LIBRARY OF ART
GREAT AGES OF MAN
LIFE SCIENCE LIBRARY
THE LIFE HISTORY OF THE UNITED STATES
TIME READING PROGRAM
LIFE NATURE LIBRARY
LIFE WORLD LIBRARY
FAMILY LIBRARY:
    HOW THINGS WORK IN YOUR HOME
    THE TIME-LIFE BOOK OF THE FAMILY CAR
    THE TIME-LIFE FAMILY LEGAL GUIDE
    THE TIME-LIFE BOOK OF FAMILY FINANCE

This volume is one of a series that chronicles
in full the events of the Second World War.
Previous books in the series include:

Prelude to War	The Battle of the Bulge
Blitzkrieg	The Road to Tokyo
The Battle of Britain	Red Army Resurgent
The Rising Sun	The Nazis
The Battle of the Atlantic	Across the Rhine
Russia Besieged	War under the Pacific
The War in the Desert	War in the Outposts
The Home Front: U.S.A.	The Soviet Juggernaut
China-Burma-India	Japan at War
Island Fighting	The Mediterranean
The Italian Campaign	Battles for Scandinavia
Partisans and Guerrillas	The Secret War
The Second Front	Prisoners of War
Liberation	The Commandos
Return to the Philippines	The Home Front: Germany
The Air War in Europe	Italy at War
The Resistance	

WORLD WAR II · TIME-LIFE BOOKS · ALEXANDRIA, VIRGINIA

BY KEITH WHEELER
AND THE EDITORS OF TIME-LIFE BOOKS

BOMBERS OVER JAPAN

Time-Life Books Inc.
is a wholly owned subsidiary of
TIME INCORPORATED

Founder: Henry R. Luce 1898-1967

Editor-in-Chief: Henry Anatole Grunwald
President: J. Richard Munro
Chairman of the Board: Ralph P. Davidson
Executive Vice President: Clifford J. Grum
Chairman, Executive Committee: James R. Shepley
Editorial Director: Ralph Graves
Group Vice President, Books: Joan D. Manley
Vice Chairman: Arthur Temple

TIME-LIFE BOOKS INC.

Editor: George Constable
Executive Editor: George Daniels
Director of Design: Louis Klein
Board of Editors: Dale M. Brown, Thomas H. Flaherty Jr.,
William Frankel, Thomas A. Lewis, Martin Mann,
John Paul Porter, Gerry Schremp, Gerald Simons,
Kit van Tulleken
Director of Administration: David L. Harrison
Director of Research: Carolyn L. Sackett
Director of Photography: Dolores Allen Littles

President: Carl G. Jaeger
Executive Vice Presidents: John Steven Maxwell,
David J. Walsh
Vice Presidents: George Artandi, Stephen L. Bair,
Peter G. Barnes, Nicholas Benton, John L. Canova,
Beatrice T. Dobie, James L. Mercer

WORLD WAR II

Editor: Thomas H. Flaherty Jr.
Bombers over Japan was prepared under the
supervision of Time-Life Books by the following
contributors:
Editors: Charles Osborne, Sheldon Cotler
Picture Editor: Peter D. Collins
Assistant Designer: Leonard Vigliarolo
Researchers: Martha J. Mader, Jane Furth,
Suzanne Odette Khuri, Kay Neil Noble, Mary K. Doris
Writers: Cathy Beason, Don Earnest,
Eric Schurenberg, Cinda Siler, E. Ogden Tanner,
Susan Hillaby Young
Art Assistant: Ellen A. Kostroff
Editorial Manager: Felice Lerner
Editorial Assistants: Keith Nislow, Nicholas Goodman

Time-Life Books Editorial Staff for Bombers over Japan
Researcher: Loretta Britten
Copy Coordinators: Ann Bartunek, Elizabeth Graham,
Barbara F. Quarmby
Art Assistant: Robert K. Herndon
Picture Coordinator: Renée DeSandies
Editorial Assistant: Andrea Reynolds

Editorial Operations
Production Director: Feliciano Madrid
    Assistant: Peter A. Inchauteguiz
Copy Processing: Gordon E. Buck
Quality Control Director: Robert L. Young
    Assistant: James J. Cox
    Associates: Daniel J. McSweeney,
    Michael G. Wight
Art Coordinator: Anne B. Landry
Copy Room Director: Susan Galloway Goldberg
    Assistants: Celia Beattie, Ricki Tarlow

Correspondents: Elisabeth Kraemer (Bonn); Margot
Hapgood, Dorothy Bacon (London); Susan Jonas,
Lucy T. Voulgaris (New York); Maria Vincenza Aloisi,
Josephine du Brusle (Paris); Ann Natanson (Rome).
Valuable assistance was also provided by Philip
Hevener (Las Vegas); John Dunn (Melbourne); David
Snyder (New Orleans); Carolyn T. Chubet, Miriam
Hsia, Christina Lieberman (New York); Jane Estes
(Seattle); Kotaro Katogawa, Masao Murata, Kazuo
Ohyauchi (Tokyo); Diane Lewis (Wichita).

The Author: KEITH WHEELER, a South Dakota newspaperman and a writer for Life, covered the war against Japan for the Chicago Daily Times and wrote of his experiences in The Pacific Is My Beat and We Are the Wounded. He has published a number of novels and nonfiction books and contributed five volumes to the Time-Life Books Old West series. He is the author of two previous volumes in the World War II series: The Road to Tokyo and War under the Pacific.

The Consultants: COLONEL JOHN R. ELTING, USA (Ret.), a military historian, is the author of The Battle of Bunker's Hill, The Battles of Saratoga and Military History and Atlas of the Napoleonic Wars. A former Associate Professor at West Point, he is the author of Battles for Scandinavia in the Time-Life Books World War II series.

LIEUT. COLONEL DAVID MACISAAC, USAF (Ret.), is a graduate of Trinity College, Yale University and Duke University. A former professor of history at the United States Air Force Academy, he has also served as visiting professor of strategy at the Naval War College; as chief, history of warfare studies, at the Air War College; and as a resident fellow, Woodrow Wilson International Center for Scholars. He is the author of Strategic Bombing in World War II: The Story of the U.S. Strategic Bombing Survey.

ALVIN D. COOX, who holds degrees from New York University and Harvard University, is a historian best known for his work on the Japanese Army and the Pacific War. A resident in Japan for a dozen years after World War II, he is Professor of History and Graduate Coordinator of Asian Studies at San Diego State University. He is the author of Japan: The Final Agony and Tojo, and collaborator with Colonel Saburo Hayashi on the English edition of Kogun: The Japanese Army in the Pacific War.

Library of Congress Cataloguing in Publication Data

Wheeler, Keith.
    Bombers over Japan.

        (World War II; v. 34)
        Bibliography: p.
        Includes index.
        1. World War, 1939-1945—Aerial operations,
American. 2. World War, 1939-1945—Aerial operations,
Japanese. 3. B-29 bomber. 4. World War, 1939-1945—
Japan. 5. Japan—History—1912-1945. 5. Japan—History—
1912-1945.
    I. Time-Life Books.   II. Title.   III. Series.
    D790.W4118   940.54'49'73   82-5627
    ISBN 0-8094-3429-6
    ISBN 0-8094-3428-8 (lib. bdg.)
    ISBN 0-8094-3427-X (retail ed.)

For information about any Time-Life book, please write:

Reader Information
Time-Life Books
541 North Fairbanks Court
Chicago, Illinois 60611

CONTENTS

FORGING A NEW AIR WEAPON

Under guard, the ultrasecret B-29 prototype travels by barge in July 1942 from Boeing's Seattle plant to a test field otherwise reached only by narrow road.

AN EFFORT UNRIVALED IN AVIATION HISTORY

Shortly after Pearl Harbor, the U.S. Army Air Forces and the American aircraft industry urgently accelerated an existing plan to develop a new four-engined bomber. It would be the world's largest, with range, armament and destructive power heretofore barely imagined. Creating the new giant turned out to be the most massive single effort in aviation history. The War Department named the Boeing Aircraft Company as the primary contractor, and designated four major factories—two of them not yet built—to assemble components produced by a network of smaller plants.

Government purchase orders for the plane doubled and redoubled with every turn of the War, and the pressure of time required the builders to take a unique gamble. Boeing had proved with the B-17 Flying Fortress that it could make an excellent bomber, but no one had yet developed a new plane and simultaneously prepared assembly lines for its mass production. Nevertheless, the company tooled up—a year before complete blueprints were available.

By September 1942 the first B-29 was flown, and by the following summer, while flight tests of subsequent prototypes were still going on, production models of the new Superfortress began to come off the line. Haste and endless modifications in the ensuing months hugely complicated the plane's development; some changes were still being imposed when the B-29s first flew in combat. But the aircraft's basic design proved magnificent, and the gamble paid off. By 1944, America had a weapon of untold potential.

The exceptionally wide cockpit of a newly minted B-29 Superfortress resembles a greenhouse, with its windows offering visibility in three directions.

On the Boeing assembly line at Seattle, workers bolt nose cones made of nonshattering, pressure-resistant plexiglass to the forward sections of B-29s.

TRIAL BY TORTURE CHAMBER

While some Boeing engineers readied the first B-29, others put an earthbound duplicate, known as a static-test airframe, through excruciating tests. In a so-called Torture Chamber, the airframe was torn, exploded and shot apart. Instruments recorded the precise points of vulnerability.

Often, standard tests did not apply to the B-29. The usual way to verify wing strength—piling bags of lead shot on the wings—was too unwieldy and too time-consuming for a plane its size. Instead, the engineers used hydraulic jacks to apply pressures simulating every ordeal the wings would undergo—from a takeoff fully loaded to a high-speed turn in combat.

After being subjected to 300,000 pounds of hydraulic pressure to simulate the stress induced by pulling out of a steep dive, the wing of a B-29 flexed nearly 100 inches—then collapsed.

As technicians adjust stress-gauging equipment, a weighted airframe suspended in the Torture Chamber awaits a key test—a drop of 27 inches.

A 20mm cannon is positioned to fire into a B-29 fuselage. It was aimed at the interior of a gun mounting, one of the plane's most vulnerable points.

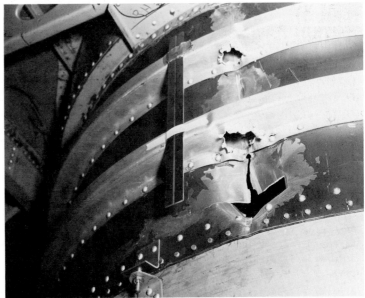

A photograph taken from inside the plane, with a ruler taped into place for scale, shows that despite shell damage the gun mounting did not collapse.

Workers thread control cables in a bomb bay at Boeing's Renton, Washington, plant. At top is the tunnel that will connect the cockpit and waist cabin.

A FLOW OF COMPONENTS FROM PEACETIME RIVALS

Because no single company could meet the Army Air Forces' demand for hundreds, then thousands, of Superfortresses, Boeing farmed out the work as it had done successfully in making the smaller B-17s. Some coproducers fabricated and assembled complete planes; more often, other companies built components of the B-29 and shipped them to the assembly plants.

To make sure that the complex feeder system worked as it should, Boeing turned over its innermost secrets to companies that had been its peacetime competitors; it supplied them with blueprints, exact specifications and even templates of the aircraft's components. But the task of ensuring a smooth flow to the assembly plants of millions of acceptable parts made by a dozen major corporations and thousands of smaller firms was beyond Boeing's capacity, and eventually the AAF assumed overall management of the program.

A prefabricated bomb bay is trucked to the assembly plant in Seattle.

In the yard outside Boeing's Seattle plant, a clerk catalogues a shipment of 43-foot-long horizontal stabilizers awaiting their turn on the assembly line.

PUTTING THE PARTS TOGETHER

To cope with the demands of time, and the B-29's unprecedented size, planes were assembled section by section at four plants in Renton, Washington; Omaha, Nebraska; Wichita, Kansas; and Marietta, Georgia—the last two constructed especially for the purpose. Wing, tail and nose sections were completed separately and were joined in the last few steps before the finished bomber rolled out of the factory.

The wartime labor shortage had left the aircraft plants staffed in part by workers who had been hastily recruited and had never before built a plane—or anything else for that matter. To compensate for this inexperience, assembly procedures were made as simple as possible. The enormous, tubular fuselage sections, for example, were simply bolted together with nuts and washers; this eliminated the need for highly skilled workmanship at the joints.

A factory mock-up of the B-29 shows how its major components were designed to come together.

Supported by wheeled jacks, wings for Superfortresses trundle down the assembly line at Boeing's plant in Renton with their engines already in place.

A wing section weighing 17 tons is lowered to join the bomb bays at Boeing's Wichita plant.

Parallel columns of forward- and rear-fuselage sections converge near the end of the assembly line at Renton. The immense factory had four such lines.

On a rainy Kansas night, glistening Superfortresses emerge from the Boeing plant in Wichita. Erected under pressing wartime conditions, the factory rolled

out its first B-29 in April 1943, and provided the planes for the first B-29 combat wing. Within two years it had produced 1,000 of the new bombers.

On November 1, 1944, the people of Tokyo gazed skyward at a glittering apparition. High above the city was the first American aircraft they had seen since Lieut. Colonel James H. Doolittle's carrier-launched raid 30 months earlier with twin-engined B-25s. This boldly uncamouflaged intruder was the *Tokyo Rose,* a reconnaissance version of the great new four-engined B-29 Superfortress, based 1,300 miles away on the island of Saipan. Tokyo's defenders responded alertly: Antiaircraft batteries opened fire and fighter planes scrambled into the air. Unperturbed, the B-29's pilot, Captain Ralph D. Steakley, circled deliberately for 35 minutes while his plane's battery of cameras shot 7,000 pictures of potential targets below. At 32,000 feet, the Superfortress was well above the reach of Tokyo's biggest guns; a few fighters approached, but did not come within range—apparently unwilling to challenge the B-29's heavy armament.

A number of Tokyo's citizens considered the appearance of the *Tokyo Rose* a portent of evil; they were correct. The reconnaissance flight foreshadowed a relentless bombing campaign by the U.S. Army Air Forces that reached its peak in the spring and early summer of 1945. By then, hundreds of B-29s were roaring over the home islands almost every day, carrying the War to Japan's streets and alleys and driving even Emperor Hirohito to the safety of a bomb shelter. In 154 days of terrible attack commencing in March, the Superfortresses burned out the hearts of 66 cities, sowed mines that destroyed more than 600,000 tons of shipping and clawed at the nation's industrial complex. So devastating was their impact that some highly placed American military leaders became convinced that Japan could be defeated by bombing alone. Indeed, the B-29s were regarded as self-contained weapons that were capable, by themselves, of demonstrating the dominance of air power; their advocates thought of the bombers as vehicles through which they hoped to establish an independent United States air force.

The aircraft that was ultimately instrumental in imposing catastrophe on Japan was a paradox; it was conceived, designed and rushed into production to carry out an entirely different mission in another part of the world. In early 1939, the Western world's most visible potential enemy was Adolf Hitler. The attention of the men charged with the air defense

THE "$3-BILLION GAMBLE"

of the United States was almost totally monopolized by the Luftwaffe, Hitler's reborn air force.

The preoccupation of American airmen with Europe became focused in April 1939, when the transatlantic pathfinder Charles A. Lindbergh returned to the United States after having inspected the Luftwaffe as the guest of its commander, Hermann Göring. Lindbergh was profoundly impressed. He told Major General Henry H. "Hap" Arnold, chief of the Army Air Corps (as the American land-based air force was called until June 1941) that in his judgment the Luftwaffe was more formidable than the air forces of all the other European nations lumped together. The only weapon the Germans lacked, Lindbergh said, was a heavy bomber as good as the American B-17 Flying Fortress, the four-engined plane whose development had begun in 1934 and which was now in production.

Responding to Lindbergh's appraisal, Arnold had the air hero commissioned a reserve colonel and appointed him to a blue-ribbon panel, under Brigadier General W. G. Kilner, assigned to study the needs of American air defense. In late June, 1939, the Kilner board declared that the United States could no longer rely solely on Naval and coastal artillery defenses to repel a potential invader.

The board warned that an enemy might well establish bases in other countries in the Western Hemisphere from which to bomb American soil. In view of this possibility, the board felt that the Air Corps needed new long- and medium-range aircraft that would be capable of attacking such bases to destroy German planes on the ground and otherwise disrupt offensive air operations. Though the B-17 was deemed an excellent plane, the board felt that it had insufficient range and bombload capacity to fulfill the nation's heightened defense needs.

The Kilner board's recommendations became more urgent barely two months later with the onset of war. When the Luftwaffe began bombing Polish cities, the widespread apprehension over German air power was confirmed. In Washington, General George C. Marshall became Chief of Staff of the Army, and firmly endorsed the Kilner report, saying, "This establishes for the first time a special mission for the Air Corps." His meaning: The United States now had full justification for pressing ahead with development of long-range bombers for defense of the hemisphere.

Just over two months after war began in Europe, the Kilner board's recommendations began to take effect. On November 10, Arnold went to the War Department with a priority request: He sought approval of contracts with the aircraft industry for preliminary studies of a very-long-range (VLR) bomber. By now a reluctant, isolationist Congress was sufficiently alarmed by events in Europe to set aside $4.7 million for bomber research.

During the first weeks of 1940, test pilots and engineers of the Air Corps Matériel Division at Wright Field in Dayton, Ohio, drew up specifications for a giant aircraft capable of flying more than 5,000 miles at 400 miles per hour while carrying a ton of bombs. In late January the specifications were sent out to four major American aircraft firms: Boeing, Consolidated-Vultee, Lockheed and Douglas.

By April, the four companies submitted preliminary designs and in June, Boeing and Consolidated were awarded contracts of $85,652 each to proceed with wind-tunnel studies. Thus was the first public money spent on an aircraft that would ultimately cost about $600,000 per plane.

The war in Europe expanded in the spring of 1940, and the appalling vulnerability of Germany's enemies became clearer. Ideas of what kind of bomber to build shifted with the changing situation. Norway and Denmark fell to the Nazi onslaught, and invading tank columns swept across Belgium and the Netherlands. In the first week in June, a broken British Army was evacuated from Dunkirk; three weeks later, France fell.

It seemed likely that the Germans would attempt to invade England before the year was out. Indeed, on Hitler's calendar the invasion, designated Operation Sea Lion, was scheduled for September 21. In August, Göring threw the bulk of the Luftwaffe against the Royal Air Force, and the Battle of Britain was joined in earnest. A force of 640 Hurricanes and Spitfires rose to challenge more than twice their number of German fighters and bombers. Although the United States was beginning to help Britain with food and weapons—even with planes—it seemed illogical that the RAF could stop Hitler's overpowering force.

American military leaders, confronted with the prospect that Britain might fall, envisioned the possibility of striking targets in Europe from North America. They speculated seriously about building a very large bomber with a range of

8,000 miles—almost twice that of the plane specified only a few months earlier. The concept was still defensive, contemplating a weapon with which to strike back should the Axis powers attempt to expand beyond the shores of Europe. (Such a possibility existed. Hitler proposed on at least two occasions to seize the Azores as a base from which to teach the Americans a lesson for helping Great Britain.)

The United States remained uneasy about being drawn directly into the European conflict. But alarm was growing, and on May 16—following the seizure of the Low Countries by Germany—President Franklin D. Roosevelt called upon the American aircraft industry to manufacture 50,000 warplanes a year.

Operation *Sea Lion* never materialized. With the aid of radar, the electronic eye that could detect German raiders long before they reached England, the RAF was a match and more for Hitler's superior numbers. Although London and other British cities suffered cruelly in the 1940-1941 German bombing campaign, which the British called the blitz, it began to seem likely that the island nation would survive and fight on.

Planners in the United States now foresaw a possible Anglo-American alliance—not just to fend off Hitler, but to defeat him; their concept of a big bomber began to veer toward its use on the offensive. The change in goals had a practical aspect, since the bombers would not need the extreme range demanded for defensive transatlantic operations from the United States: Once available, the giant planes could make their home bases in Great Britain. From there they would shuttle back and forth to Egypt or Tunisia—roughly 1,800 miles each way—bombing Axis targets both coming and going.

In these early planning stages, Germany—and its partner, Italy—were the only targets that were under serious consideration. During 1940, Washington's relations with Tokyo deteriorated steadily because of Japan's continued expansion in China and other parts of southeast Asia. But scarcely anyone in the United States thought of Japan as a potential target for the VLR bomber that was still gestating on the drawing boards. One exception was Colonel Carl ''Tooey'' Spaatz, General Arnold's Chief of Staff. As early as September of 1939, Spaatz had suggested that, should the need arise, the proposed bomber might be loosed against Japanese industry from bases in the Philippines, Soviet Siberia or the Aleutian Islands.

Tooey Spaatz's view proved prophetic. But even that far-seeing air commander could not guess the full truth: that the VLR bomber would never be used in Europe and that Japan would be its only target.

By September 1940, the plane's design studies had advanced far enough for the Army Air Corps to award contracts of $3.6 million to Boeing and Consolidated for two prototypes each. Later the orders were increased to three. Now the builders confronted a gargantuan task. The American aircraft industry would be required to explore new frontiers of the plane builders' art. Moreover, with Hitler bent on what seemed like world conquest, the builders were asked to carry out the job in great haste. Ordinarily, the development of a new military plane was expected to take five years; for this revolutionary machine the work would be accomplished in four.

Both companies' prototypes were plagued by birth pains, caused in no small measure by the constant alterations imposed by the Air Corps's changing concept of mission. Consolidated's plane, designated XB-32 and designed to carry a 10-ton bombload 1,250 miles and return, was evaluated by the Air Corps as the less desirable. Its development was impeded by technical defects, and by the time it was ready for full-scale testing in the autumn of 1944 the Army Air Forces had lost interest. Only 15 of the B-32s were deployed to the Pacific combat zone, where they performed unimpressively during the short time before the War ended.

Both the Consolidated and the Boeing designs were circumscribed by the dual demands for extreme range and large payload. Aircraft designers often had asked themselves how big and how heavy they could make an airplane before it became unflyable or unmanageable by its pilot. Boeing's proposed plane, designated XB-29, appeared to strain these limits. Its wing span was to be 141 feet 3 inches; its fuselage, 99 feet long, was to carry a tail fin towering more than 27 feet high, the equivalent of a three-story building. The designers originally intended to build the craft with a weight, unloaded, of 74,500 pounds and a maximum of 114,000 pounds with full fuel and bombload. Eventually it would fly into combat weighing up to 142,000 pounds, making a midget of its forerunner, the B-17, which weighed in at a mere 54,000 pounds fully loaded. So enormous was the new plane that engineers determined from the start that runways at fields where the new aircraft was to be used would have to be strengthened to withstand the landing and takeoff pressures.

It was clear from the outset that the new plane would demand more engine power than any previous flying machine, and Boeing's planners believed they knew where to find it. Since 1936, the Wright Aeronautical Corporation had been working to perfect a complex new engine, the Cyclone R-3350. The Cyclone was the most powerful of a line of air-cooled radial engines, each mounting two rows of nine cylinders, closely packed around a circular crankcase. It carried two turbo-superchargers to pump air at high pressure, boosting the amount to be ignited with gasoline in the cylinders, and thus increasing power at high altitudes where the air is thin. Each engine would turn a four-bladed propeller 16½ feet in diameter and produce 2,200 horsepower—twice the output of a B-17's engine. On paper, the R-3350 was a miracle power plant, approaching the long-sought goal of a full measure of horsepower for every pound of engine weight; the giant propellers, the superchargers and lightweight construction—incorporating magnesium —promised an engine of unparalleled efficiency.

The overall design of the new plane, like that of its engine, entailed engineering advances even beyond its great size, speed and range. It was to carry a new radar navigational system—the forerunner of the sophisticated guidance devices adapted decades later for space exploration. The system was intended to let a navigator know precisely where he was above the surface of the globe, no matter how bad the weather.

The B-29 was intended to fly for long hours at high altitudes. To ease the strain on its 11-man crew, the plane's interior was to be pressurized, providing a heated "shirt-sleeve" environment at altitudes up to 30,000 feet. The crews of other planes capable of flying that high had to breathe bottled oxygen and wear warm clothing against the –50° F. cold. The oxygen requirement involved the use of cumbersome masks and other equipment and could generate such problems as "aviator's bends"—an accumulation in the bloodstream of nitrogen bubbles that could block tiny

blood vessels, causing excruciating pain. To avoid having to pressurize the entire fuselage of the B-29, with its yawning bomb bays, the engineers designed separate sealed cells for the six men who would be stationed in the nose, the three gunners and the radar operator in the waist, and the tail gunner aft (drawing, page 33).

In May of 1941, as Hitler's armies crouched for the invasion of Russia, the B-29 was still a primarily paper airplane. About 8,000 drawings represented two years of work by thousands of aeronautical engineers and draftsmen. The only three-dimensional clue to the plane's existence was a full-scale wooden mockup at the Boeing company plant in Seattle, Washington.

Responding to pressure as Germany grew more aggressive, the Army Air Corps abandoned its cautious precedents for procuring expensive new equipment. The B-29 became the first military aircraft ordered into industry-wide production straight off the drawing board before the first prototype had been built, much less flown. On June 16, 1941, the Air Corps signed a contract with Boeing for 14 Superfortresses, with delivery to begin in January 1943. In September the or-

Pioneers in the development of strategic air power, Lieut. General Henry H. "Hap" Arnold and newly promoted Brigadier General James H. Doolittle confer in 1942 shortly after Doolittle's historic carrier-launched bombing raid on Tokyo with twin-engined B-25s. As commanding general of the Army Air Forces, Arnold in 1944 persuaded the Joint Chiefs to assign control of the B-29s to a headquarters unit, the Twentieth Air Force, rather than to a theater commander; this move was a major step toward the creation of an independent air force.

der was increased to 250 bombers. By that time, Boeing had begun work on a new plant in Wichita, Kansas, to manufacture the plane.

In December the Japanese attacked Pearl Harbor, and war for the United States was no longer a matter of speculation. A month later, orders for the new bomber were doubled to 500, and by the time the prototype flew in September of 1942, the manufacture of 1,664 B-29s had been authorized.

As the orders multiplied, it became evident that the program would be too much for Boeing—which also built the B-17—to handle alone. The Bell Aircraft Company and the Glenn L. Martin Company were enlisted to build B-29s under the guidance of Boeing engineers in plants at Marietta, Georgia, and Omaha, Nebraska. Boeing converted still another plant, at Renton, Washington, from Naval aircraft manufacturing to B-29s. When the program achieved full gear, the Chrysler Corporation, the Fisher Body Division of General Motors, the Goodyear Tire and Rubber Company and dozens of other firms were part of its unprecedented production team.

By 1942, so much money had been committed to the development and production start-up of the B-29 that the newly constituted Army Air Forces began to think of the plane as its "$3-billion gamble." Many times in the frustrating months ahead it would seem that the gamble was lost.

To hedge their bet, the AAF planners kept tinkering with specifications—and frustrating the civilian builders. "A new airplane is like a Christmas tree," grumbled Wellwood Beall, a Boeing vice president deeply involved in the B-29 project. "People are tempted to keep hanging things on it and changing things around."

Before the first test flight, no fewer than 900 major and minor modifications were decreed. Some changes that the AAF wanted were basic. The officers from Wright Field complained that Boeing's wing design would result in unacceptably high landing speeds. The problem, which went to the heart of the craft's aerodynamics, arose from a concept called wing loading. As the name implies, wing loading is defined as the number of pounds supported in the air by each square foot of wing surface, or the total gross weight of an aircraft divided by its total wing area.

Wing loading is an important aerodynamic factor in the ability of a plane to take off, remain in the air and land safely; the greater the weight each square foot of wing must bear, the faster the plane must travel to take off and stay airborne. By the same token, such high speeds can be perilous on landing—the heavier the plane, the greater the danger.

Solving the problem in the B-29 meant decreasing the wing load; this would enable the plane to remain under control while landing at reasonably safe speeds. It would also allow the plane to take off at relatively slow speeds, which in turn meant that it could be based on airfields equipped with runways only somewhat longer than normal.

Boeing designers, however, fumed at the prospect of changing their wing design. They had devised a long, narrow wing intended to permit the high air speed that the Air Forces had asked for. But the price was a wing loading of 70 pounds per square foot, almost twice that of the B-17. The landing speeds were bound to be troublesome.

The wing dispute was settled by compromise. Boeing designed a set of wing flaps that were larger than the entire wings of most pre-Pearl Harbor fighter planes. When extended, the flaps increased the B-29's wing area by 20 per cent, permitting shorter takeoff runs and the same landing speed—about 100 miles per hour—as the B-17. Because they still had no B-29 on which to test the flaps, Boeing engineers built a set of miniatures and tested them successfully on a small trainer. But no one really knew how the flaps would perform on a full-sized bomber.

Other problems arose from conflicting demands on the B-29's performance as an aircraft, and its ability to fight and survive. The AAF had paid close attention to Britain's experience fighting the Luftwaffe. The RAF had lost many of its best bombers, Vickers Wellingtons, because the Wellington's three power-driven gun turrets failed to stave off German interceptors. On some missions, half the Wellingtons were shot down. The fault seemed to lie in the Wellington's defensive equipment, so the AAF demanded protective armor for the crew of the B-29 and tremendous firepower in its manned turrets.

Here was true meat for the argument between airworthiness and fighting capability. Boeing was striving for a "smooth" aircraft, an airframe as streamlined as ingenuity could produce. The engineers protested that manned turrets would burden the slick outer skin of the airplane with bulky speed-reducing bulges; moreover, with their swivel mounts, the turrets would compromise the pressurization system.

Yet the engineers knew that adequate firepower was vital. "When I put myself in the place of the guy in the cockpit, I can see his point," conceded Boeing's Wellwood Beall. This time it was engineers of the General Electric Company who solved the problem, and the B-29 ultimately emerged with the most sophisticated defensive armament ever devised for an aircraft.

The Superfortress had manned guns only in the tail; but four low-profile, unmanned gun turrets were grafted into the outer skin of the fuselage, at points remote from the pressurized waist compartment. In General Electric's design, each turret was power-driven, operated by remote control by a gunner in one of three plexiglass sighting blisters in the waist compartment or by the bombardier in the nose. The turrets were electrically interconnected so that any gunner who happened to have the best view of the enemy could fire two or more turrets at once. All sighting and firing information for the turrets passed through a so-called "black box," a computer that automatically cranked in corrections for speed, distance, temperature, altitude, the direction of the target and the velocity of the gunner's own plane. With eight—and later 10—.50-caliber machine guns mounted in the four turrets, plus two more .50s and—for a time—a 20mm cannon in the tail stinger, the B-29 became a formidable fighting platform.

Another concern over the new plane's combat efficiency focused on the bomb-bay doors. As a high-level precision bomber, the B-29 needed to hold a rock-steady course and speed in the final moments of a bombing run. But these requirements could not be fully met with bomb-bay doors that opened slowly, imposing a gradual reduction of speed that could hamper a bombardier's calculations. To avoid this difficulty, the engineers devised an air-operated trigger that snapped the doors open in $7/10$ of a second and closed them in three seconds.

These changes required thought, ingenuity and engineering time. They also added a great deal of weight to the airplane. By the time the airmen and the engineers finished hanging things on Boeing's Christmas tree, a B-29 weighed

The XB-32, an experimental rival to the B-29, taxis down a runway at the Consolidated-Vultee Aircraft Company in San Diego. The prototype flew in early September, 1942, two weeks before its Boeing competitor, but development was slowed by aerodynamic flaws and shifts in the Air Forces' specifications. Much redesigned, the first production B-32s were delivered in late 1944; by then, however, the B-29's demonstrated capability had eliminated the need for a second superbomber.

about 105,000 pounds (without bombs), 30,000 pounds more than had been intended.

The development process gained momentum through the summer of 1942. Full-scale components of the aircraft were fabricated—then subjected to torture. The engineers took a completed fuselage and shot it full of .50-caliber and 20mm shell holes to see how much punishment it could take before disintegrating. To test the integrity of the pressurized crew compartments, the engineers injected gradually increasing amounts of compressed air until the cabins burst. (Though the gunners' plexiglass blisters passed such tests, they later blew out repeatedly in the air. The blister had to be redesigned again and again to withstand the extreme stresses encountered at high altitudes.)

Other systems demanded their share of attention in the shakedown process. The new radar navigational equipment, based on technologies developed by the British, required constant testing and tinkering before it could be trusted in the B-29. The aircraft had no fewer than 150 electric motors to operate parts ranging from guns to landing gear. The motors needed so much electrical power that a new type of generator had to be devised to furnish sufficient current.

At last, a whole airplane was assembled at the Boeing plant in Seattle. But instead of taking it out and flying it, the engineers first piled aboard weights simulating a full combat load; then, to test the strength of the plane's structure, they hoisted it to a height of 27 inches—and dropped it. Everything held together.

Difficult and time consuming as were the problems of developing the B-29's airframe, they paled compared to the headaches caused by its Cyclone R-3350 power plant. To economize on weight and improve streamlining, Wright's engineers had created an extremely compact and lightweight engine assembly. But the economies were proving costly—and in some ways deadly. Magnesium, a metal one third lighter than aluminum, was employed wherever the engineers thought it would serve. But magnesium crankcases proved too brittle to take the pounding of 18 powerful cylinders. They eventually had to be abandoned, though the builders continued to use magnesium for parts that came under less stress—and were less likely to catch fire.

Indeed, fire was a hazard so persistent and apparently in-

Experimental gun mountings built into the fuselage of a specially modified Superfortress are shown at right. Doubts about the dependability of the B-29's new remote-controlled weapons system led to the testing of a manned upper turret and a hand-operated waist gun (top), a retractable belly-mounted ball turret (middle) and twin nose-gun pods (bottom), to be fired by a single remote control. All these approaches were discarded when the central fire-control system proved workable.

curable that for months it threatened to abort the entire $3 billion gamble that the B-29 represented. The Cyclone R-3350 had a stubborn tendency to overheat and burst into flames. The basic cause was evident: The engine was so compact, its parts so closely jammed together, that not enough cooling air reached its cylinders. Knowing the cause, however, did not produce an immediate solution, and engine fires plagued the plane throughout its development phase and well into its operational life.

The prototype Superfortress rolled out of Boeing's Seattle plant on September 11, 1942. At 3:40 in the afternoon, the company's chief test pilot, Edmund T. Allen, eased open the throttles and took the plane up for the first time. He landed 75 minutes later and announced, "She flies." Coming from the notoriously laconic Allen, the statement amounted to effusive praise. It was a verdict confirmed the next day when Colonel Donald Putt, the AAF's project officer, flew the prototype and reported that it was "unbelievable for such a large plane to be so easy on the controls." It was easier to fly, said Putt, than a B-17.

The B-29 had flown—and well—but it was still a long way from being an operational aircraft. Five months after its maiden flight, the B-29's major problem—its engines—was tragically demonstrated at Boeing Field in Seattle. On February 18, 1943, test pilot Allen and 10 of Boeing's flight engineers took off at noon in the second prototype for a two-hour test of power-plant performance.

At 12:16 p.m. Allen radioed the Boeing tower and reported his position as 20 miles south of Seattle at 5,000 feet. Five minutes later he called again and calmly asked for landing clearance. "Number one engine is on fire, trouble not serious," he said.

Three minutes later, Allen reported himself at 1,500 feet, descending, and made no mention of the fire. But one minute after that, through a fluke of electronics, a controller in the Seattle tower overheard someone speaking on the plane's intercom system:

"Allen, better get this thing down in a hurry," the voice said. "The wing spar's burning badly." Then Allen's unexcited voice came up again on the plane-to-tower channel, asking the controllers to mobilize fire-fighting equipment. "I'm coming in with a wing on fire," he added.

Forty-five seconds later, power failed at Boeing Field. The B-29 had ripped through a transmission line and plunged into the fifth floor of a nearby packing plant. All 11 men on board the plane and a score of plant workers were dead.

The cost of the crash to the B-29 program was devastating. The elite among Boeing's design and testing personnel had perished with the plane. Allen himself, as chief of the company's Research Division, had known more about the giant aircraft's mechanical intricacies than any other man. Production was stalled for months. General Arnold ordered a searching investigation into the Cyclone engine's fatal tendency to burn. Senator Harry S. Truman of Missouri, chairman of a war-production watchdog committee, launched his own inquiry and issued a scathing report that spared neither the engine builder nor the AAF.

To the investigators it seemed likely that the use of magnesium in the engines, long identified as a problem, had contributed to the destructiveness of the fire. Magnesium is a combustible metal; once ignited, it burns fiercely, at very high temperatures. Thus, a fire of any duration in an overheated engine would probably reach magnesium engine parts; after that, the fire would be out of control. It would take only about 90 seconds to burn through the engine fire wall and into the wing structure; before long, the wing would break away from the fuselage.

Out of the crash investigations came a decision by the Army Air Forces to take direct control of the entire B-29 program: production and flight testing, as well as the training of combat crews. Brigadier General Kenneth B. Wolfe, commandant of the Matériel Division at Wright Field, was put in charge of the B-29 Special Project, as the integrated program was called; Colonel Leonard "Jake" Harman was appointed his deputy.

Striving to get things moving again, Wolfe and Harman visited Boeing headquarters in Seattle in late May of 1943. While there, Colonel Harman narrowly averted a second B-29 disaster. He was to take up a prototype Superfortress for a test flight; at the head of the runway, he opened the throttles and the big plane roared to life. But moments later, with the aircraft surging forward at nearly takeoff speed, the right wing unaccountably dipped and the B-29 slewed off the runway. Harman wrestled it to a shuddering stop. When General Wolfe and Boeing's executives arrived, they found the aircraft intact—and Harman livid with rage: Human error had added to the plane's mechanical shortcomings. A careless worker had unaccountably managed to reverse the aileron control cables. With the cables crossed, a movement of the controls intended to raise the right wing lowered it instead.

Maddening as the succession of delays, malfunctions, accidents and modifications was, it appeared as 1943 progressed that the first B-29s would soon be ready to send against the enemy, perhaps as early as the following January. The time was growing near when the Air Force would have to decide precisely what to do with the Superfortresses, and exactly who the enemy was. The decision was high on the priority lists, and it was a concern even of President Roosevelt.

Roosevelt or his chief advisers met six times with other Allied leaders in 1943: at Casablanca in January, at Washington in May, at Quebec in August, at Cairo in November and again in early December, and at Teheran in late November. At each top-level conference, and at lower levels between meetings, the disposition of the Superfortresses became increasingly important. At Casablanca, it was still expected that the first 24 operational groups would be sent to England, probably to be used as shuttle bombers flying to North Africa via targets in Germany.

Major General Ira C. Eaker, Commander of the Eighth Air Force in Britain, proceeded on this assumption through the early months of 1943. But when he learned that he could not expect the Superfortresses before 1944 and found out how much work and money could be required to enlarge and strengthen runways in England to accommodate them, Eaker decided that his fleets of B-17s and B-24s could finish the job in Europe well enough.

Axis fortunes in Europe had begun to decline after the Allied landings in North Africa in the autumn of 1942 and the Battle of Stalingrad in the winter that followed. Before the end of 1943, the Joint Chiefs of Staff had ruled out sending B-29s to the European theater, a decision that was confirmed at the Cairo Conference in December.

Unlike Eaker, commanders in the war against Japan had long been clamoring for the Superfortresses. They needed a bomber with the B-29's great range in a theater that was dominated by the huge distances of the Pacific Ocean and the Asian land mass.

In the Southwest Pacific, Major General George C. Kenney, boss of the Fifth Air Force under General Douglas MacArthur, thought his outfit was clearly entitled to the first delivery of operational planes. Kenney had worked on the B-29 program in 1941 and 1942 while stationed at Wright Field. He proposed to base the bombers in Australia; from there, he would send them against Japanese shipping and oil installations in the Netherlands East Indies.

The U.S. Navy had its own ideas about how to use the powerful planes. By changing the strategic assignment of the B-29 to reconnaissance and antisubmarine warfare, the Navy felt it could find ample bases. It laid claim to a share of the planes to perform these tasks. The AAF resolutely opposed the Navy's proposal. General Arnold had long since decided that control of the new bombers was to be restricted to his headquarters in Washington; by no means was it to be dispersed to local Air Force commands around the world, let alone shared with the Navy.

What is more, the leaders of the Army Air Forces had only

Boeing's leading test pilot, Edmund T. Allen (above), leans from the cockpit of the second prototype XB-29, in which he and 10 other members of the B-29 development team died on February 18, 1943. With one of its engines on fire, the 50-ton bomber crashed into a meat-packing factory near the Boeing field in Seattle and exploded. At right, pigs stand atop their smashed pen while fire fighters try to help plant workers who are trapped inside the building.

one mission in mind: the destruction of Japan itself. The momentum of the War had overtaken the potential value of using the new weapon against even the best of targets outside the Japanese home islands.

General Spaatz had once suggested that B-29s might be able to hit Japan from bases in the Aleutians. But by 1943, as a result of its unhappy experience with the wretched climate in those northern islands, the AAF had given up that idea. American aircraft attempting to harass the Japanese on Attu and Kiska in the island chain had been forced to contend with sudden, unpredictable storms and what amounted to perpetual fog.

One other immediate vantage point from which Japan might be vulnerable to the B-29s was mainland Asia. From bases in central China, for example, the Superfortresses could just manage the 3,800-mile round trip to southern Japan. No such bases existed, but the China option had an attractive political side. As early as the Casablanca meeting in January, President Roosevelt had made it clear that he was determined to do something substantial for China in order to persuade the wavering Generalissimo Chiang Kai-shek to

stay in the War. General Marshall had suggested that American air power could strike Japanese industry in Asia from China. Roosevelt agreed, reflecting that the presence of American bombers would surely boost Chinese morale. From that point on, the idea of basing the B-29s in China picked up speed.

Bombing from China would be a costly and difficult operation. To begin with, no seaport was available for the delivery of supplies to a bomber force. In 1943, the Japanese held every city on the Asian coast, from Manchuria in the north, around the curve of the continent southwest through Burma to the fringe of India. Food, fuel, bombs, spare parts, ammunition and manpower all would have to come to Chinese bases by air from India—over the Himalayas. Pondering the supply problem, Roosevelt may have been the first to suggest a partial solution: to locate rear bases for the B-29s in the region of eastern India, around Calcutta, with forward bases in China for launching the actual attacks.

British airfields, built in the neighborhood of Kharagpur, 70 miles southwest of Calcutta, were available for the Indian bases. But differences arose among the planners over the

ANATOMY OF A HEAVYWEIGHT

Modifications imposed even during production made each new B-29 a little different from the last. The cutaway portrait on these and the following pages is a composite of the first 100 Superfortresses produced. The tail markings are from one of these early planes, nicknamed *Wempy's Blitzburger* after its pilot, Major Neil W. Wemple. It was assigned to the 40th Bomb Group in India, and took part in the B-29s' first combat mission.

Wempy's Blitzburger differed from its sister B-29s in some ways—such as the precise arrangement of its electrical wiring—but it resembled them all in the superlatives required to describe it. With a wingspan of 141 feet, 3 inches and a weight, unloaded, of 74,500 pounds, the B-29 was the largest and heaviest airplane that ever had been mass-produced. Its four 2,200-hp engines, the most powerful in aviation, turned the world's largest propellers, each 16½ feet in diameter. It was the first plane to have its guns coordinated by a central fire-control system, and its crew compartments were the first on a combat plane to be pressurized. The B-29's performance capability was equally prodigious. It could carry up to 10 tons of bombs, four tons more than its predecessor, the Boeing B-17; its top speed of 357 mph at 25,000 feet was 55 mph faster than the B-17 and

1	Bombardier's gun sight	10	Navigator's map table	19	Communications tunnel
2	Norden bombsight	11	.50-caliber machine guns	20	Fuel transfer lines
3	Copilot's instrument panel	12	Radio receiver	21	Outer wing fuel tank
4	Pilot's instrument panel	13	Radio operator's desk	22	Inner wing fuel tank
5	Throttles and trim controls	14	Pressure bulkhead	23	Turbocharger inspection
6	Forward landing gear	15	Pressure door		panels
7	Control column	16	Forward bomb bay	24	Wing center section
8	Bombardier's seat	17	Radio direction finder	25	Compressed air duct
9	Flight engineer's control		antenna	26	Rear main wing spar
	panel	18	Turbocharger	27	Left main landing gear

its 3,800-mile range was double that of its elder sister.

The B-29's body had five basic segments: three crew cabins (inset), a midplane bomb-bay section and a rear storage and utility compartment.

At the front of the nose cabin, or "greenhouse," was the bombardier's post, with the top-secret Norden bombsight. Aft of the bombardier were twin seats for the pilot and copilot, facing a panoply of instruments; behind them were the flight engineer's post, from which the engines and the fuel supply were monitored, and the navigator's foldaway desk.

Dividing the mid-plane section into fore and aft bomb bays was a wing center section, where two massive structural spars of aluminum alloy bisected the fuselage. Fuel storage tanks in the center segment were connected by vacuum lines to the wing tanks, which fed the engines.

Compressed air for the cabins flowed from superchargers on the inboard engines through a duct into the communications tunnel, and thence to the nose and waist cabins. From the waist, where the fire control center and radar were housed, ducts carried air through the utility compartment—with its camera equipment and the auxiliary generator—to the rear gunner's isolated post in the tail.

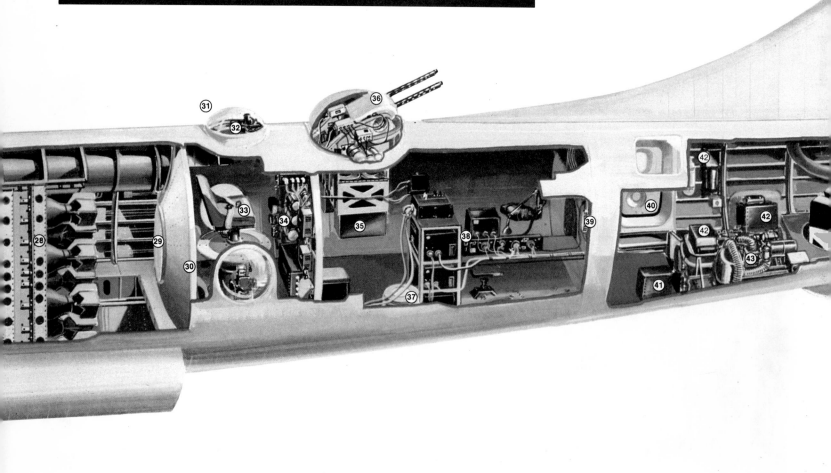

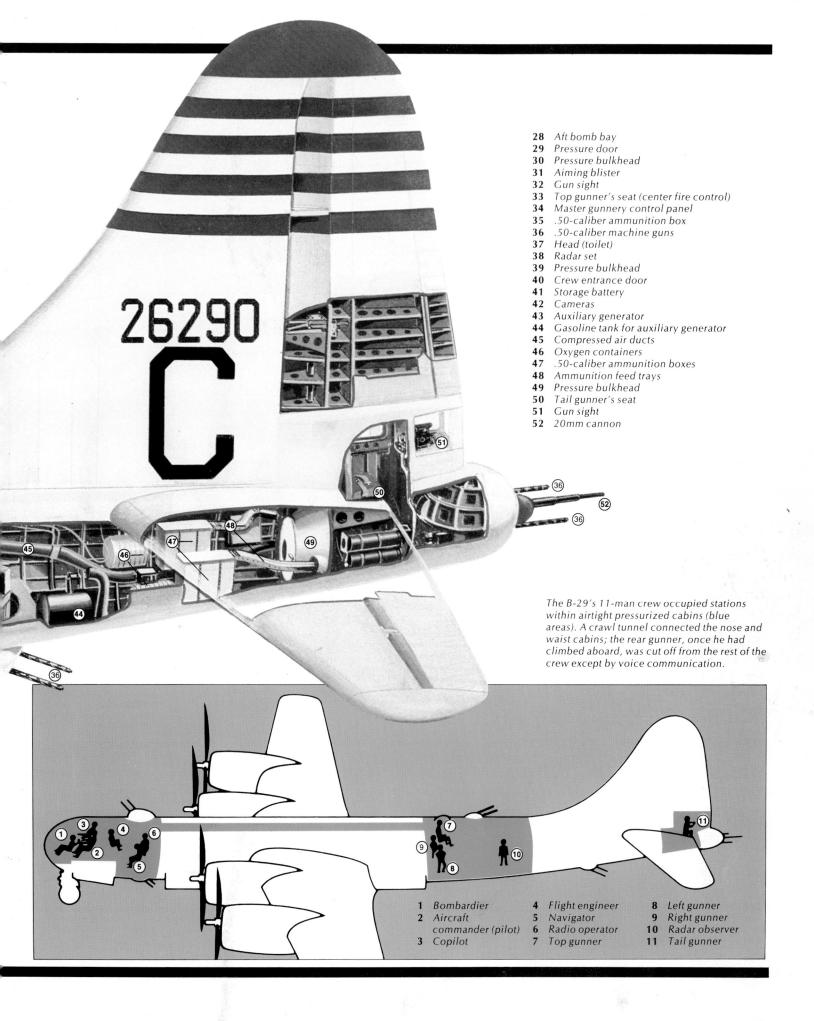

28 Aft bomb bay
29 Pressure door
30 Pressure bulkhead
31 Aiming blister
32 Gun sight
33 Top gunner's seat (center fire control)
34 Master gunnery control panel
35 .50-caliber ammunition box
36 .50-caliber machine guns
37 Head (toilet)
38 Radar set
39 Pressure bulkhead
40 Crew entrance door
41 Storage battery
42 Cameras
43 Auxiliary generator
44 Gasoline tank for auxiliary generator
45 Compressed air ducts
46 Oxygen containers
47 .50-caliber ammunition boxes
48 Ammunition feed trays
49 Pressure bulkhead
50 Tail gunner's seat
51 Gun sight
52 20mm cannon

The B-29's 11-man crew occupied stations within airtight pressurized cabins (blue areas). A crawl tunnel connected the nose and waist cabins; the rear gunner, once he had climbed aboard, was cut off from the rest of the crew except by voice communication.

1 Bombardier
2 Aircraft commander (pilot)
3 Copilot
4 Flight engineer
5 Navigator
6 Radio operator
7 Top gunner
8 Left gunner
9 Right gunner
10 Radar observer
11 Tail gunner

locations of the attack bases in China. Major General Claire Chennault, whose gallant Flying Tigers had become the U.S. Fourteenth Air Force, supported a plan to build a string of bomber strips around Kweilin in southeastern China. This was the home of the Fourteenth, whose experienced fighter pilots could protect the Superfortresses from Japanese air attack. And at Kweilin, the B-29s would be within range of southern Japan.

Lieut. General Joseph W. "Vinegar Joe" Stilwell, the American officer whom F.D.R. had assigned as Chiang Kaishek's chief of staff, objected to this proposal. Stilwell argued that it would take 50 American-trained Chinese divisions to defend bases in that region from eventual Japanese ground assault. Stilwell also asserted that because Japanese forces were within 340 miles of Kweilin, they could mount air attacks against the bases with ease.

In September 1943, General Arnold directed General Wolfe, as overall commander of the B-29 project, to work up an operations plan for bombing Japan from China. Wolfe's plan, code-named *Matterhorn*, basically agreed with Stilwell's approach. Instead of building airfields near Kweilin, the plan envisioned placing the forward bases 550 miles northwest in the region around Chengtu, in Szechwan Province. There they would be removed from both ground and air assault. The price for such security was the greater distance to potential targets—although Chengtu was within B-29 range of Japanese steel and aircraft plants on Kyushu, southernmost of the major home islands.

Wolfe's *Matterhorn* plan was accepted by the Joint Chiefs of Staff, despite the logistical problems they foresaw in ferrying enormous quantities of supplies to China over the Himalayas from India. Until some better roost became available as American forces advanced island by island through the western Pacific, China would be home to the B-29s.

If the bombers were to operate out of India and China, they would need airfields in areas not under American control. Before the Cairo conference in November 1943, F.D.R. asked British Prime Minister Winston Churchill and Chiang Kai-shek to assist in making land and labor available to build the necessary bases. General Arnold foresaw that damaged B-29s flying home from Japan might need emergency refuge, and at Teheran, Roosevelt asked Josef Stalin for landing privileges in Siberia. The Soviet Premier stalled.

Russia had its hands full with Germany in the West, and needed to preserve its uneasy truce with Japan.

Meanwhile, General Chennault, long the dominant U.S. air commander in east Asia, demanded control of all activities there, including B-29 operations out of China. From India, Britain's Lord Louis Mountbatten, who was Supreme Allied Commander, Southeast Asia, made a similar request. Arnold, with the Joint Chiefs' support, had no intention of yielding control of the B-29 armada to either of them.

In July 1943, the first production B-29s rolled off the assembly line at the new plant in Wichita. By the end of August, 14 B-29s had been delivered to the AAF and General Wolfe began to think about selecting and training crews for an operational B-29 unit. He need not have hurried. Six months later, the manufacturer had delivered only 97 Superfortresses, and of these only 16 were in condition to fly. The rest needed as many as 54 modifications apiece, including tires strong enough to withstand the strain of more than a few landings.

By now, even Roosevelt was becoming edgy. He had promised Chiang that B-29s would be in China by January 1944. When he learned that the bombers would not be ready to go before March or April at the earliest, he wrote indignantly to Chief of Staff Marshall, expressing his disgust with the situation and offering a solution of his own. "The worst thing is that we are falling down on our promises to China every single time," the President wrote. "I do not see why we have to use B-29s. We have several other types of bombing planes."

Roosevelt knew full well that the United States had no other aircraft with the range to reach Japan. But his frustration over the progress of the B-29 program was all too real. Everyone was worried. Air Force Chief Arnold was annoyed not only about the planes, but also about the lagging pace of base construction in India and China. He called on his favorite troubleshooter, General Wolfe, telling him to "get over there yourself." Wolfe arrived in New Delhi on January 13, 1944, and proceeded to the base construction area near Calcutta. He found chaos.

"We wanted runways," Wolfe said later. "We found a bunch of Indians making mud pies."

What Wolfe saw were thousands of peasants, male and

female, trying to move 1.7 million cubic yards of earth in wicker baskets balanced on their heads. He found the American colonel in charge of construction desperate for both heavy machinery and the skilled personnel to use it.

Wolfe flew to General Stilwell's headquarters in the Burmese jungle and borrowed a battalion of black American construction engineers who had been working on the Ledo Road, the land supply link between India and China that Stilwell was building through Burma.

The GI builders turned the situation in Calcutta around. "They came with a battery of concrete mixers and put on the damnedest exhibition of instantaneous concrete laying you ever saw," Wolfe said in admiration. Thereafter, the putting down of five concrete strips went on apace, each strip 8,500 feet long and 10 inches thick to handle the heavyweight bombers.

Wolfe flew on to Chengtu, 1,200 miles nearer to Japan. There he found that progress was being made but under conditions even more difficult than in Calcutta. Two hundred thousand well-organized Chinese laborers were hard at work. However, they had no concrete; instead, they were building four runways 8,500 feet long and 19 inches thick out of hand-crushed rock. The rocks, broken into tiny pieces by men and women using hammers, were being moved to the runway sites in wooden wheelbarrows or in buckets slung at either end of a shoulder pole.

"The wheelbarrows squeaked," recalled Lieut. Colonel Carey L. O'Brien Jr., a construction officer. "Thousands of squeaking wheelbarrows can get on the nerves, so one day when the Chinese were out having their lunch of rice, our engineer had his boys grease all the axles."

When the next shift began and the barrows failed to squeak, the Chinese workers declared a strike and went home. The baffled engineer called in an interpreter who explained that he had committed a blunder: "No squeak in wheelbarrow means devil will come. Squeak keeps devil away. No squeak—no work." After a laborious degreasing job had restored amicable labor relations, the work resumed—noisily.

Once the rock bed of a runway at Chengtu was in place, it was coated with a sealant of tung oil—an oil extracted from an indigenous tree and generally used in varnish. Then the runway was packed with great stone rollers, each

weighing as much as 10 tons and requiring hundreds of workers to pull it. Once a roller got momentum, it was hard to stop. Occasionally one of the people pulling the roller would stumble and fall; and sometimes the stone juggernaut would crush the unfortunate into the runway before he could scramble away.

To American ears, the hand-hewn bases that were taking shape had exotic, unpronounceable names: in India, Piardoba, Dudhkundi, Kalaikunda, Kharagpur and Chakulia; in China, Sintsing, Pengshan, Kiunglai and Kwanghan. Corps of laborers were still working on them when the Superfortresses began to arrive in the late spring of 1944.

Primitive though they were, the airfields had been expensive. In India, the AAF had spent about $20 million by the time construction neared completion in September 1944. The costs in China could be termed exorbitant. Although the laborers—260,000 of them at the peak—received the equivalent of scarcely nine cents a day, Generalissimo Chiang Kai-shek placed his own value on the fields, demanding $2 billion (Chinese) for the land and labor; he also insisted on Roosevelt's personal guarantee that the bill would be paid. The President agreed, provided the exchange was figured at the 1943 rate of $100 (Chinese) to $1 (U.S.). Chiang held out for an exchange rate of 20 to 1 that would have yielded him $100 million in U.S. currency. The American negotiators refused this demand as unreasonable. A compromise was reached: The work would go on, the exchange rate to be determined later. Washington eventually found the compromise a bad bargain; when the bill was finally paid in July 1944, it came to $210 million.

General Arnold wanted to have 150 combat-ready Superfortresses and 300 eleven-man crews ready to ship overseas by March 1, 1944. To establish an active combat organization, at least on paper, the XX Bomber Command was brought into being. It was to be commanded by General Wolfe. Colonel Jake Harman, Wolfe's field deputy, was put in command of the unit's first bombing wing, the 58th, which at full strength was to comprise 120 planes, 3,045 officers and 8,099 enlisted men. A second combat wing, the 73rd, was also established on paper but never actually became an element of the XXth.

To conduct a training program, Wolfe named Brigadier

General LaVerne G. "Blondie" Saunders, a veteran combat pilot who had flown B-17s against the Japanese during the battle for Guadalcanal in 1942. Potential crews, rigorously selected for skill and experience, were recruited from throughout the AAF. Arnold set an exacting standard for pilots: Only men with at least 400 hours' flying time in four-engined aircraft could apply.

Recruits for the 58th Wing began assembling at Smoky Hill field near Salina, Kansas, in the summer of 1943, and Wolfe moved his headquarters there in November. The program began to make progress—at least in the classroom.

Every crewman was expected to learn not only his own difficult assignment, but also be capable of doubling in another. Gunners had to master the Superfortress' formidable armament system and learn how to maintain the new and intricate computerized fire-control system. They also had to know their way around the plane as electricians or engine mechanics. Bombardiers were required to learn the rudiments of navigation, and vice versa. Radio operators were called upon to have a working knowledge of radar.

One of the most demanding assignments aboard a B-29 was that of the flight engineer. It was his responsibilty to

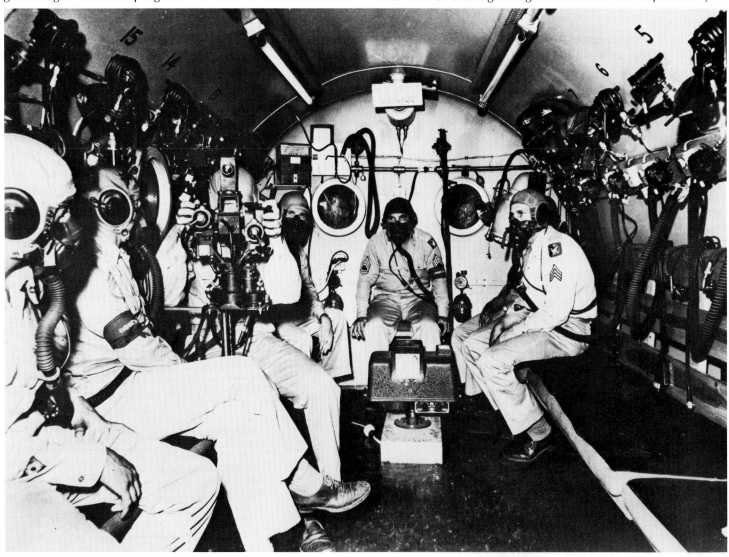

At simulated high altitude in a test chamber at Smoky Hill field in Kansas, a gunner practices with a gun sight while other trainees wait their turns. The pressurized cabins introduced on the B-29s eliminated the need for oxygen masks under normal conditions, but the crews wore them while drilling to be prepared for an emergency loss of air pressure.

monitor the performance of the Wright engines and oversee all the hydraulic and electrical systems of the aircraft. Mastering the details of that job alone could take nearly a year of study. At the same time, the engineer was supposed to know how to fly the plane in a pinch, should the pilot and copilot become casualties.

The opportunities to learn flying were slim, however. While ground school progressed, flight training suffered from lack of aircraft. For three weeks, the 58th Wing had just one B-29, an overworked machine that was frequently grounded for repairs. During the rest of 1943, the wing never had more than a dozen planes available. A semblance of flight training was arranged by using B-17s, which had some of the characteristics of the B-29 and could make long-range, high-altitude flights. In one important aspect, however, the Flying Fortress could not serve as even a makeshift substitute. The B-29 was designed with a new tricycle landing gear—two sets of wheels under the wings, a third set under the nose—that scarcely resembled the B-17, which had its short third wheel under the tail. The B-29 landing gear, supporting the nose and holding the fuselage level when on the ground, required a landing technique entirely different from the B-17, which completed its touchdown with its tail lower than its nose.

The Martin B-26 medium bomber had a tricycle gear comparable to that of the Superfortress, and using it to train B-29 pilots in landing was an obvious suggestion. It turned out, however, to be a bad idea. The only B-26s available were early models manufactured at the Martin plant in Maryland. The fliers called them "Baltimore whores" because, they said, the planes had no visible means of support; with very short wings, they landed at excessive speeds. A number crashed on landing and killed the crews.

When pilots did get a chance to fly one of the new B-29s, they found the experience exhilarating—and unnerving. The pilot's compartment in the plane's greenhouse nose, made up of 26 variously shaped panes of plexiglass, was both a delight and a puzzlement.

Captain James Pattillo, who climbed into the pilot's lefthand seat for the first time in October 1943, was struck by a vast sweep of forward and upward visibility that he had never expected to find in any airplane. But there was a catch: Sitting far to the left in the greenhouse, Pattillo looked out at an angle; he found that he had trouble judging distance on landing because some of the glass panels, their optics influenced by shape and curvature, distorted the perspective of his view ahead. On one of the first landing attempts, with his squadron commander, Lieut. Colonel James B. Edmundson, sitting in the cockpit to check his performance, Pattillo was fooled by the glass. He guessed wrong on his distance from the ground and dropped the aircraft 50 feet onto the concrete. The impact did no more than jar loose the bombardier's gun sight from its restraining socket, but it was a bad moment, and Pattillo was afraid he would be sent back to training school. His commander said nothing, however, and on his next try Pattillo landed the plane without trouble.

A related landing problem for Pattillo and other novice B-29 pilots was the plane's seeming tendency to drift leftward off the center line of the runway just before touchdown. Pattillo eventually decided that the fault was his, not the airplane's. He concluded that, sitting so far to the left in the greenhouse and straining to gauge the distance to the ground through the greenhouse, he unconsciously lifted the right wing a little, inducing the leftward drift.

With only a handful of Superfortresses available—and given the unreliability of the Cyclone R-3350 engine—pilots in training had to be extremely conservative. They were under strict orders, in the words of squadron commander Edmundson, to "fly it by the book. Don't play around. Remember, the B-29 hasn't been proven like the B-17. Save it for the Japs."

The pilots were expressly forbidden to attempt three-engine takeoffs, which were sometimes undertaken in training to find out how a plane would react. Such power-short takeoffs were dangerous because the engines were not adequately broken in and were likely to quit—with calamitous results, particularly if a second engine shut down on the same side as the idle one. On duty one day in the control tower at Smoky Hill, Pattillo watched a friend, one of the most experienced pilots in the program, violate the rule and die. Taking off on three engines, the aircraft made an extraordinarily long run before leaving the ground; then, as soon as it was airborne, it went into a shallow right turn. The bank steepened to 35 degrees and—still turning—the plane stalled, plunged to the ground and exploded. The end had come swiftly when a second engine quit on the same side as the one shut off purposely—which was too cold to start when it was needed.

Pattillo considered himself lucky to log 25 hours of B-29 time in his first month at Smoky Hill; many of his colleagues were getting as few as 18 hours. By the end of January 1944, just one month before Arnold's deadline for the China takeoff, Smoky Hill had graduated only seventy B-29 command pilots.

By now Superfortresses were at last moving off the production lines with some regularity, but they were complete airplanes in name only. In October 1943, it had been decided at last to freeze the design and take care of urgently needed modifications after the planes were finished. Modification centers had been established at Kelly Field, Texas, and at Pratt, Walker and Smoky Hill in Kansas, the Bell plant in Marietta and the Martin works in Omaha. But so many changes had to be made in each aircraft that the centers found the task next to impossible, and the program had fallen into total disarray.

There were a few people in the United States with the necessary expertise to restore order. At 2 o'clock on a midwinter night in early February 1944, Major Victor Agather, a member of the B-29 project team who was working on the problem of engine fires, was wakened by the telephone in his quarters at Wright Field. On the line was his superior,

Colonel Erik Nelson. "Vic, get your tail in the saddle," Nelson said, "and get out to Salina immediately with a list of all serial numbers of B-29s and the modifications required." An airplane was standing by to take the major to his assignment.

Agather spent the next five days and nights at Pratt Field in Salina, Kansas, cataloguing the condition of every B-29 there. With his list in hand, he flew to Wichita and dragooned 400 specialists from the Boeing production line. As each man was selected he was chauffeured immediately to the airport and flown to Pratt, while someone else went to his home to notify his family and pick up a few clothes.

Back at Pratt, Agather worked alongside his shanghaied specialists inside the B-29s until it seemed to all of them that to be grease-smeared and exhausted was a permanent state. At one point, a mechanic climbed into the plane where Agather was working to tell him that a visiting general was outside the aircraft and wished to have a few words with the major.

"If he wants to talk to me, tell him to climb up here," Agather said. He paused long enough to look out a window and see his message being delivered to an officer in an immaculate uniform. When the general wheeled and stalked away, Agather did not have to be told that his invitation had been taken badly. He soon learned that the visitor had cited him for insubordination and was threatening a court-

martial. However, Agather's assignment overrode normal military protocol and he escaped censure.

For all the efforts of Agather's team and others like it, the modification work went on with agonizing slowness. One obstacle was a lack of maintenance equipment. At Pratt Field alone, 100 engines needed changing, but Pratt's shop had no gear for hoisting engines in and out of their nacelles. Somebody remembered that mobile scaffoldings fitted with block and tackle—called engine slings—were available in Erie, Pennsylvania. A civilian airliner was commandeered, its passengers bumped, and the plane flown to Erie, where welders cut the bulky slings into pieces small enough to be stowed on top of the passenger seats. At Pratt, other welders put the slings back together. The engines were changed.

The sheer newness of the B-29s continued to cause problems. Parts were found to be missing, and replacing them was complicated by the way the original manufacturing contracts had been parceled out among many small companies. Records to indicate which subcontractor had made which part had to be tracked down before the needed components could be ordered and installed. Moreover, design alterations had been made in such profusion and haste that they were built successively into production models as they moved along the assembly line—making each aircraft a little different from the last. A case in point was the bomber's maze of electric wiring, which on each plane became a unique mystery that could only be unraveled when individual wires were traced and new wiring diagrams drawn.

Despite the disorder, General Arnold convinced himself that the first 175 B-29s would be ready to go to war by March 10, 1944, and cabled this information to General Wolfe in India. Acting on his own prediction, Arnold arrived at Salina on March 9 to witness the first historic departures. He was told that not a single Superfortress was yet ready to go. The Army Air Forces' commanding officer erupted in rage and demanded to know who was in charge of the anticipated send-off. "I'll do it myself!" he shouted.

In informal Air Forces annals, the ensuing crisis became known as the Battle of Kansas. Arnold turned to a senior aide, Major General Bennett E. Meyers, and told him to remain on the spot in Salina as his deputy, to coordinate the work there and get it done. Another general was dispatched to Wichita to draft an additional 500 trained mechanics from Boeing. Telephones rang all over the country as subcontractors were ordered to put all other work aside and concentrate on turning out the missing parts for the waiting Superfortresses. A stream of transport planes, trains and trucks began arriving in Kansas from every point of the compass, bringing the necessary material.

It was frantic work and bitter cold. The Kansas plains were in the grip of a late winter freeze, soon made worse by a raging blizzard. Because little hangar space was available, most of the work had to be done in the open, on planes parked along the wind-lashed flight line. The teams of mechanics, even though bundled in high-altitude flight suits, had to be relieved every 20 minutes.

But the Battle of Kansas was being won. In the middle of March, Colonel Frank Cook took off in the first combat-ready B-29 and flew to England by way of Miami and Newfoundland. This first long, roundabout, overwater flight by a Superfortress was intended to disguise the fact that the B-29s were now intended to bomb Japan. Cook's decoy flight may have been modestly successful; a mere 45 minutes after the plane landed in England, it was photographed by a German reconnaissance pilot. But it is unlikely that the Japanese were confused. Their intelligence had reported that outsized airfields were being built in India and China, obviously meant for planes larger than B-17s or B-24s.

The big planes were coming. In the predawn dark of March 26, the Kansas fields came alive with the whine of starting engines that soon deepened to a shuddering roar. The first 11-plane contingent of Arnold's Superfortresses was ready to go. Colonel Jake Harman, the wing commander, had the left-hand seat in the greenhouse nose of the lead plane. His course would take him first to Gander in Newfoundland, then 2,700 unbroken miles to Marrakesh at the foot of North Africa's Atlas Mountains, and from there to Cairo. He would span the Near East to Karachi, and finally come down in the steamy heat of Chakulia, near Calcutta—11,530 miles from the icebound fields of Kansas.

Indian laborers carry dirt in baskets from the unfinished site of a B-29 base near Kharagpur in 1944. Because the local contractors were paid according to the depth of the excavation, cones of earth have been left untouched to mark the original level of the field. Once the amount of payment was confirmed, the cones were removed.

A PERILOUS LEAP INTO COMBAT

Flying the Hump in 1944, a B-29 bomber crosses the Himalayas, transporting gasoline and other supplies from India to a forward airfield in southern China.

FIELD TRAINING
FOR FLEDGLINGS

When the first Superfortress task force assembled in India in April 1944, its members discovered that their mission was aptly named Operation *Matterhorn,* after the formidable Alpine peak: Before they could begin flying combat missions, the airmen had a host of imposing obstacles to surmount.

An advance party under the direction of the task-force commander, Brigadier General Kenneth B. Wolfe, was already at work on the most pressing problems. Former British airfields near Kharagpur in northeastern India were taken over as the principal bases for the B-29s, and the advance party had to extend their runways to handle the big planes and construct living quarters for the crews. At the same time, forward bases for the B-29s were nearing completion under American supervision near Chengtu in south-central China. The landing strips there had to be built from scratch by filling in rice paddies.

The fields in China brought the bombers within striking distance of Japan. But supplying them was the most intimidating problem of all. Every bomb, every spare part, every gallon of fuel had to be flown into Chengtu over the Hump—that part of the mighty Himalayan mountain range, rising to 23,000 feet, that separates India and China. Unpredictable, often violent weather, poor communications and occasional enemy fighters made flying the Hump so hazardous that crews making the transport run were given credit for combat time.

The untried B-29s themselves were a problem. Their newly designed engines overheated, and the planes were prey to a host of other maladies as well. One B-29 required 30 major alterations in a single week. The crewmen, barely acquainted with the complexities of their new aircraft, had to unravel the mysteries of coordinated defensive gunfire and bombing by radar. And while the fledgling outfit struggled with its numerous problems, the pressure from Washington for Operation *Matterhorn* to begin lashing out at Japanese targets grew more relentless by the day. "We are just barely able to crawl," lamented General Wolfe, "and they call on us to do the 100-yard dash."

At the controls, a young pilot prepares for takeoff on the first B-29 combat mission—a raid on Japanese-occupied Bangkok on June 5, 1944.

Perched on an engine hoist, an airman in India paints the tail of a B-29 with four stripes that identify the plane's unit, the 40th Bombardment Group.

With little to keep them busy between missions, off-duty crew members sprawl on the porch of their quarters at an air base near the city of Kharagpur.

Aircrewmen display a python seven feet long and a monitor lizard that were killed in their living quarters.

SETTLING IN ON HELL'S HALF-ACRE

The American bomber crews arrived at the beginning of India's hottest season— a time when a searing wind blowing from the Great Indian Desert in the northwest raised choking clouds of dust that were relieved only by afternoon rain squalls. The men at one field called their base Hell's Half-Acre. Midday temperatures of 115° F. affected airmen and aircraft alike, effectively limiting takeoffs to early morning and late afternoon.

Engine maintenance was carried out at night under lights that attracted swarms of flying insects. More dangerous annoyances were cobras and malaria-carrying mosquitoes that made it necessary for the men to sleep under nets.

By July, however, most of the new living quarters—straw-thatched huts that the Indians called *bashas*—had been completed. They were ready just in time to provide shelter against the region's next season: the summer monsoon.

Local workers unload straw to finish
thatching a roof on one of the huts that were put
up for housing, offices and recreation at the
American bases in India.

Three months after their arrival, airmen from the 40th Bombardment Group celebrate the opening of an officers' club on the Fourth of July in 1944.

During a stopover at Chengtu, three B-29 crewmen have their picture taken with a Chinese officer and a rifle-carrying soldier, members of a unit assigned by Chiang Kai-shek to protect the American fields.

A work crew of Chinese soldiers, carrying tool baskets slung from shoulder yokes, crosses a B-29 airfield near Chengtu. The fields were built largely by conscripted civilians, but for security reasons soldiers did most of the maintenance work after the bases became operational.

A VITAL SPRINGBOARD IN CHINA

Constructed in the area of China under the Nationalist government of Generalissimo Chiang Kai-shek, the four B-29 bases that sprang up in 1944 around the old university town of Chengtu were an amazing accomplishment.

Each field had an 8,500-foot runway of hard-packed rock and clay that rose six feet above the surrounding rice paddies; all were built in just over three months by 300,000 Chinese workers using shovels, wheelbarrows and human muscle.

At the Chengtu bases there were even fewer amenities than in India. Men stationed there or laying over between supply runs were billeted in Chinese-run hostels and ate local food. Anything that had to be flown over the Hump was in short supply; the Chengtu beer ration was two bottles per month, compared with 24 in India.

Airmen went sightseeing and learned to take local customs in stride, with one tragic exception: Chinese civilians would sprint across the runways in front of landing or departing planes, and during the first few weeks seven of them were killed. Many Chinese, it turned out, believed that the moving planes could brush away evil spirits. The suicidal practice was halted only by posting guards on the runways.

A market street in the city of Chengtu bustles with rickshaw and bicycle traffic in this snapshot, which was taken in 1944 by a visiting American aviator.

A camera-carrying American flier pauses on a Chengtu street to watch the work of an open-air butcher, whose wares are displayed hanging from a pole.

SHAKEDOWN UNDER FIRE

Few fliers have ever taken off on a combat mission without feeling a certain amount of tension. But the operations flown out of India and China were nerve-racking in every respect. These long-range missions were in effect training flights on which the green Superfortress crews learned under fierce enemy fire how to handle the planes and their complex equipment. The flights were also shakedown runs during which any of the 50,000 parts that made up the still-unproven B-29s might give out with no warning.

The only predictable outcome of the early raids was that many of the bombers would be unsuccessful. On the first mission—a strike against Bangkok in early June, 1944—one fifth of the 98 planes involved developed severe mechanical difficulties. The pilots either turned back or ditched their planes in the Bay of Bengal. With some exceptions, the 1-in-5 failure rate remained distressingly steady during the next two dozen missions.

Just as troubling were surveillance photographs of the targets after each raid that showed only a minimal amount of bomb damage. Most of the blame for these repeated failures was laid to inexperience: It would take six hard months before the American air and ground crews grew confident that they had mastered their powerful but balky new fighting machines.

Outside the operations shed on one of the airfields at Chengtu, officers and ground crews gaze intently skyward, straining to count and identify the B-2

A gunnery officer delivers last-minute instructions on fire control to an attentive group of gunners before a raid on Bangkok. On their previous mission one week earlier, the Superfortresses had encountered strong resistance from Japanese fighter planes.

An intelligence officer (left) debriefs a crew just back from the first B-29 attack on Japan on June 15, 1944. The results of the raid — against Yawata steel plants — were mediocre.

Superfortresses that are on their way back from a bombing mission.

Fire consumes four B-29s in India after a massive explosion that killed eight men when a fragmentation bomb was accidentally released during loading.

At an emergency landing strip near Chengtu, airmen inspect a pair of B-29s that did not quite make it home; the man standing on the fuselage at right

HEAVY LOSSES ON HOME BASES

At first, the B-29s were their own worst enemy, and they were most likely to come to grief on or near their home bases. Like all bombers, they were in constant danger from their explosive cargoes. On one occasion in India, a bomb mishandled during loading wiped out four B-29s *(left)* in a matter of seconds.

The planes were most vulnerable during takeoff, when each carried up to 8,500 gallons of fuel and two and a half tons of bombs. In order to conserve fuel and avoid overheating the engines, the bombers had to lift off with clockwork precision, one right after the other, with no margin for hesitation or mishap. The crashes that often resulted—along with in-flight failures and accidents on landing—claimed more lives than did Japanese air defenses.

Only the tail section and a port engine remain of a bomber that exploded and burned after crashing in a watery Indian field just after takeoff from the base at Chakulia.

examining the partially dismantled tail section for possible reuse. The waist gunners' blisters and gun turrets on both planes have already been salvaged.

51

2

The men of the 58th Bombardment Wing, XX Bomber Command, were the first B-29 crews to go overseas, arriving at the new bases in India brimming with optimism. All too quickly, however, they discovered that they were only beginning a long, dangerous and sometimes humiliating apprenticeship.

Merely to position themselves within range of the enemy, the American airmen had already endured an exasperating ordeal. The first of 150 B-29s began leaving Kansas on the 26th of March, 1944. Taking off at the rate of nine or 10 per day, they soon were strung out all the way from Gander to the new bases near Calcutta, with stops in between at Marrakesh, Cairo and Karachi. Not until May 8 were the first 130 planes safely down on the new Indian airfields; most of the others had gotten as far as Marrakesh. Seven B-29s were lost to various causes on the way, one at Marrakesh, one at Cairo and five in a single week at Karachi.

The plane at Marrakesh refused to lift, ran off the end of the runway and piled up in flames. Crews of other B-29s experienced a baffling loss of power while trying to reach and maintain the 16,000-foot altitude needed to cross the Atlas Mountains on the run between Marrakesh and Cairo.

Captain James Pattillo managed to get his aircraft off the ground at Marrakesh, but it refused to climb until he ordered the engine cowl flaps closed to reduce drag; closing them reduced dangerously the amount of cooling air that reached the cylinders. Pattillo watched his instrument panel gauges tensely as temperatures in the cylinder head rose to 644° F., a temperature 166° hotter than the engines were designed to tolerate. The engines kept working beyond reasonable expectations.

No such luck favored the five B-29s that went down at Karachi. After the losses, which included one B-29 that vanished without a trace over the Arabian Sea, the Superfortresses were grounded until some method could be devised to curb the tendency of the Wright Cyclone R-3350 engine to overheat and then consume itself. To correct the overheating, engineers made modifications that provided at least a partial answer to the problem. Among other changes, the upper flaps on the engine cowl were cut back three inches; control linkages were installed that made it possible to open and close these flaps from the cockpit and thus admit more cooling air around the cylinders. Such corrections

APPRENTICESHIP IN ASIA

were worked out by engineers at Wright Field, and specialists were dispatched to India to modify the planes that were already there.

The crews in India were painfully green. Their preparation for B-29 duty had been confined largely to classroom work and training flights in B-17s; few of them had received more than two hours' training in their intended function—high-altitude precision bombing, carried out while flying in formation. Nor had the pilots and engineers learned the nuances of cruise control—the combination of delicate engine adjustments and flying techniques calculated to wring the greatest possible mileage out of time aloft. (Ideally, this maximum was 4,100 miles in about 20 hours, from a load of 8,000 gallons of high-octane fuel.)

Living conditions at the new bases were raw. India's heat was relentless. Transport problems curtailed the availability of U.S. Army rations, and the unfamiliar local food and impure drinking water soon made stomach disorders endemic among the crews. And there were exotic terrors to be endured. One day Captain Pattillo, squatting on his bed—a network of rope laced over a wooden frame—was startled by a rustling noise. He looked up to see an 18-inch lizard strike at something unseen; then the victim, a black, yellow-legged centipede, nine inches long, tumbled out of the thatch overhead. A few days later, another officer killed a cobra beside his bunk.

Worse hazards lurked just ahead. Major General Henry Arnold had conceived of his B-29s as a global strategic air force that would be not only independent of local command control, but also self-sustaining in the field. If the Superfortresses were to bomb the Japanese from the forward fields around Chengtu, in China, they would have to haul their own supplies; this included gasoline, for which the B-29 had a voracious appetite. The Indian bases drew their fuel from Calcutta by a pipeline laid the previous winter by American engineers employing Indian civilian labor; but no pipeline ran to China.

Chengtu lay more than 1,000 miles northeast of Calcutta and the route led over the notorious "Hump," the loftiest air-transport route in the world—planes had to climb to more than 24,000 feet in order to clear the perpetually snow-covered peaks and gorges of the Himalayas. The Hump was not only high, but was a breeder of vicious weather: bitter cold, sudden storms and violent downdrafts that could knock a plane out of the sky like a rock.

To mount the first two raids, the 58th Bombardment Wing had to airlift 700,000 gallons of gasoline to China. Brigadier General Kenneth Wolfe, the commanding officer, ordered fuel tanks installed in the Superfortresses' bomb bays; some were also stripped of all armament except rear guns and basic radar equipment, more than doubling the amount of gasoline that could be ferried.

Brigadier General LaVerne Saunders, Wolfe's training officer, helped to pioneer the route by taking a B-29 over the Hump on the 24th of April. Saunders flew into the Kwanghan field at Chengtu—and received a formal welcome from Chinese dignitaries and Major General Claire Chennault, commander of the U.S. Fourteenth Air Force, based in China. The ceremonies were enlivened by 75,000 Chinese laborers who shouted "Ding hao!"—an expression of congratulations.

It was a nice day and Captain William O'Malley, the navigator in Saunders' plane, had enjoyed the view on the way from India. "The flight over the Hump was by-God amazing," O'Malley later wrote of the event. "Perfect weather, incredible mountain valleys and gorges, tiny villages on the lesser mountains."

So pleasant an excursion turned out to be rare. Two days after Saunders' trip, Major Charles Hanson was above the Hump carrying 2,000 gallons of aviation fuel to Chengtu. Over the India-Burma border at 16,000 feet, Hanson sighted a dozen small aircraft off his right wing; they were about five miles away, 2,000 feet below him and clearly identifiable as Japanese fighters. As Hanson yelled a warning to his crew, six of the Japanese planes broke formation and began a rapid climb. Once level with the B-29, the single-seated Nakajima Ki-43 fighters fell into formation on either side of the bomber. For 15 tense minutes they flew alongside, just out of range of .50-caliber machine guns and 20mm cannon, studying and perhaps photographing the American plane. So far as was known, they were the first Japanese to see a Superfortress.

At length, the Japanese flight leader broke away and attacked Hanson's plane from behind and below. Muzzle blasts flamed along his wings as he closed to within 400 yards. His explosive shells began to hit; miraculously, none ignited the B-29's gasoline cargo, but a gunner shouted that he had been wounded.

At this moment the Superfortress' unreadiness for war made itself dangerously evident. The tail gunner's cannon refused to fire; simultaneously, the machine guns in the tail and three of four guns in the upper turrets jammed. While the gunners struggled to free their weapons, two more enemy fighters dived in from the rear. Their fire missed. Hanson put his plane into a climb, hoping to shake off his antagonists. Another Nakajima came up from behind and closed to within 90 yards—too close for his own safety. The tail gunner, Sergeant Harold Lanham, had managed to free his machine guns. His burst at close range sent the Japanese plane smoking down into the overcast, a probable kill. After several more passes, the remaining fighters departed.

It had been the B-29's first exposure to combat. Hanson, in his debriefing, placed much of the blame for the near disaster on the unreadiness of the crew, however willing they may have been. The tail cannon, for example, was activated by a spring-loading device; investigation showed that somebody had forgotten to wind the spring.

Such gasoline runs as Hanson's became a severe test of the independence of the B-29 force. It soon appeared that General Wolfe's idea of moving the fuel to China in Superfortresses would not be enough. Day in, day out, the weary crews hauled their burdened ships over the Hump and down to Chengtu, some planes burning 12 gallons for every one they deposited in the Chinese fuel dumps. Wolfe was forced to call for help from the Air Transport Command, the U.S. Army's hard-pressed air-freight service.

The assistance was furnished—and it was crucial—but it came grudgingly, since the Air Transport Command already had its hands full. In all of May only 1,950 tons of supplies crossed the Hump to the B-29 bases at Chengtu. Of this, two thirds were hauled by C-46 Curtiss Commandos of the ATC. The rest still had to be carried in B-29s. The arithmetic became staggering. It was apparent that for every plane that flew out of Chengtu against the home islands of Japan, a freighter B-29 would have to fly at least six supply missions over the Himalayas, transporting everything from bombs to toilet paper.

The plane crews tried to put a bright face on their predicament: For each round trip a camel's hump was painted on the fuselage. "Here's to the XX Bomber Command—a goddamn trucking outfit," one weary airman announced in a mock toast. But "trucking" the Hump was more than drudgery; it was dangerous. During the early months of hauling supplies across the mountains, the command lost a dozen B-29s and the ATC lost half that number of C-46 transports. Some crews were able to bail out over the mountains, but only the luckier ones eventually made it home.

The old engine problem continued to plague the missions over the Hump. One day early in June, Lieutenant Leslie J. Sloan and his crew off-loaded a cargo of gasoline at the Pengshan strip in China. On the return to India, they were over the headwaters of the Yangtze River when the No. 3 engine blew a cylinder head and a violent explosion shook the ship. Sloan tried to feather the propeller, adjusting its blade edges to offer the least wind resistance; but his efforts failed, and the propeller ran wild, windmilling and braking the aircraft. The engine caught fire, and the B-29 began losing altitude fast; Sloan gave the bail-out order at 22,000 feet. Ten men got out but the left waist gunner, though last seen with his parachute on and preparing to jump, inexplicably never left the plane.

Three of the crew had trouble with their chutes. The flight engineer, Lieutenant Robert F. Casey, struggled with a rip cord that was stuck and would not yield until he yanked on it with both hands. The tail gunner, Sergeant John Moore, got out of the plane in good order but his chute refused to open. Working in frantic haste, he ripped off the cover and pulled out the canopy with both hands. The right gunner, Sergeant Virgil Bailey, was pinned against the side of the fuselage by the slip stream until at last he kicked himself free. Bailey fell fast and landed hard; one silk panel of his chute had been torn.

The other men who jumped came down safely. Lieutenant Sloan landed in a tree 20 feet off the ground and had to swing himself over to grab the trunk before he could unbuckle his harness and make his way to the ground. Once down, he paused to wonder what came next. He and his men had been flying over country inhabited by mountain tribesmen called Lolos, reputedly unfriendly and fierce. Nobody knew where the loyalties of the Lolos lay and, it occurred to Sloan, they could be bounty hunters eager to earn

At a base near Chengtu, Chinese workers roll 55-gallon drums of high-octane aviation gasoline onto a platform from which it will later be put in storage tanks. To fuel one bomber for a raid on Japan, more than 7,000 gallons—representing six trips by B-29s stripped and refitted for carrying gasoline—came 1,200 miles over the Himalayas from bases in India.

the 300-rupee reward the Japanese were said to be paying for captured American airmen.

From the rocky ground where he had landed, Flight Engineer Casey watched apprehensively as a group of armed men approached. The men indeed were Lolos—shorter, heavier and much darker in appearance than the Chinese that Casey was familiar with. They wore turbans and long, heavy cloaks of goat hair, and they stank. The Lolos made gestures that Casey interpreted as threatening; one indicated that he would like to have Casey's .45-caliber side arm. Casey gave it to him—seeing surrender as a better bargain than having the weapon taken from him by force.

The Lolos led Casey to a village of mud huts and turned him over to a man who was evidently the village chief. The other American airmen from the B-29 were brought in, most already having surrendered their watches and jewelry. One crew member who had hoped to keep his canteen lost it when a Lolo neatly slashed it from his belt with the 10-inch blade of his knife.

The prisoners' prospects brightened a bit when the chief proffered a meal of stewed goat and rice. Repelled by the food's aroma, the Americans refused; by the second day, however, they were hungrier.

When night came, the village elders sat in a circle smoking opium and hospitably offering a pull at their communal pipe to the airmen, who politely declined.

For 11 days the Americans were held as the Lolos' guests. They were allowed to visit their wrecked plane and bury the dead gunner. When they grew sufficiently dirty and louse-ridden to be in urgent need of baths, they were permitted to strip, plunge into an icy mountain stream and then scour themselves with sand. The scrubbing provided much amusement for the Lolos, one of whom had become friendly and was even learning the words to American cowboy ballads from one of the airmen.

On the 11th day, the chief at last appointed an escort and sent the refugees off down the mountain. Before their departure, he presented them with a supply of gummy raw

opium with which to barter their way back to Chengtu.

Moving from village to village, the party descended to lower ground. The guides kept changing. The Americans paid their way with the opium and with Chinese and Indian money that Sloan had managed to hold onto. As the party traveled northeastward, the villagers they encountered became more Chinese in appearance. Once the group was fired upon from across a river by Lolos unknown to the guides. On another occasion, the guides, by now predominantly Chinese, killed two Lolo bandits encountered on the trail; they beheaded one and took the head along as a warning to others.

The fliers sensed that their ordeal was nearing an end when they reached the ancient Chinese town of Leipo. The mayor ordered hot baths for the travelers, provided them with clean clothes to wear while their own tattered garments were cleaned, furnished American cigarettes and laid a banquet of eggs, chicken, peaches and tea. In Pengshan, a retired Chinese general provided another banquet and quarters for the night; the next morning, he sent them on their way—the two strongest aviators still walking, the others in bamboo sedan chairs carried by bearers.

On the 28th day following their crash, Lieutenant Sloan and his crew arrived back at Chengtu. They had covered an estimated 250 miles and had lost from 15 to 35 pounds per man. After a short period of convalescence, they went back to flying the Hump.

As the gasoline stores slowly accumulated in China during the late spring of 1944, General Arnold in Washington kept demanding immediate, massive action against the Japanese home islands. In India, General Wolfe temporized; he still did not have enough fuel at Chengtu to mount a substantial, sustained assault. The Japanese had made his situation more precarious by launching a great land offensive in eastern China. They were aiming toward Kweilin, 250 miles northwest of Canton—perhaps believing B-29s were to be based there, alongside the planes of Chennault's Fourteenth Air Force. The Japanese also meant to threaten Kunming, a city about 400 miles south of Chengtu that was the hub of all American efforts in China.

The Fourteenth Air Force desperately needed supplies from over the Hump in order to stave off the Japanese at-tack; General Chennault even sought to expropriate what fuel Wolfe had managed to stockpile at Chengtu. Thus, in spite of General Arnold's demands, the realities of warfare in China moved B-29 operations ever lower on the list of Allied priorities.

Since Japan was beyond his immediate reach, General Wolfe scheduled the first combat strike of the XX Bomber Command as a partial training mission against a somewhat closer target: the Makkasan railroad shops and yards near Bangkok in Japanese-held Thailand, 1,000 miles from the B-29 bases in India. The raid was scheduled for June 5, at the beginning of the monsoon season.

Laden with five tons of bombs and 6,486 gallons of gasoline each, 100 Superfortresses began taking off from their fields near Calcutta at 5:45 a.m. Wolfe, aware of his crews' inadequate training in daylight formation flying, had scheduled a night mission, with the planes making their bomb runs one by one. But Arnold, in Washington, overruled Wolfe; it seemed to him imperative that the airmen learn their job quickly by doing it. That meant bombing visually during the day from high altitudes in four-plane, diamond-shaped formations.

Ninety-eight of the B-29s succeeded in getting off the ground. One flight was aborted on the runway. Another plane bumped awkwardly along the strip, staggered into the air, dipped its left wing into the ground and plunged forward in a flaming cartwheel. Bombs exploded in the bay, tearing the fuselage apart. One member of the crew survived. At various stages of the outbound flight, 14 planes turned back with mechanical failures; seven others never found the target.

Weather thickened on the 1,000-mile run to Bangkok, breaking up the formations. The B-29s came over the target area stacked at altitudes from 17,000 to 27,000 feet, in visibility so poor that any possibility of achieving what Arnold wanted—a precisely timed and executed parade of destruction—was out of the question. Instead, confusion ruled in the air over Bangkok. Coming at the target helter-skelter in singles, pairs and threes, the B-29s were in far more danger from collision with one another than they were from the inaccurate flak or the nine cautiously flown fighters that the Japanese sent to attack them. Seventy-seven B-29s unloaded their bomb bays, most of them sighting by radar, with which the crews had no more expertise than they had with formation flight.

The ragged fleet turned for home, but trouble lay ahead. The weather was growing worse. Engines were malfunctioning and fuel was running low. One pilot, Major Booth G. Malone, tried to nurse his fuel for an emergency landing at Kunming, but ran dry 60 miles short of his destination. He and his men bailed out and were rescued by Chinese. Others ran into problems over the Bay of Bengal. Out of fuel, Captain J. N. Sanders ditched his plane in a sea that was glassy smooth. Two of his men were lost during the ditching, but the other nine were picked up by British air-sea rescue motorboats. A day later the Superfortress itself floated to shore, evidently buoyed by its empty fuel tanks.

Another B-29 crossing the Bay of Bengal still had gasoline in its tanks, but the transfer system that pumped fuel from tank to engine had been damaged. Major Alex N. Zamry, the pilot, jettisoned his remaining fuel and came down in a hard, dead-engine ditching that broke the fuselage in half. Zamry and his radioman were killed. Eight other men aboard succeeded in inflating their two rafts. Two men, both wounded, floated all night in their Mae West life jackets. When their companions found them the next day and pulled them aboard a raft, one of the men was delirious; he had been badly bitten by crabs. After another day and night at sea, the two rafts and the men in them washed ashore near Calcutta. Thirty additional planes, afflicted by the monsoon weather and a variety of other problems, got lost on their way back from the raid and landed at fields all over southeastern India.

Subsequent photoreconnaissance of Bangkok revealed that the first B-29s sent against the enemy had accomplished very little. Only 18 bombs had fallen in the primary target area. Some had missed the target by as much as two miles. The blooding of the XX Bomber Command had not been a rousing success.

Arnold waited just one day to apply the pressure again. The Joint Chiefs, he told Wolfe by dispatch, urgently wanted the B-29s to hit Japan itself—soon and hard. Arnold cited two reasons: to take some of the Japanese pressure off Chennault's airfields in east China, and to coordinate their action with an unnamed but important Navy operation in the Pacific—which turned out to be the invasion of Saipan. Wolfe replied that, with great effort, he might be able to fly 50 B-29s off the Chengtu fields by June 20. Arnold instructed him curtly that it would have to be at least 70 planes, launched not later than June 15.

Faced with an outright order, Wolfe bore down hard, assigning more B-29s to the fuel run and putting the 312th Fighter Wing, which had been assigned to defend the Chengtu fields, on a bare-bones fuel ration. By June 13 he had enough gasoline on hand to send 75 planes against Kyushu, southernmost of the main Japanese islands. Two days later, as Arnold had ordered, the aircraft took off from Chengtu, each carrying two tons of bombs.

They had been assigned what the Joint Chiefs considered a prime strategic target: the coke ovens of Japan's largest steel plant, the Imperial Iron and Steel Works at Yawata in northern Kyushu, which produced one fourth of the Empire's rolled steel. Word of the mission attracted a number of American newsmen, who got permission to come along. Somewhat reluctantly, Arnold agreed that the mission be flown at relatively low levels—between 8,000 and 18,000 feet—for the sake of accuracy, and at night for protection against flak and fighters. This time Wolfe had pleaded successfully that his green crews could not be expected to hold formation for the 3,200-mile round trip.

Once more, taking off was the most perilous moment of the mission. Of the 75 planes, one crashed and burned on the field, but the crew miraculously scrambled out of the flaming wreck alive. Six B-29s aborted their takeoffs. Four turned back soon after takeoff. That left 64 planes heading for Japan through the late-afternoon dusk. The expedition was commanded by General Saunders, the only general officer Arnold would allow to risk his neck.

Only 47 of the B-29s found the target. At 11:38 p.m. China time, the first of them arrived over Yawata, a blacked-out city from which the roving beams of searchlights reached up to pin the silver planes against the dark sky. Then Saunders radioed the code word, "Betty! Betty! Betty!" Colonel James Garcia, the intelligence officer, had chosen his wife's name as the signal that Saunders had unloaded the first B-29 bombs on Japan.

It was a harrowing few minutes for the men in the planes. Flying through the searchlights, which were coordinated in

As a crew member looks on from the hatchway, an ordnanceman inserts
the propeller fuse into a 500-pound demolition bomb before the first B-29
raid against Japan in June 1944. In its two bomb bays, the Superfortress
could carry up to 10 tons of payload—the equivalent of 40 of the bombs
shown here—but because of the weight of the extra fuel needed
for this 3,200-mile mission, each B-29 carried only two tons of bombs.

multiples like gun batteries, proved an unnerving experience, at least at first. "One full battery caught us in its fierce, savage beam. Our whole cabin was lit up like Madison Square Garden on hockey night," reported Roy Porter, a radio newsman who accompanied the mission. "Still the lights blazed—and though we dodged and dipped, we could not avoid them. We climbed a bit—we dropped a bit—and all this time the cold steel was spattering against the outside of the cabin. Then suddenly, as if nothing at all had happened, the pilot leaned back and said, 'We are very well out of that,' and as he spoke the lights died away."

On the ground, the perspective was understandably reversed. A Japanese reporter wrote: "The propeller noise of the enemy planes spread over the whole sky. I could see clearly the figures of the enemy planes. At once, antiaircraft began to shoot. The guns shouted like lightning. But the hateful enemy planes flew on. Then came big black things from the white bodies of the planes . . . . And boom! boom! boom! The devils, the beasts!"

Free of the flak and shaking off the pursuing searchlights, the B-29s turned toward home. Several of them had been hit over the target and on the way to Chengtu three planes crashed. All aboard were killed, including *Newsweek* correspondent Robert Schenkel. One plane, flown by Captain Robert Root, was carrying *Time* correspondent Harry Zinder. It malfunctioned and made an emergency landing on a Chinese strip near the front lines. Root's radio call for assistance was intercepted by the Japanese. Aided by the Chinese, Root and his crew were working on their plane, trying to get it ready to take off again, when the enemy intervened.

"Two fighters were streaking across the low mountains," Zinder later wrote. "We saw the Rising Sun on their sides. We yelled to the others and rushed for a shallow ditch 50 yards away. The fighters roared across, pulled up and then turned down on our ship. They spattered bullets across the fuselage and the wings, then started a little fire on the left side. We hugged the ground closer as bullets kicked up dust and grass alongside the ditch. They made many passes. When the fire was fully blazing, they left."

About all the mission to Kyushu accomplished was to demonstrate that Japan's home islands were now vulnerable to B-29 attacks. Practical results were scant. Seven planes had been lost, and photoreconnaissance of the target area showed that some bombs had missed their mark by as much as 20 miles; the bomb falling nearest to the steel plant's coke ovens, the aiming point, had wrecked a small building three quarters of a mile away.

Relations between Arnold in Washington and Wolfe in India grew increasingly strained. Two days after the planes returned from Yawata, Arnold demanded a series of missions, including an attack on the big Showa Steel Works at Anshan in Manchuria—specifically, the company's coke plant. Wolfe had to reply that he had only 5,000 gallons of gasoline remaining at Chengtu, not enough to fill the tanks of even a single B-29.

Angry and frustrated, Arnold relieved Wolfe on July 4, bestowed another star on him and in effect kicked him upstairs as head of the Army Air Forces Matériel Command. The transfer was probably sensible: Wolfe was a specialist at building aircraft; before going to India, he had never held a combat command.

General Saunders took over the XX Bomber Command and accomplished what Wolfe had not. In July his command hauled 2,998 tons of supplies, primarily gasoline, to Chengtu, and ATC transports fattened the stockpile with an additional 976 tons. On July 29, General Arnold got his mission to Manchuria.

Arnold wanted at least 100 planes to hit the Showa works, which produced one third of the Empire's metallurgical coke. Saunders' overworked B-29s had been reinforced in twos and threes, but the planes were deteriorating rapidly in India's heat and humidity, and were increasingly difficult to maintain. By hard work and good luck, Saunders got 107 Superfortresses to Chengtu, losing one aircraft and eight crewmen en route. On the day of the strike one entire group was mired by rain on one of Chengtu's four fields, but 72 planes got off from the others. One crashed shortly after takeoff, killing eight of its crew. Seventy-one flew on toward Anshan, 1,600 miles to the northeast.

For the first time, the B-29s performed the way they were intended. Eleven of the planes were unable to find Anshan, but the remaining 60 arrived over the city at 25,000 feet in perfect bombing weather, still in their tight four-plane diamonds, and dumped 160 tons of high explosives on the Showa plant. They were on target. Subsequent intelligence evaluation of the mission indicated that the coke ovens had suffered substantial damage.

Fighter opposition over Anshan was generally insignificant, and the antiaircraft fire, although heavy, was mostly inaccurate. Not all of the bombers, however, were able to escape without damage. Captain Robert T. Mills was leaving the target area when flak knocked out his No. 2 engine. Then the plane, crippled and losing altitude, was jumped by five fighters—one of them a captured American P-40 still bearing the insignia of the Chinese-American Composite Wing, Fourteenth Air Force. When the fighters knocked out another engine, Mills ordered his crew to bail out. Eight men parachuted safely, were sheltered by Chinese guerrillas and made it back to Chengtu a month later. Pilot Mills was not one of them.

A very different experience awaited Captain Howard Jarrell and the crew of a B-29 named *Ramp Tramp*. Jarrell's crew bombed Showa without incident, except for one near-miss burst of flak that at first appeared not to have harmed their plane. But when the engineer reduced power to bring them down from bombing altitude, the No. 3 engine ran wild. Jarrell was unable to feather the propeller, and even after its power was shut off the engine continued to windmill at 2,700 rpm's. As Jarrell later recalled, "The old bird came downhill so fast that in no time at all we were all alone, and getting more so."

Jarrell had a decision to make. He calculated that with the power settings necessary to keep the crippled *Ramp Tramp* airborne, in no more than four hours he would have to set the ship down, wherever he was. Four hours to the south lay the Japanese Army. Less than two hours northeastward lay Vladivostok in Soviet Siberia. Jarrell banked the *Ramp Tramp* around and set his course to the northeast.

In previous briefings the B-29 crews, contemplating possible places of refuge in time of trouble, had considered Siberia. It seemed logical enough. The Russians were not at war with Japan, but they were allies of the Americans in the war against Germany, and therefore at least fairly likely to be hospitable.

In case they were not, the *Ramp Tramp's* crew got busy and prudently shredded every piece of confidential paper on the aircraft—including coded memoranda and operating manuals. Since they could not jettison this trash without depressurizing the inside of the plane, they stuffed the shredded paper in the nose-wheel well, tucking it around the wheel; they figured that when the landing gear was lowered as they approached the airfield, the paper would scatter and blow away.

Jarrell sighted Vladivostok on schedule and thankfully began letting down toward a long concrete strip near the city. He never reached it. A covey of 14 Russian fighters came up to intercept the *Ramp Tramp;* they formed a huge circle and took turns firing bursts across the nose of the crippled plane. Finally, they herded it down to their own grass field near the Pacific Ocean, a strip woefully short for landing a B-29.

"Hanging on the props," Jarrell said later, recalling the episode, "we came over the fence at 90 miles an hour, chopped the throttles, touched down, hit the brakes and slid almost to the water's edge."

On the ground, Jarrell and his crew were cross-examined by a Russian general. He wanted to know what secret weapon—the scrap paper in the wheel well—they had dropped when the wheels came down; what kind of aircraft the *Ramp Tramp* was, how many the United States had, how many bombs it could carry; and what, above all, the airmen were doing in Siberia. Receiving no useful answers, the general at first scowled fiercely, but then he grinned and clapped Jarrell on the shoulder.

The Russians fed and housed the Americans and toasted them with vodka, but it was 11 days before they heeded Jarrell's request to be taken to the American consul, and about seven months before the crew got home, evacuated from the Soviet Union by way of Iran. They never saw their airplane again. However, a year or so later the Russians produced a new heavy bomber, described as the brainchild of A. N. Tupolev, the renowned Soviet aircraft designer; it looked very much like a B-29. "Since then," Captain Jarrell later reflected, "I have been known as the guy who gave Ivan the bird."

Along with Anshan—and Japan itself—a target high on the B-29 priority list was the Plaju refinery at Palembang, Sumatra. The big plant was believed to produce 22 per cent of Japan's fuel oil and a whopping 78 per cent of its aviation gasoline. The bait was tempting. However, Plaju had one drawback as a target: It was too far away for even the B-29s to reach from India. To bring the refinery within range, a decision was made to stage the planes through the island of Ceylon off the southeastern tip of India, about 1,900 miles from Palembang.

Provisions were made to extend four British airstrips on the island to accommodate the B-29s. As it turned out, only one strip was finished—at China Bay near the port city of Trincomalee—in time for the mission. Fifty-six Superfortresses were staged there early in August; on August 10 they roared down the long, specially built runway and took off for Sumatra.

The Palembang strike was the longest thus far undertaken by the B-29s. The round trip of nearly 4,000 miles would be pushing the far edge of their range. The crews approached the mission with misgivings. One pilot, Major Thomas Vaucher, had trouble believing what he heard when a briefing officer advised plane commanders that "General Arnold is prepared to sacrifice every B-29 on the mission to achieve success." Having dropped that bombshell, the briefing officer went on to say that because the target lay at the outer

limits of a B-29's capacity, extraordinary measures had been taken to ensure that the crews got back alive. These measures, he said, consisted of a British cruiser, three destroyers, three submarines and several flying boats stationed 600 miles out along the expected return route.

Upon reaching the vessels, the briefing officer told the crew members, "You should know whether you have fuel enough to make it all the way. If not, ditch near the ships and you'll be picked up."

The crews took off from Ceylon with this admonition in mind. Vaucher's plane almost did not make it into the air. Well down the runway, too late to abort, he noticed that flags along the strip were blowing in the same direction that he was going. Using standard procedure, he had taken off into the wind, but the wind had suddenly backed around. Vaucher was making a downwind takeoff in an aircraft loaded to its absolute limit—a circumstance that certainly called for the extra lift of an upwind takeoff. At the end of the runway, Vaucher hauled back on the wheel. The B-29 refused to lift; it roared across the apron and out over the

A heavily laden Superfortress taking off from Kiunglai airfield near Chengtu in August 1944 clears a too-typical hazard—a B-29 that crashed on takeoff. Part of the wrecked plane's tail has already been knocked off by the landing gear of a bomber that failed to climb quickly enough.

sea, flying only inches above the water. Still the plane would not lift, and a side gunner shouted that spray was flying onto his blister.

A small island loomed ahead. Vaucher was too low to dare banking around it and he could see the end of his life straight ahead. Then, just about to crash, the airplane began to climb. Later, Vaucher understood that flying over the little island was what saved him and his crew; a phenomenon called ground effect, a greater compression of air over land than over water, had furnished just enough extra lift to permit the straining plane to rise.

Of the 54 Superfortresses that got off at China Bay, 14 carried 1,000-pound mines to be dropped at strategic bends on the Musi River, which led from the sea to Palembang's port. The 40 remaining Superfortresses carried bombs intended for the Plaju refinery.

As it turned out, Palembang was another jinxed mission. One plane had been designated to reach the target area first and drop flares to illuminate the scene. The pilot of the flare plane aborted—there was no backup—and the bombers came up to the target blind. Thirty-one of them bombed either by radar or by sighting on fires set by earlier arrivals.

Despite the airmen's belief that they had inflicted considerable damage to the refinery, reconnaissance photographs later revealed that only one small building in the target area had been destroyed.

The planes that were carrying mines had better success. Briefed by a Dutch ship captain who was familiar with the port, they followed pilot lights up the Musi River at very low altitude and dropped the mines. Equipped with parachutes to prevent them from exploding on impact and to safeguard their fusing mechanisms, the mines were sowed at bends in the stream where a single wrecked vessel could block the

channel. It was ascertained later that the mines had sunk three ships, damaged four more and tied up traffic at the oil port for a month.

Major Vaucher, who had almost crashed on takeoff, lost an engine on the way home. By the time he raised the rescue flotilla in the middle of the Indian Ocean, he felt that he had things under control, and his aviator's instinct told him to stay with his plane as long as it would fly. If he did have to ditch, he would at least be nearer home. A few hours later, Vaucher landed at China Bay, his three remaining engines coughing on the last few gallons of fuel. One other plane on the mission ditched 90 miles short of China Bay and lost one of its crewmen at sea. The rest of the planes returned safely to Ceylon.

On the day of the Palembang strike—and 3,000 miles away—two dozen B-29s flew from Chengtu to Nagasaki, on Kyushu, and dropped 63 tons of incendiaries and fragmentation bombs on that city's shipyards. On the way home, Captain Stanley Brown got lost, ran low on fuel and looked for a place to make an emergency landing. He checked the condition of four airstrips near the Chinese front lines, chose one, and landed. The plane immediately became mired in mud. Nevertheless, Brown had made a lucky choice; the other three strips he had considered were held by the Japanese.

Brown radioed for protection and the 312th Fighter Wing, based 400 miles away at Fenghuangshan, dispatched a flight of P-40s. Japanese fighters got to Brown first. Strafing the B-29, they wrecked two engines before the P-40s arrived and shot down three of the Japanese. For almost two weeks the P-40s, flying daily patrols over the Japanese airstrips, kept the enemy at bay while new engines were flown in and the B-29 was stripped of all superfluous weight. Chinese laborers brought 4,500 railroad ties to pave an improvised takeoff strip through the mud. With his ship slimmed down to 86,000 pounds and only four crewmen aboard, Brown gunned his engines, bounced along the railroad ties and flew the B-29 home.

The next daylight mission was a disaster. With the approval of the Joint Chiefs, General Saunders scheduled a return to the coke ovens at Yawata on August 20. As had happened before, the trouble started with the takeoff. Although

Pillars of smoke from the Japanese city of Yawata rise toward a B-29, one of 61 that hit the steelworks there on August 20, 1944. The raiders met heavy resistance from enemy fighters; 14 of the B-29s were lost.

63

68 planes got up from three of the Chengtu fields, a plane taking off from a fourth field at Kiunglai crashed on the runway, blocking it. Later in the afternoon, with the runway cleared, eight planes took off tardily from Kiunglai; en route to the target, they joined five planes that were late in taking off from other bases.

The earlier groups had reached Yawata in daylight and ran into intense antiaircraft fire and aggressive opposition by fighters—Nakajima Ki-43s and two-seated Kawasaki Ki-45s. Of the first flight, 61 planes managed to bomb the target area. For the first time, a B-29 was rammed, probably deliberately. A fighter came in on a four-plane formation from dead ahead, banked tightly and knifed its wing vertically into the wing of the outboard B-29 in the formation. Both planes blew up; their debris smashed into the trailing B-29 of the formation and sent it spinning down.

Another Japanese fighter shot down the Superfortress flown by Colonel Richard Carmichael, a Texan who commanded the 462nd Group. Most of the crew bailed out, but the radio operator mysteriously failed to jump. One man, wounded before he jumped, fell to his death when his parachute failed to open. Japanese fighters strafed and killed another as he floated down.

Carmichael and the other seven members of the crew were taken prisoner. For months they were systematically starved and beaten, and kept in cages too small for lying down or even for sitting. When he was liberated at the end of the War, along with all his fellow crewmen, the muscular, 220-pound Texan emerged weighing 140 pounds.

Of the 13 late starters, 10 reached Yawata that night. One was so severely damaged by flak that the pilot took it toward Siberia, seeking refuge. The crewmen bailed out near Khabarovsk and, like Jarrell's crew before them, they were interned by the Russians. The raid had inflicted little damage on the coke ovens, and its cost was high: 14 B-29s lost and 95 airmen reported dead or missing.

The second strike at Yawata symbolized the frustrations of the XX Bomber Command. Although the unit's situation, at least in the airlift of gasoline and supplies to Chengtu, had improved under Saunders, Arnold was far from satisfied. Late in June he had reached out to the U.S. Eighth Air Force in Europe to recruit the commander he wanted: Major General Curtis E. LeMay, commanding officer of the 3rd Bombardment Division and at the age of 38 the youngest two-star general in the flying service.

LeMay reached B-29 headquarters at Kharagpur, India, late in August of 1944, bringing with him a reputation as a tough and innovative practitioner of strategic-bombing techniques. He had stopped off at Grand Island, Nebraska, in order to learn to fly a B-29, and he did not enjoy the experience. Later, LeMay would describe the B-29 as "the buggiest damn airplane that ever came down the pike."

Before leaving the United States, LeMay asserted that he could not run his new command properly until he had some personal knowledge of its problems; he wanted to fly missions himself. LeMay won Arnold's reluctant permission to fly one mission, and only one. For this single shot, he picked the first big raid on Saunders' schedule, a daylight return to the Showa works in Manchuria. "The main reason I chose it," LeMay said later, "was that the Japs were alleged to have their best fighters up there. If I was going to learn anything about repelling the enemy fighter attack, I ought to be along when and where the B-29s were up against a well-mounted and well-disciplined attack."

LeMay was aboard one of the 108 Superfortresses that took off from the fields at Chengtu on the morning of September 8, and his plane was one of the 95 that reached Anshan, flying at 25,000 feet in another spell of fine bombing weather. He did not get a chance to evaluate a first-class Japanese fighter attack, however, because the defenders failed to live up to their reputation. The Japanese tactics, LeMay later advised Saunders, "were stinkin'. They were up there, in a position to make a beautiful attack on us, and then they turned the wrong way! Only one guy got a fleeting shot but the rest of them never could catch up." He sounded almost regretful.

Although the tactics of the enemy may have disappointed him, General LeMay could not complain that his trip was dull. While flying over the target his aircraft was struck by antiaircraft fire; bits of flak hit the radio operator and the crew member in charge of the central fire-control system that coordinated the plane's defensive guns. "The radio operator was kind of crouched down, back there in that hole where he worked," LeMay later recounted in his memoirs, "and he had a most peculiar look on his face. He was examining his flak vest, and also examining the fragment of shell which had hit him. It was a slice of flak three and a half or four inches long, and the vest had stopped it cold. All he'd felt was a big sock on the back."

Free of other duties, LeMay went to check the wounded CFC, or central fire-control gunner. A fragment had hit the handle of a piece of equipment that the man had been holding "and just stung the hell out of CFC's hands," as LeMay described the situation. "The hide wasn't even broken. So that was *his* wound. After we got on the ground it was funny. It wasn't funny up there in the air."

The mission to Anshan had cost the XX Bomber Command four planes—through accidents on takeoff and forced landings in China—but only one man was killed. Compared with earlier B-29 performances, the strike was a success. After evaluating reconnaissance photographs, the analysts advised LeMay that the two Anshan strikes combined had cost the Showa works about 35 per cent of its coking output. Nevertheless, LeMay was not much more impressed by the showing of the Superfortresses than he had been by

the Japanese fighters. He decided that henceforth things would be done in a new way.

LeMay began by reprimanding his pilots. "You're just getting your feet wet over here," the general told them, and so far he considered their efforts amateurish. LeMay then challenged his men with an imposing list of changes to come. To get the most from the B-29s' sophisticated radar gear, bombardiers and radar operators would learn to work as a team, in good weather as well as bad, fixing the exact point of drop by simultaneous, synchronized tracking with both the cross hairs of the bombsight and the impulses, reflected from the ground, of radar.

The old four-plane diamond would be discarded, LeMay decreed, to be replaced by a 12-plane box formation that he had used successfully in Europe. The planes would not bomb individually; they would drop their bombs on signals from the lead planes, manned by the most expert fliers. Beginning immediately, lead crews were to undergo a period of intensive training.

Some pilots and engineers, said LeMay, had a lot to learn

With their Chinese helpers, a maintenance crew uses a makeshift tripod to remove a damaged bomber's propeller. The B-29 crash-landed returning from a raid on aircraft factories in Japan in October 1944.

A bizarre booby trap, the silhouette of a B-29 in trouble, painted on the ground with lime, is intended to lure American planes into the range of antiaircraft guns at an airfield in Indochina. Smoke appears to be billowing from one engine in the silhouette, which is scaled to look from the air like a plane flying at an altitude of several thousand feet. The Japanese hoped that B-29 pilots would descend to protect their sister ship; there is no record that anyone was ever deceived.

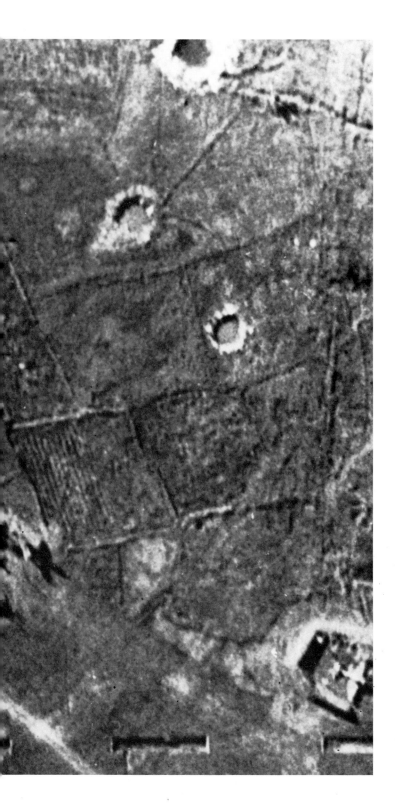

about conserving fuel. Citing examples, he pointed out that a crew that burned 7,600 gallons of gas on the Yawata run could surely profit by pointers from a crew that burned only 6,100 gallons on the same mission.

While LeMay hectored his fliers in early September 1944, the target analysts in Washington had been questioning the wisdom of their earlier priorities. Smashing steel plants in Manchuria and refineries in Sumatra appeared to lack purpose when one considered that Japan no longer had enough ships to carry the steel or tankers to transport the oil. Moreover, General Douglas MacArthur was about to invade the Philippines. Might it not be wise to ease his way by assigning the Superfortresses—in cooperation with carrier strikes by the Navy—to wreck the Japanese aircraft industry? The change in priorities was so ordered.

At this juncture it began to appear that either the XX Bomber Command's luck was changing or LeMay's retraining program was beginning to pay off. Or both. On October 14, the B-29s struck the Okayama aircraft complex on Formosa; the raid was in support of MacArthur's anticipated landings on Leyte in the Philippines. LeMay launched 130 Superfortresses, and each plane carried a bomb load of 6.8 tons, more than three times heavier than most previous loads. Using their new box formation, 104 of the planes arrived over the combined air base and assembly and repair plant at Okayama. The strike, added to carrier attacks on the two preceding days, left only six small buildings standing at the plant, flattened seven hangars and 16 other buildings on the air base and wrecked 116 aircraft on the ground.

The B-29 strike force's luck held up after the bombs were away. No planes were lost over the target. Twelve had to make emergency landings in friendly areas of China; but only one crashed, with the death of a single airman.

On October 25, with the gasoline stockpile partially replenished, LeMay again hurled his raiders at Japan's aircraft industry, this time against a factory at Omura on the island of Kyushu. The 59 planes that reached the target inflicted substantial damage. On the way home, however, the crew of a plane called the *Heavenly Body* experienced an ordeal of extraordinary dimensions.

The *Heavenly Body* was clear of the target and passing over Nagasaki when the pilot, Captain Jack Ledford, heard the CFC gunner shout that a fighter was coming in at two o'clock high. Seconds later, a 20mm shell exploded in the cabin and Ledford felt a smashing blow against his side. He did not know it yet, but he had a fractured hip bone and his side was sliced open so that one kidney was exposed. The cockpit was full of wreckage—smashed instruments and electrical gear, including the intercom. The *Heavenly Body* began losing altitude.

Ledford tried to reach the radio at the rear of the cabin to call for assistance. "Take the controls," he shouted to his copilot. "I'm going to contact the formation leader! We need help—and fast!"

Ledford never sent his message. As he struggled out of his seat, he saw that the flight engineer, Master Sergeant Harry Miller, was down and unconscious. A shell fragment had pierced his helmet and inflicted a serious head wound. Air inside the greenhouse cabin grew opaque with mist as the plane depressurized through the shell hole; the mist was caused by the rapid cooling of the air in the cabin, resulting in condensation.

Ledford called the bombardier to fit an oxygen mask on the unconscious Miller, while he himself took the engineer's station so as to keep the B-29 aloft. The fighter plane's attack had destroyed the No. 3 engine and now No. 1 was coughing, running out of fuel. At the engineer's post, the control panel was wrecked. Ledford dragged himself into the bomb bay to make manual adjustments to transfer fuel to engine No. 1. Then for an hour he nursed the faltering engines until, too weak to attend them any longer, he turned over the engineer's station to the tail gunner. Another crewman applied surgical dressings to Ledford's wound and offered him morphine to deaden the pain. Ledford refused the relief; he wanted to stay alert.

Ledford intended to land the *Heavenly Body* on an emergency field in an area of China unoccupied by the Japanese, where he hoped to find medical help for Miller. But the plane kept drifting lower as the fuel gauges dropped. It was evident that the crippled B-29 would not be able to manage the 12,000-foot altitude needed to clear the mountains that lay between it and the emergency field. Ledford advised three gunners to bail out to lighten ship. They did—and lived to tell about it—but their departure was not enough. It became clear that every man would have to jump.

Bailing out might save all but the unconscious Harry Miller. Sergeant Gilbert Rodeneal had an idea. There was a spare parachute aboard; they could tie one of its shroud lines to Miller's rip-cord ring and drop the unconscious man through the nose-wheel well, using the line to jerk the rip cord when Miller was clear of the plane.

So far, so good—but Captain Ledford was worried about what would happen once the men reached the ground. "I'm going along with Harry," he said. "I want to be near him when he lands."

They bailed out. The shroud-line trigger worked and Miller's parachute opened. But despite Ledford's efforts to stay near him, they drifted apart. Miller vanished behind a low hill. Ledford landed in a rice paddy and staggered out of it, stunned and weak, covered with mud and blood. A group of curious Chinese approached, but they could not understand as Ledford kept repeating, "*Ding hao!* American flier!" using the only Chinese phrase he knew. He desperately wanted to send someone to look for Miller, but could think of no way to communicate until a small man, wearing spectacles, elbowed his way to Ledford's side, and introduced himself: "Mr. Yung, village postmaster. Speak good English."

"Where am I?" Ledford asked.

"Seventy miles from Laohokow. Five hundred miles from Chungking, eight miles Japs close by," the postmaster said.

"Are the others all right—the wounded man, too?"

"Wounded one in hospital. Others on way over here."

The town physician, who was Japanese-trained, arrived and dressed Ledford's wound. Through the postmaster, the doctor voiced his opinion that the pilot was in critical need of an operation. At first Ledford declined, hoping it might be possible to have an American doctor flown in, primarily to take care of Miller. But when the crew had assembled and the grievousness of their situation became fully evident, he changed his mind. Miller, it turned out, was already dead—having died shortly after landing. But under the care of the rural Chinese physician, Jack Ledford recovered; once he was able to travel, the Chinese made arrangements to transport the pilot and his crew back to their base.

For the most part, as they showed in their treatment of Ledford's crew, the people of the Chinese countryside controlled by the Nationalists under Chiang Kai-shek were both

AN UNEXPECTED HAVEN

The unstinting help and hospitality accorded downed B-29 aircrews by Chinese Communists came as a pleasant surprise to the Americans. While the Communists under Mao Tse-tung waged war on the Japanese, they also were at war with Chiang Kai-shek's Nationalist government, which the United States supported.

Late in 1944, a B-29's crew bailed out over contested territory after a strike on Japanese-held Nanking. Major Francis B. Morgan and four other survivors were given refuge by Mao's men. For the 16 weeks that Morgan and his companions spent with the Communists awaiting evacuation, the guerrillas did everything possible to make them feel at home, including serving elaborate meals on Thanksgiving and on Christmas. When the airmen finally were escorted overland to rendezvous with an evacuation plane, they were greeted as heroes in Communist-held villages.

In fact, the chief danger to Morgan's men and other rescued airmen seemed to be from the Nationalists, who refused to negotiate with the Communists even for the airmen's return. The American evacuation planes, landing at Communist-held fields, whisked the men out of China, concerned that Chiang's secret police might kill the rescued fliers lest they speak well of their treatment at Mao's hands.

Crowds displaying exuberant banners lettered in English greet rescued American airmen upon their arrival in a Communist-controlled town in China.

An invitation in Chinese and English bids Major Francis B. Morgan to dine with Communist regional-government officials.

While on his way out of China in 1945, a bearded Major Morgan is escorted by one of Mao Tse-tung's division commanders.

hospitable and generous. They sheltered B-29 crews and did their best to escort them to safety. But General LeMay, conscious that part of northwest China was under Communist control, thought he might improve the overall prospects for rescue by making overtures to the Red leader Mao Tse-tung, in remote Yenan. LeMay sent an envoy to Yenan in a C-47 transport with a load of electronic equipment and orders to seek permission to establish a radio station in Mao's stronghold. The Communist leader turned out to be cooperative. The station was quickly set up and tied in with Mao's own network, so that word of the whereabouts of downed American airmen could be relayed quickly to Chengtu.

Once the relationship was established, LeMay sent Mao another plane loaded with modern medical supplies.

"I should not pretend that this was all sweetness and light on my part," LeMay subsequently recalled, "and that I was making so free with our U.S. taxpayers' sulfanilamide that I needed to furnish it to any Communists, Chinese or otherwise. But I wanted to be damn sure that there were medical supplies in those areas when my own people came in, busted up or wounded."

The long-distance relationship between the fire-eating American general and the leader of the Chinese Communists continued to flourish. They exchanged letters and gifts: a Japanese samurai sword to LeMay, a pair of binoculars to Mao. When LeMay suggested it might be a good idea to improve and extend the Yenan airstrip, Mao approved and even spent one day a week working on the project himself.

"We were able to keep track of a lot of our crews this way," LeMay wrote. "I remember one bunch: The B-29 went down on the south shore of the Yellow Sea. It was in a region more or less controlled by Mao's people, but right next to the Japs. Next thing you knew there was a pitched battle going, over that airplane and crew. As I remember it, the Communists rescued all the crew except one man, who fell into the hands of the Japanese."

For all the progress LeMay had made in China, Arnold was delighted when American forces secured the Mariana Islands in late summer of 1944. Even before the fighting stopped, air bases long planned for the islands were rapidly being built on Saipan, Tinian and Guam. By late November, more than 100 B-29s were stationed on Saipan.

With the bases on the Marianas in hand, the difficult operation out of India and China could be wound down. LeMay had concluded that "there can be no sustained and intensive effort by any bombers who have to feed their own fuel to themselves." General Chennault also wanted the Superfortresses removed from China; they could do almost nothing for him tactically, and at the same time they nearly monopolized the tonnage flown over the Hump that he needed for his Fourteenth Air Force.

Until the following March, however, B-29 activity continued in the old bases around Calcutta and Chengtu. When sufficient gasoline was available in Chengtu, the XX Bomber Command ran strikes against airfields on Formosa, against the aircraft plants at Mukden in Manchuria and Omura in Japan, and against shipping at Nagasaki. From India, the bombers struck at Japanese targets all over southeast Asia: Rangoon in Burma, Bangkok in Thailand, Saigon, Camranh Bay and Pnompenh in Indochina, and Kuala Lumpur and Singapore in Malaya.

The first strike against Singapore was a most unusual mission—an extreme-range, 3,800-mile round trip from India. The prime target, only 10 feet wide and 200 feet long, was the gate to the King George VI Graving Dock, the largest dry dock in the Orient. The B-29s struck on November 5. One bomb hit a ship inside the dock and another, exploding within 50 feet of the aiming point, strained the gate enough to let in a flood of water that put the dock out of commission for three months.

Three months later Lord Mountbatten, the overall theater commander, ruled the King George VI Graving Dock out of bounds for subsequent attack; he wanted it usable when and if the British returned to Singapore.

The last raids out of India and China produced instances of heroism—and avoidable tragedy. At 21,000 feet over the Mukden aircraft plant on December 7, with the B-29s under heavy fighter attack, the open bomb-bay doors jammed on a plane piloted by Captain Carl T. "Shorty" Hull. Without a parachute, but carrying a tool kit and a portable oxygen bottle from which to breathe, Technical Sergeant Nathan Dyer crawled into the gale whistling through the open bay. He worked there for 40 minutes in temperatures of –42° F., and, though his hands grew so numb that they were nearly immobilized, he managed to disconnect a faulty motor from the front-bomb-bay doors and replace it with a good one from the rear bay. Dyer won a Silver Star and promotion from gunner to flight engineer.

Not all the episodes had happy endings. Committed to a raid on Rangoon on December 14, the crewmen protested bitterly and some even threatened mutiny. They had made the discovery that their bomb bays were loaded with 1,000-pound bombs slung just above instantaneously fused 500-pounders packed with a new, extremely powerful and unstable explosive. If two of the new bombs should happen to collide in the air close to the plane after the drop, the men argued, they would all be blown out of the sky. They took off reluctantly after the group commander threatened them with courts-martial.

The apprehension of the crewmen was justified. Lieutenant Marion Burke was navigating the lead aircraft of an 11-plane formation that came over Rangoon through medium flak and unloaded its bombs. The plane shuddered violently and Burke heard the tail gunner scream, "My God! The sky has turned red."

What they had feared had happened. Bombs released by a nearby plane had collided and gone off, blowing up the plane and showering the rest of the formation with meteorites of debris. Three other planes were ravaged, including Burke's. He turned to his navigation table. It had vanished. He looked at the radioman, Richard Montgomery. His left hand had been nearly chopped off and hung by a thread of tendon. The flight engineer yelled, "Number three's gone!" The No. 3 engine had not merely stopped; it had been torn completely out of the wing and now the wing was crumpling. It was time to bail out.

Burke's crew landed in the middle of a Japanese Army training camp and all the airmen were captured. From British prisoners who had watched the raid from the ground they learned that two of the stricken B-29s had crashed in the city proper, one falling on a loaded troop train and killing 700 Japanese soldiers. The British prisoners of war were detailed to bury the dead.

One of the last strikes staged by LeMay out of Chengtu was a raid on Hankow, in northeast China, the major supply depot for Japan's China-based armies. For months, General Chennault had been urging an incendiary strike on Hankow in order to slow the powerful land offensive the Japanese

had launched in the spring of 1944. The Japanese had taken Kweilin in November and were closing in on Kunming, threatening the bases of Chennault's Fourteenth Air Force. Chennault had the support of General Albert Wedemeyer, who had replaced General Stilwell in command of U.S. forces in the China area. LeMay, however, had a long list of targets he considered more important than Hankow; he questioned the mission—and Wedemeyer's authority to order the B-29s anywhere. Wedemeyer eventually went to LeMay's superiors—General Arnold and the Joint Chiefs—to get approval for the mission, and despite confusion that was brought about by abrupt and unexpected changes in the timing of the raid, it was a success. The bombers hit Hankow on December 18 and burned out almost 50 per cent of the target area.

The incendiaries that set fire to Hankow were loaded in the B-29s in clusters that if not properly packed were as dangerous to the planes and their crews as the explosives used on the Rangoon raid. Three fire-bomb clusters jammed in their racks in the open bomb bay of one B-29 over Hankow. Staff Sergeant John D. Austin climbed into the bay and was terrified to discover that the fuse spinners, propeller-like mechanisms on the bomb noses that were supposed to whirl in the air during the drop and arm the bombs, had somehow come unlocked. They were whirling in the blast of wind that was roaring through the bays. Knowing that the bombs would be ready to detonate in 35 seconds, Sergeant Austin locked the whirling spinners with his hands. Next he managed to nudge a manual lever that dumped all the bombs out of the bay. Then, from relief and a lack of oxygen, the sergeant fainted.

Less than a month after the Hankow strike, in January 1945, General Arnold again reached out for LeMay, ordering the burly flier to take over the XXI Bomber Command in the Mariana Islands.

Operating from the new fields on Tinian, Saipan and Guam, the XXI Bomber Command was having problems living up to Arnold's expectations. "All we'd heard was that the new B-29s over there in the Marianas didn't seem to be earning any merit badges," LeMay wrote. And he paraphrased the challenge set by Arnold: "Here's another great big bear for you. Come and grab it by the tail."

AN ISLAND TRANSFORMED

An aerial view of unfinished Northwest Field on Guam in early June of 1945 shows the jungle bulldozed to create runways and taxiways for B-29 bombers.

A SUPERBASE RISING ON GUAM

No sooner had U.S. amphibious forces captured the Marianas in the summer of 1944 than a crash program got under way to transform the islands into forward bases for the B-29s. The installations on Guam—at 216 square miles the largest of the Marianas—were conceived as the equals of any in the United States, a sprawling complex of paved airstrips, hardstands and taxiways, maintenance and supply depots and a headquarters facility.

From the outset, however, the builders on Guam had problems more reminiscent of a Western frontier settlement than a modern air base. Several thousand Japanese who had refused to surrender still roamed the island's dense jungles. More a nuisance than a threat, they had to be hunted down by American patrols—and a few managed to hide out for years. Torrential rains made a mockery of construction schedules; some mornings, the men woke in their tents to find water lapping at their cots. But the Army Air Forces engineers and their Seabee partners responded to the challenge. Officers and men worked side by side in the tropical heat. Together they bulldozed the jungle aside to make room for almost eight million square feet of runways, and covered an additional 600,000 square feet of coral with storage and maintenance buildings.

By February of 1945, Guam's North Field was in operation, to be followed by Northwest Field in June. By then everything that the B-29s needed, short of a complete engine overhaul, was in place. The construction teams found time as well to build churches, theaters and baseball diamonds, and the civilian population on the island shifted from its prewar agrarian economy to providing services for the U.S. military.

Despite the jungle holdouts, the War sometimes seemed very far away from Guam—a place where a general could fly into a rage because the headquarters ice-cream freezer was out of order. But once the B-29s started flying in February, the harsh reminders of combat were frequent enough: a B-29 crashing on takeoff, or returning with engines shot out and wounded men aboard—or not coming back at all.

Assisted by a Guam civilian (left rear), a sign painter from the U.S. Navy adds an admonition to banana poachers to his growing stock of placards.

Seabees on Guam assemble a Quonset hut, a prefabricated structure of corrugated metal named for Quonset Point, Rhode Island, where it originated.

A crew of Seabees watches as a crane operator lowers a tractor into line at the salvage yard on Guam, where it will wait its turn for reconditioning.

MIRACLE OF THE "BIG SCOOPS"

A Japanese captured during the invasion of the Marianas steadfastly maintained that his countrymen would soon return and throw the Americans out. But as the weeks went by and he watched the new airfields materialize as if by magic, the prisoner's optimism evaporated. Asked why, he replied bitterly: "It's the big scoops!"

The scoops were on the business end of bulldozers and power shovels—supplemented by cranes, trucks and carryalls—that Americans shipped into the islands in a seemingly endless flow. At the peak of construction, more than 1,000 such machines were running day and night.

Some of the equipment was imported to solve special problems: In one instance, heavy-duty drills were needed to bore the 12,000 holes required for a single gigantic dynamite blast to break up the coral for a runway. And the main repair depot on Guam had to be fitted with a small factory for the rehabilitation of truck and airplane tires, shredded by the sharp coral surfaces of the islands.

Not all the machinery employed in the Marianas came ready-made. In order to move 2.6-ton B-29 engines from flight line to repair shop, construction engineers improvised their own trolleys—using wheels scavenged from abandoned amphibious landing craft.

A bulldozer attacks a stubborn tangle of stumps during the building of Guam's North Field, while in the background a ground crew services a B-29.

Rubber molds line the center of Guam's tire shop, where a dozen experienced workers and their trainees recapped and repaired 3,000 tires every month. Sets of B-29 tires were good for only 10 to 15 landings.

At an outdoor dump, ordnance men draw bombs for a mission from a stockpile of high explosives.

Mechanics check B-29 engines at North Field. Maintenance done on Guam tripled an engine's use before it had to be sent to the mainland for overhaul.

In June of 1945, with facilities fully operational, an overflow of supplies is stacked outside the Quonset huts that constituted Guam's vast storage area.

A PROBLEM OF SUPPLY

The fighting for control of Guam still raged when the first U.S. Navy transport arrived carrying maintenance gear for B-29s. A harbor master, concerned only with combat logistics, barked at the vessel's captain: "I'll give you 24 hours to get that ship out of here!" The captain unloaded his cargo in a hurry. But with no one to receive it, the gear that soon would be badly needed was abandoned in the jungle.

The loss was the earliest in a series of supply problems to plague the B-29 units that arrived in the Marianas two months later. From the outset, the Navy shipped in abundant food and fuel and—usually— enough bombs. But replacement parts to keep the planes working were low on the Navy's priority list and the AAF had to fly them in from the United States.

The Navy's selection of Guam as a major forward base contributed to a shortage of service troops and construction crews as well as supplies. Even after the maintenance depot was completed in April 1945, there was not enough shelter and mounds of equipment had to be left outdoors, exposed to both rain and dust.

By early summer, however, a logistics system for the B-29s had been forged out of experience and sweat. On any given day, only two planes in 1,000 were likely to be grounded for lack of a crucial part.

THE STURDY HUT OF MANY USES

Guam in 1945 became a veritable metropolis, inhabited at its peak by 65,000 Air Forces and 78,000 Navy personnel and 59,000 Marines. Island life centered on the ubiquitous Quonset hut, which provided living, storage and work space.

The round-roofed buildings, based on the British Nissen hut of World War I, were usually erected in their simplest form —corrugated sheets of metal over arched ribs. Designed to be rigid, they could withstand even hurricane-force winds.

The metal huts often became unbearably hot inside, but their adaptability and portability made them indispensable. And for special purposes, they could be insulated: Guam had 68,000 cubic feet of refrigerated Quonsets for the storage of such perishable supplies as medicine and food.

The Quonsets' uses were legion. One served as Guam's bank; another housed a crucial link to the outside world—the western Pacific's busiest post office. The Navy built a two-story version for its fleet headquarters, and when a herd of cows was imported to provide precious milk for military hospitals throughout the Pacific, their barns, naturally, were Quonsets.

Inside Guam's main post office, mail is sorted for distribution to the Marianas and other Far East bases, and to units of the U.S. Pacific Fleet.

In a Guam Quonset hut, communications specialists man a bank of Teletype consoles connecting B-29 headquarters with other air bases on the Marianas.

An off-duty airman shaves (foreground) while his fellow crew members pass the time in the cramped quarters of their Quonset-hut barracks.

80

Preparing dinner, an AAF cook stirs a kettle of corn. Food was plentiful, but anything fresh was a luxury; some men tried growing vegetables.

A sailor who was a farmer in civilian life forks feed into troughs for dairy cows, part of a small herd of livestock that was sent to Guam in late 1944.

Military personnel and civilians patronize Guam's Navy-operated bank, one of two such banks in the Pacific theater. The other was on Samoa.

The lights of Guam glitter in the Pacific twilight. The picture was taken from a hill overlooking installations supporting the North Field complex.

An asphalt-laying machine spreads blacktop on a smooth base of crushed coral. A porous and self-draining substance, coral made an ideal roadbed.

Looking like a nestful of enormous hornets, B-29s sit poised on their hardstand

ACRES OF ASPHALT AND A FOUR-LANE HIGHWAY

Once completed, the wartime transformation of Guam was almost beyond imagination. An American possession until the Japanese captured it two days after Pearl Harbor, it had been a sleepy tropical outpost—with a population of 22,000 and an economy based on copra, coffee, tobacco and bananas. The high points of its week were the refueling stops of Pan American's flying boats on their Pacific crossings.

By 1945, only Guam's tropical climate had not changed—giant zinnias planted there and in the other Marianas grew larger than any ever seen in North America.

Guam's quiet harbor was bursting with ships—some waiting days to be unloaded—and 100 miles of paved roads crisscrossed the island. Route 1, which linked busy North Field (below) with AAF headquarters, boasted four asphalt lanes that were wider—and more congested—than contemporary U.S. highways.

Most dramatically, Guam represented the fully developed warmaking potential of the United States. From North Field alone in the final six months of the War, the B-29s flew 6,339 sorties to Japan and dropped 34,494 tons of bombs.

at North Field. Six miles of taxiways linked the hardstands to the runways at upper left, and the finished air base could accommodate more than 200 planes.

TENSE HOURS IN AN ISOLATED WORLD

The men who flew the B-29s to Japan and back had the most rigorous—if not the most dangerous—duty of any combat crews in World War II. A mission from China typically took 16 hours and covered 3,200 miles; a strike westward from the Mariana Islands consumed 15 hours and traversed 3,000 miles. For the 11 men in each Superfortress, the flights were an eternity of tension broken by moments of mortal danger.

On each mission there were two brief periods when the airmen were in certain danger. Everyone was apprehensive about the takeoff, a lumbering 40-second roll down the 8,500-foot runway with a full load of fuel and bombs that required the synchronized efforts of pilot, copilot and flight engineer to coax the 65-ton machine aloft. The other time of extreme hazard—perhaps five or 10 minutes long—occurred when the plane reached the target area and came under attack from antiaircraft gunners and enemy fighter pilots—some of whom were willing to commit suicide to bring the bombers down.

Apart from these perilous moments, the flights were exercises in endurance. Considering the time spent in briefings before and debriefings after the mission, the crews could count on almost 24 consecutive hours of duty. And despite all the tensions, it was often difficult to remain alert. Chronic drowsiness was the enemy of every Superfortress crew, and the airmen fought it, not always successfully, with such stimulants as Benzedrine and coffee. "My first experience sleeping was also the last," recalled a pilot. "When I woke, I found the entire crew asleep and the ship ghosting along on autopilot." To remain awake, he inhaled pure oxygen through his mask and listened to Tokyo Rose on the radio.

For all the tension, boredom and fear, the long missions afforded some uniquely rewarding moments. Noting that the flight nearly always included a sunrise and a sunset, one pilot later wrote: "The variations in light and color in the Pacific were fantastically beautiful. They softened our own strain and our anxieties."

Moments before departure, a B-29 crew on Guam lines up for a briefing by their pilot-commander. Life jackets were required during the mission.

Cruising above a bank of broken clouds, a waist gunner looks out through his plexiglass blister at the B-29 flying alongside in loose formation.

A SUPREME TEST OF NAVIGATION

The navigator of a B-29 flying from the Marianas faced an unprecedented challenge: guiding his aircraft over vast expanses of open water to a target 1,500 miles away, and home again to a tiny island base. He relied on a combination of dead reckoning (charting his position by course, speed, time and drift caused by wind), celestial navigation employing the sun and stars when the weather permitted, and reports from the radar operator.

If Japan was covered by clouds, the radar operator had another task when the plane was close to its destination: to locate the target for the bombardier by studying the radar reflections on his viewing screen.

Bent over a desk behind the pilot, a navigator uses pencil and calipers to plot his plane's position against his preflight plan on a Mercator's chart.

A radar operator stares at a small circular screen on which reflected radio waves reveal the outlines of land masses and the intended targets below.

A flight of B-29s on its way to Japan from the Marianas flies above a carpet of almost unbroken clouds—a condition commonly encountered on such missions

A FEARSOME ARRAY OF DEFENSIVE SYSTEMS

Until fighter escorts became available, the B-29s had to rely solely on their own defensive armament to beat back enemy attacks—and the combined firepower of 10 to 12 heavy machine guns on each plane could be devastating.

Three pairs of guns firing from the B-29's waist and tail usually discouraged attacks from the rear, so many Japanese fighters chose to attack head on, closing at a dizzying rate of more than 600 mph. Then a B-29's best response was a quick change of direction and a burst from the four guns in the two forward turrets. In later models, the upper turret was fitted with two extra guns, for a total of six throwing a curtain of lead ahead of the plane.

A gunner checks the gun sight at his blister in the plane's midsection.

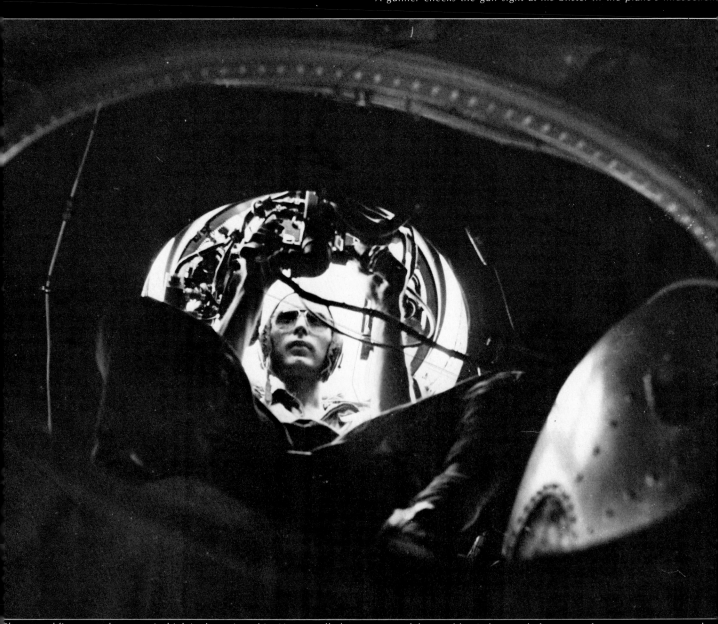

The central fire-control gunner sits high in the waist cabin. He controlled a master panel that could switch control of any turret from one gunner to another.

Protected by thick bulletproof glass in his small rear compartment, a tail gunner adjusts his sight, which controls a pair of .50-caliber machine guns.

Framed in one of a B-29's cockpit windows, a Japanese fighter screams in for a frontal attack during a daylight raid on Yawata on August 20, 1944.

A pilot bites his tongue in tension as he steers his plane into the bomb run.

From the nose, the bombardier sees the target, smoking from earlier hits.

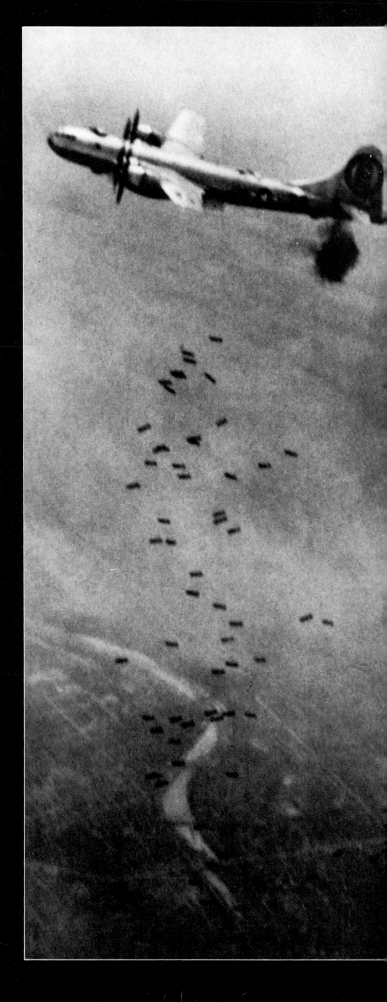

90 SECONDS THAT SEEMED FOREVER

The bombing run itself took at least 90 seconds, and for the crew, they were an eternity. Near the target, the assigned bombing altitude was fed into the automatic pilot; the bombardier was responsible for holding the plane's heading steady, controlling its course through his bombsight, while the pilot kept a constant speed.

The bombardier used the bombsight, an instrument that combined optical aiming with a calculating mechanism, to determine the exact moment to release the bombs. But a plane flying straight and level became easier for enemy ground defenses to track, and a B-29 was never more vulnerable than when it was locked on course during a bomb run—illuminated by searchlights and with flak exploding around it. For all hands, the cry "Bombs away!" came as an immense relief.

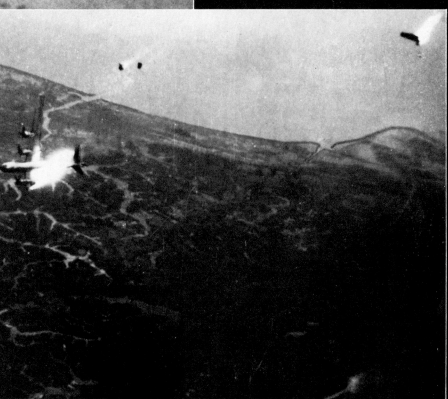

Victim of a direct hit by enemy flak, a B-29 explodes in midair during a bomb run in June 1945 over aircraft factories in Nagoya.

As flak bursts around them, a formation of B-29s simultaneously release clusters of incendiary bombs over a Japanese city

Its right outboard engine trailing smoke, a battle-damaged B-29 begins the difficult journey home

Getting a B-29 home, once the bombs were away, was seldom a joy ride. Any number of problems—from bad weather to mechanical failures—could turn the return flight into a struggle. If the plane was damaged, nursing it over 1,500 miles of ocean or enemy land became a nightmare.

Fuel was precious in the best of circumstances, with reserve for a scant half hour's extra flying time. Gasoline in shot-up tanks had to be quickly transferred to sound tanks. And compensating for a dead engine required great skill on the part of pilot and flight engineer.

If damage was serious enough, the crew would have to bail out or make an emergency landing, in which case their survival often depended on how close they were to home. Rescue parties could not move far through Japanese-occupied lands, and air-sea searches initially had limited range. Capture usually meant arduous imprisonment or death. However, the B-29s were remarkably sturdy planes, and many that seemed destined to ditch limped back to their bases with one or two engines gone, with gaping holes in the wings or with half the tail blown off.

Once it raised the field, a damaged aircraft had priority in landing. But the others had to cope with a sky congested by returning planes. The solution was to beat the crowd if you could: "There was always an informal competition to get home first," said one bomber pilot. "After leaving Japan, it was every man for himself."

Enduring the long flight back to base, the gunners snack or sleep or watch the radar operator, who is still monitoring his scope in the midship cabin.

Wearing his Mae West, a returning crewman naps in the pressurized tubular crawlway connecting the B-29's forward and waist compartments.

Returning Superfortresses approach Guam's North Field. In sight of home, pilots still had to worry about their tanks running dry before their turn came to land.

3

The capture of the Mariana Islands in the western Pacific in June and July of 1944 sealed the doom of the Japanese Empire. Such was the judgment of Prince Higashikuni, commander in chief of Japan's Home Defense Headquarters. After the War, Higashikuni told Allied interrogators that the arrival of B-29s at the newly established bases on the Marianas had for all practical purposes put an end to his nation's hope of victory.

"We had nothing in Japan," the Prince said, "that we could use against such a weapon. From the point of view of the Home Defense Command, we felt that the War was lost and we said so."

The Prince's pessimism was well founded. Guam, Saipan and Tinian in the Marianas, lying 1,300 miles southeast of Tokyo, were within B-29 range of every militarily significant portion of Japan. At particular risk was the highly industrial island of Honshu, which was also the site of the capital.

This, of course, had been the objective of American strategic planners from the outset of the western Pacific campaign. And proponents of the B-29 greeted the capture of the islands with elation. Possession of the Marianas at last gave the senior officers of the Twentieth Air Force a clear opportunity to prove the overall merits of the Superfortress as a strategic weapon—not only to the enemy, but to skeptics within the U.S. armed forces.

Yet as matters turned out, misfortune continued to dog the Superfortress even when it was operating from bases that were tailor-made for it. Persistent trouble with the engines, compounded by unforeseen weather problems over Honshu, prolonged and intensified the B-29s' frustrating inability to deliver bombing results of the dramatic sort demanded by Army Air Forces' chief Hap Arnold.

The upshot was a crisis in the fate of the great bomber—and in the careers of its partisans—exacerbated by the success of the U.S. Navy, whose carrier-based fighters and light bombers hit Japan in a series of raids in February. Overcoming the crisis would require radical measures that would include the denial of hallowed strategic doctrine and the turning of the B-29s' original mission profile upside down.

Mop-up squads were still rousting Japanese snipers out of Saipan's rugged terrain on October 12, 1944, when the first gleaming Superfortress droned out of the sky to land on the

A ROOST IN THE MARIANAS

island's Isley Field. The bomber, jauntily dubbed *Joltin' Josie*, received a VIP welcome from American personnel on Saipan, some of whom were still working on the runways and the aircraft parking areas, called hardstands. The facilities were intended to accommodate the newcomer and 179 additional B-29s from the 73rd Bombardment Wing of the XXI Bomber Command.

So far, little more than the intention was manifest: The runway length specified for a B-29 was 8,500 feet, but the only runway that was suitable for B-29s was just 7,000 feet long, of which barely 5,000 feet had been paved. Except for a bomb storage dump and a few tank trucks to haul fuel, there were no other facilities—no living quarters, no repair shops, no command complex. However, preparing the base was only part of the Army Air Forces' problems.

At first, the mere fact that the B-29s now were based in the Marianas made their mission seem clear, and eminently practical. In theory, they could be adequately supplied by ship without the perilous and wasteful flight over the Hump to the Chengtu bases in China. And from their island bases they could operate according to the tenets of massive strategic bombing: Flying above the reach of most fighter planes and antiaircraft fire, they would hold formation and systematically obliterate Japan's war industry with precision bombing. Their attacks would be guided by the Norden bombsight, backed up by the B-29's radar navigational system, designated APQ-13.

The responsibility for making this concept work rested on the man who had landed the *Joltin' Josie* on Saipan. He was Brigadier General Haywood S. Hansell Jr., nicknamed Possum, newly chosen by General Arnold to run the XXI Bomber Command. Hansell came to the job with impressive credentials. He had long been a disciple of the heavy-bomber theories of Brigadier General William "Billy" Mitchell, an early champion of an independent air force and of the power of strategic bombing. Shortly before the United States went to war, Hansell had served on a four-officer board that had been set up to advise President Roosevelt on the number and types of combat aircraft the nation would need to win the War, if engaged.

After Pearl Harbor, Hansell commanded a heavy-bomber wing in the European theater. Brought into the B-29 program by General Arnold, Hansell helped to plan the Superfortress deployment in India and China. Until he was assigned to the Marianas, he had been Arnold's chief of staff for the Twentieth Air Force, the command center for all B-29 operations. It was Hansell's conviction that the only proper role for the Superfortress was high-level precision bombing from formation.

Hansell had been among the first to identify the Mariana Islands as the best potential home for the big bombers, so his assignment there satisfied a certain logic. Yet he knew that the job facing the XXI Bomber Command was formidable. It was still a long trip to Tokyo and back, 15 or more hours in the air, virtually all of it over empty ocean. Planes that left the Marianas for Japan had to get back on their own—or be written off. The nearest alternate airfield in American hands was Kwajalein, 1,200 miles to the southeast—much too far away to be reached from Japan.

Planes that failed to make it home, either because of battle damage or all-too-frequent mechanical breakdowns, were doomed to come down at sea. To recover downed crews, an air-sea rescue organization composed of submarines, destroyers and Navy and Army Air Forces planes was coming into being but was still far from complete.

The Marianas presented problems of their own. Plans for the island bases called for five operational fields—one on Saipan, two on Tinian and two on Guam. Additional facilities were to include a maintenance depot on Guam. But in the confusion of combat during the American recapture of Guam, the maintenance depot's complicated and expensive equipment was inadvertently dumped in the jungle, where it rusted and rotted for weeks before anyone had time to think about recovering it.

The first runway at Isley Field on Saipan was completed to its full 8,500 feet on October 19. But it had a taxiway at only one end, which meant that planes could take off and land in only one direction, and the timetable for improving the airfields had been delayed—primarily by the fierce Japanese resistance.

Yet the B-29s kept coming, a few more every day. On the 20th of October, Brigadier General Emmett "Rosey" O'Donnell arrived to take command of the 73rd Wing, and immediately sat down with Hansell to plan the campaign against the home islands. In Washington it had been decided that obliterating the Japanese aircraft industry would win the War sooner than destroying the steel plants that had originally been the prime targets of bombing missions from China. One flaw in this concept was that nobody on the target-selection committee or in the XXI Bomber Command knew much about the disposition or defenses of Japan's aircraft manufacturers.

"We had almost no information upon which to base the initial raids," Hansell said later. "We had to go to Japan to get it." On November 1, the photoreconnaissance plane nicknamed *Tokyo Rose* took off in clear weather and returned 14 hours later, after spending about 30 minutes of that time taking pictures over Tokyo.

The *Tokyo Rose's* principal mission was to pinpoint the location of the Nakajima engine works in the suburb of Musashino, about 11 miles northwest of downtown Tokyo. The works at Musashino was an inviting target because it turned out 30 to 40 per cent of the military-aircraft engines produced in Japan.

Hansell scheduled a strike on the Musashino factory for mid-November, to coordinate with an attack by Admiral

William F. "Bull" Halsey's carrier air groups. When the Navy operation was canceled—most of the available carrier planes were committed to covering the invasion of the Philippines—Hansell decided to attempt the mission anyway. He was unwilling to have it appear that his B-29s needed outside help, and in fact was eager to go it alone.

Planning the Tokyo raid, however, was an anxious time for Hansell. He wanted to mount a high-altitude, daylight, precision operation in formation. That was the doctrine he believed in. But then, forwarded from Arnold, came a letter written to Twentieth Air Force headquarters by Lieut. General George C. Kenney, chief of MacArthur's air forces, forecasting disaster. If the B-29s went over Tokyo in daylight and in formation, Kenney predicted, they would be shot down like so many clay pigeons. The warning from such an experienced air officer gave Hansell pause. And a note appended by Arnold was little help: If Hansell thought he could bring off the raid, "Good luck and God be with you."

Hansell then received a disturbing handwritten message from his senior wing commander, General O'Donnell, the Brooklyn-born Irishman who would be leading the flight; it

said the mission as planned had little chance to succeed. Hansell summoned O'Donnell, who rattled off a list of the problems—unfinished training, distance to target, untrustworthy engines. O'Donnell suggested that it would be the better part of valor to dispatch this first raid at night, in flights of single planes, instead of in formation in the revealing light of day.

Hansell appreciated the dangers as keenly as O'Donnell and the others. But he also sensed the larger consequences of retreat. If he switched to a safer, more cautious course he would be admitting that the Twentieth Air Force could not, or dared not, perform the strategic mission for which it had been created. O'Donnell finally agreed that the Tokyo mission was the kind of job they had come to the Pacific to do.

By early November, Hansell and O'Donnell did not yet have the minimum of 100 Superfortresses they felt the raid required. The commanders used the days remaining to sharpen skills that the crews still clearly lacked. Three training missions were dispatched to bomb Truk, Japan's once formidable—but now bypassed and nearly impotent—stronghold, about 600 miles from the Marianas.

Most of the B-29s were out on the third Truk raid when their base on Saipan was subjected to a surprise attack. A flight of twin-engined Mitsubishi bombers slipped in at low altitude to escape radar detection, swept over Isley Field and dumped their bombs. The raid inflicted only minor damage on some B-29s parked on the hardstands, but it was a warning that the Superfortresses were not inviolable in their home roosts.

Hansell responded by sending his next two training raids against the island of Iwo Jima, halfway between Saipan and Tokyo. Iwo Jima had two operational airfields and it seemed certain that the relatively short-range Mitsubishis must have staged there. But the B-29 raids failed to put the airfields out of business, and the Japanese continued to use them for attacks on Saipan.

By November 17, Hansell at last had enough Superfortresses to hit Tokyo. More than 100 B-29s, each laden with 8,070 gallons of gasoline and 2.5 tons of bombs, waited at dawn on the hardstands of Isley Field. But they did not fly. For most of the year, the trade winds in the Marianas are as dependable as the calendar. From January to June, they blow from the west; from July to December, they blow from the east. But during the autumn typhoon season, the winds can be perverse. The day began in heavy rain; as the flight was preparing for takeoff the easterly wind died, then reappeared from the southwest.

Loaded to 138,500 pounds, the planes could not risk taking off downwind. To take off into the wind, however, they would have to proceed to the runway's far end by taxiing one at a time down the runway itself. That meant a delay of about five minutes between takeoffs and an unacceptable consumption of fuel by the planes as they waited their turn. Hansell reluctantly canceled the mission.

The decision to abort turned out to be incredibly lucky. By the next day Saipan was in the grip of a typhoon portended by the changing wind; had the B-29s flown, on their return they would have had no place to land. The weather on Saipan remained bad all week and the tensed-up aircrews, despite their narrow escape, began to grumble that the B-29 was "the best airplane that never left the ground."

Not until the 24th of November did an east wind bring a fresh, clear morning. The B-29s were ready. At 6:15 a.m. General O'Donnell advanced the throttles and his plane, the *Dauntless Dotty*, began to roll. O'Donnell used all 8,500 feet of paved runway now available—as well as part of the coral apron beyond—before the *Dotty* lifted and its wheels tucked up. One hundred and ten Superfortresses followed, and headed north.

Over Tokyo, the bombers were met by heavy but inaccurate flak and about 40 cautiously flown fighters. Eight B-29s suffered some damage, but only one was lost in battle. A Kawasaki flown by an exceptionally aggressive—or suicidal—pilot slashed past three other B-29s and crashed into the tail of one flown by Lieutenant Sam P. Wagner. Both planes went down in nearly vertical dives; no parachutes were seen to open. Another Superfortress ditched on the way home, but a search plane spotted the crewmen in their rafts and all 11 were picked up by a destroyer the next day.

The casualties of the first Tokyo raid were fewer than Hansell or anyone else had dared to expect. But as the crews had approached the target, they made a mystifying—and discouraging—discovery. It was a natural phenomenon so overwhelming that it all but destroyed the cherished American concept of high-altitude precision bombing.

The B-29s made their runs in formation, stacked between 27,000 and 33,000 feet, and turned into their final approach over Japan's famed volcanic peak, Mount Fuji. Making the turn, the airmen felt their planes drifting sideways at an astonishing rate. Then, coming out of the turn and heading east toward the target, they found themselves passing surface landmarks at ground speeds of about 445 miles per hour. Up there, almost at the boundary between troposphere and stratosphere, the bombers were riding a wild western wind blowing at least 150 miles per hour. At such velocity, a bombardier had almost no time to identify a target before his aim had to be fine-tuned in the Norden sight and the bombs released. The planes had run afoul of the jet stream, a substratospheric hurricane that no one had foreseen and no one yet knew how to counteract.

As though the jet stream were not enough to deal with, the bombardiers also found themselves contending with ordinary bad weather churning between their planes and the targets, six miles below. Only a few bombardiers caught even a glimpse of the Musashino plant as they sighted down through almost solid cloud cover. Just 24 planes were able to make out enough of the target by sight, by radar or by hunch to drop their bombs in the approximate vicinity of the plant. The others, unable to find the primary target, unloaded over what they hoped were the Tokyo docks and other urban targets.

The results were mediocre. If the raiding planes had not suffered grievously, neither had they inflicted much harm. Reconnaissance photographs failed to show appreciable damage, and after the War it was learned that of nearly 1,000 bombs dropped, only 48 had fallen in the general area of the Musashino works. Three of them were duds.

At least Tokyo had been bombed for the first time since the landmark Doolittle raid in 1942. In Washington, General Arnold issued a highly positive statement: "Tokyo's war industries have been badly hurt." He assured President Roosevelt that "No part of the Japanese Empire is now out of range." To the enemy, he warned: "Japan has sowed the wind; now let it reap the whirlwind."

Three days after the first raid, Hansell sent 81 Superfortresses to bomb Musashino again. He hoped this time to demolish the manufacturing complex. The hope was doubly vain: Tokyo was veiled in clouds, and in making the turn

over Mount Fuji the crews discovered that on the first raid the jet stream had merely been teasing them. This time it was blowing at a rate of 220 miles per hour and produced a ground speed over the target of nearly 500 miles per hour. Once again, the Musashino plant survived a B-29 raid virtually unscathed.

On subsequent missions, the B-29 crews found that the jet stream was dangerously unpredictable, shifting direction with demonic abruptness. Sometimes it gusted so hard that B-29s approaching the coast were brought to a standstill, as measured by ground speed; some crew members claimed they were pushed tailfirst back out to sea.

This phenomenon suggested an alternative to riding the race-horse stream too fast for the bombardier to use his bombsight. The option was to make the bombing run in the opposite direction, flying west toward the target instead of east. Flying into the wind would give the bombardiers time to compute their complex aiming formulas. The flaw in this solution was that it also offered Japanese antiaircraft gunners time to work out the equations on their aiming devices. The aircrews detested the prospect of the reverse run, which could in effect make them almost stationary targets.

The B-29 pilots made up their minds to suffer the jet stream at bombing altitude, but their bombardiers had another problem: The eccentric course of their bombs, buffeted by other kinds of weather on the way down, made precision bombing a nearly hopeless proposition. A cold front tumbling out of Siberia, for example, might move in from the northwest and collide with the warm, wet Pacific Ocean air. The result was a witches' brew of cloud and contrary winds from the surface to as high as 40,000 feet. On the worst days, a bomb released at 30,000 feet would fall through as many as five layers of wind flowing in varying directions at different speeds. The bombardier faced an impossible exercise in ballistics. To begin unraveling the pattern, Hansell ordered three planes to fly over Japan every night; their only mission was to report on the weather.

Stung by the first missions out of the Marianas, the Japanese tried to cut them off at the source. Early on the morning of November 27, while most of the B-29s were being loaded for their second futile pass at Nakajima's Musashino plant, two twin-engined Japanese bombers from Iwo Jima swooped low over Isley Field, destroying one of the Superfortresses and damaging 11 more. Later that day, a dozen

AN ENDURING MIX-UP

Commander Robert H. Isely of the U.S. Navy *(right)* was killed leading a bombing attack against the Japanese garrison on Saipan on June 12, 1944—three days before American forces invaded. Once Saipan was captured, its airfield was made the first B-29 base in the Marianas—and was named in honor of Commander Isely.

The AAF got Isely's name right at first, but along the way a misspelling—Isley— began to appear in official references to the field. Even the sign above the base operations building *(far right)* was altered to the new, incorrect spelling—which in the wondrous ways of military bureaucracy became the field's permanent name.

The name of Commander Robert Isely (above) is misspelled at the base on Saipan named in his memory.

Parked alongside a newly paved runway, B-29s are ready for their first combat mission out of Isley Field on Saipan in October 1944. Tents and half-built Quonset huts in the foreground attest that the field's conversion from a rudimentary strip for Japanese fighters had only begun.

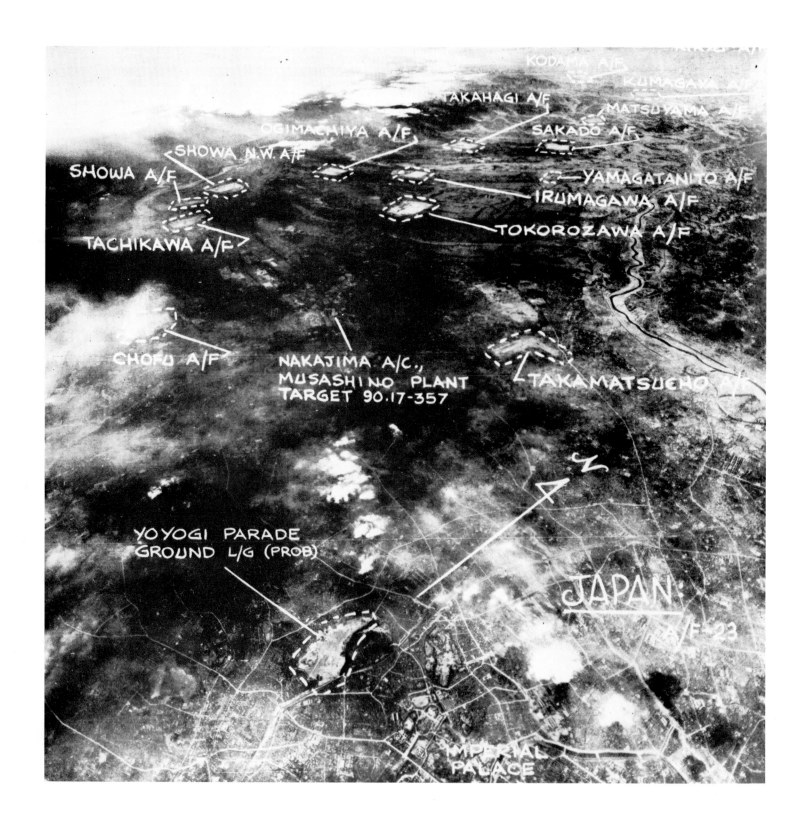

KODAMA A/F
KUMAGAYA A/F
TAKAHAGI A/F
MATSUYAMA A/F
OGIMACHIYA A/F
SAKADO A/F
SHOWA N.W. A/F
SHOWA A/F
YAMAGATANITO A/F
IRUMAGAWA A/F
TOKOROZAWA A/F
TACHIKAWA A/F
CHOFU A/F
NAKAJIMA A/C.,
MUSASHINO PLANT
TARGET 90.17-357
TAKAMATSUCHO A/F
YOYOGI PARADE
GROUND L/G (PROB)
JAPAN
A/F-23
IMPERIAL
PALACE

An aerial photo of the northwest environs of Tokyo, with markings that
were added by an Army Air Forces analyst, centers on a major B-29 target,
the Nakajima aircraft plant in the suburb of Musashino. The plant is
surrounded by a complex of airfields and a parade ground (dotted lines),
the latter designated L/G as a potential emergency landing ground for
American fighter planes. The first of the numerals (9) in the code number
assigned to the Nakajima plant identifies it as an industrial target.

single-engined fighters swept over Saipan and destroyed three more B-29s and badly damaged two others. The first attack came as a surprise, revealing how rudimentary the islands' defenses still were: The radar equipment was still in crates, and the garrison authorities had somehow counted on the 720 miles between Iwo Jima and Saipan as a margin of safety. By the second raid the defenders were ready. Anti-aircraft guns shot down six Japanese fighters, and American interceptors, which had been stationed on the Marianas since their capture, accounted for another four.

In order to protect the sitting-duck B-29s, the Navy stationed radar picket destroyers north and west of Saipan to pick up incoming Japanese planes before they could sneak beneath the land-based radar screen. General Hansell also struck back with his own measures. Twice in December he sent his B-29s, in combination with B-24 Liberators of the Seventh Air Force, newly arrived on Saipan, to attempt to neutralize the airfields on Iwo Jima. The strikes were partially successful, but the Japanese diligently patched their bombed airstrips and continued to retaliate with small raids, particularly on moonlit nights.

The Japanese attacked through early January; all told, they destroyed 11 Superfortresses and damaged 43 more. The last significant raid—and one of the most destructive— came on Christmas night, 1944. Twenty-five enemy planes slipped in, scattering strips of metal-foil chaff that blurred the radar screens and confused the operators.

The raid caught engineer construction crews working the late shift under floodlights. Small bombs and strafing destroyed two Superfortresses, damaged 13 more and wiped out an engineering outfit's headquarters. One Superfortress, loaded for a mission with 8,000 gallons of gasoline and three tons of incendiaries, blew up and set off a raging fire that ignited a trailer containing 2,200 gallons of fuel.

"The engineers stepped into the breach," Hansell reported, "and they did one of the finest jobs I have ever seen. Although the Jap 'Bettys' were dropping many small antipersonnel bombs and there was quite a bit of confusion, they brought up their heavy equipment, rode right at the exploding wreckage, piled the burning B-29s into big heaps with their bulldozers, brought up dirt and threw it on top, and then drove over the whole mass to squash the fire out."

Hansell had little occasion to praise his bomber crews as he had his engineers. The B-29s' successive failures over Nakajima's sprawling Musashino engine works could reasonably be written off to inexperience, weather and bad luck. After two raids, the plant was still virtually intact. Hansell scheduled it again for December 3, but this third strike was the least productive so far. Of 86 planes launched, all but 10 reached Tokyo. However, only 26 bombs dropped in the target area and damage to the works was negligible.

Once again the problem was the jet stream, which raged at 180 miles per hour at the selected bombing altitude. This time, too, Japanese fighters were lying in wait, and they were aggressive. They shot down six American planes and heavily damaged another half dozen.

One of the downed planes carried the flight leader of the 500th Bombardment Group, Colonel Richard T. King, and a wing staff officer, Colonel B. E. Brugge. Along with most of the plane's crew, King survived capture and months of brutality. Brugge died soon after he was made prisoner. Another badly shot-up B-29, flown by Captain Francis J. Murray, ditched in the ocean on the way home. All but one of the crew made it to the life rafts. They had drifted for 10 days when a Navy patrol plane spotted their last remaining flare and summoned a rescue ship.

Yet another B-29 called *Long Distance* scored a notable loser's triumph by demonstrating what a sturdy fighting machine the B-29 was—so long as at least three of its engines could be kept running. Over the target, the *Long Distance's* gunners fought off an incredible 131 separate fighter attacks. Then a Japanese plane rammed the bomber, ripping the No. 3 engine out of the wing. The *Long Distance* and its crew seemed done for; but Captain Donald J. Dufford regained control of his crippled ship and nursed it all the way back to Isley Field.

Musashino had begun to look like a jinx. So far, the Marianas-based air fleet had experienced little but failure. Hansell decided that a change of target might bring a change of luck. He selected the Mitsubishi Aircraft Engine Works at Nagoya, Japan's third-largest city, and on the 13th of December sent 90 B-29s to destroy it. Seventy-one of them reached Nagoya and each dropped 2.5 tons of high explosives and incendiaries. The Japanese fighters were aloft, and again they were fiercely combative. Four Superfortresses were shot down and 31 more were damaged.

For the first time, however, the results of the raid seemed worth the sacrifice. Strike photographs showed almost one fifth of the huge plant's roof area blown in. (Scrutiny of roof areas following a raid was the prevailing method for measuring results, on the assumption that if the roof was gone, whatever it had covered must also have suffered grievous harm.) In truth, the damage was more severe than the photographs indicated. The plant's production was cut from 1,600 engines per month to 1,200. Some vital parts of the plant had been completely destroyed, and 246 Japanese workmen were killed.

Yet Hansell was far from satisfied. When General O'Donnell called a meeting of his lead crews and squadron commanders and praised them warmly for their accomplishments and their courage, Hansell stepped up at the end to say a few words. "I'm in sharp disagreement," he said in a voice bristling with anger: "In my opinion you people haven't earned your pay over here. Unless you do better, this operation is doomed to failure."

Hansell's sensitivity to the shortcomings of his command was exacerbated by smoldering resentment against what he took to be a harmful change of basic B-29 policy in Washington. His ire was triggered when Brigadier General Lauris Norstad, who had replaced him as Chief of Staff for the Twentieth Air Force, instructed him to run a 100-plane incendiary raid against Nagoya. The Twentieth's top command, Norstad explained, had been considering the possibility of trying to burn out Japanese cities and wanted some practical data on which to base its plans.

Hansell's reply reflected his indignation. "We have with great difficulty implanted the principle that our mission is the destruction of primary targets by sustained and determined attacks using precision-bombing methods both visual and radar," he wrote. "Now that this doctrine is beginning to get results on the aircraft industry, you are exerting pressure to divert my forces to area bombing."

Thus the battle lines were drawn for a new high-level controversy: precision versus area bombing. Faced with Hansell's unwillingness to change his methods, Norstad temporized. He conceded that smashing Japan's aircraft industry was still a top priority, but he also wanted his big fire-

raid test as soon as Hansell found it convenient. Hansell agreed to the compromise.

On December 22, Hansell ordered 78 B-29s loaded with incendiaries for a return visit to the Mitsubishi engine works at Nagoya. As it turned out, the raid proved little about fire bombing one way or the other. The target was solidly overcast and only 48 planes dropped bombs on the plant, using radar from high altitude. Very little damage was evident in the subsequent photographs.

The year 1944 was almost over. For the XXI Bomber Command and Hansell it held one more disappointment. By now the Nakajima plant at Musashino, near Tokyo, had become something of an obsession for every man in the outfit. Hansell made it the target for the last raid of the year, on December 17. But the jinx held firm, and the results of the fourth raid over Musashino were the sorriest of all. Of 72 B-29s launched, only 39 found the massive engine works and only 26 bombs fell anywhere near it. One bomb hit a hospital, providing the Japanese with evidence to support their propaganda claims that the Superfortress crews were interested only in killing helpless civilians.

For the crews, their own casualties were a more immediate concern. They were growing accustomed to watching helplessly as their friends died. Few men died more stubbornly than Major John E. Krause and the crew of the *Uncle Tom's Cabin*, who perished during the last fruitless mission of 1944. Flying the lead plane in his formation, Krause made the turn over Mount Fuji and had locked into the bombing run when 30 enemy fighters appeared. One of the fighters went into a ramming dive on the lead plane of a higher-flying formation, missed it by 100 feet, came close to another B-29, then slammed a wing into the right side of Krause's fuselage, slicing it open. Flames spewed from the gash as equipment fell out and went tumbling earthward. The *Uncle Tom's Cabin* should have gone down with its attacker, but Krause regained control and his gunners kept firing at their assailants.

Another Japanese fighter put a burst into the B-29's No. 4 engine, which began to smoke and spray oil. The Superfortress lost altitude, but Krause held it in the bombing run. Then a second fighter rammed the cripple and exploded, tearing the B-29's No. 3 engine out of its housing. Incredibly, with both engines gone on the starboard side and the fuselage ripped open, Krause got control again and held to the bombing course.

Then the *Uncle Tom's Cabin* was rammed for a third time. Making a pass from below, a fighter overshot and drove his nose into the bomber's belly. After taking enough punishment to destroy four planes, the B-29 sloughed into a spin. It seemed to be finished, yet it was not. Once again, at low altitude, Krause hauled the *Cabin* out of its spin and for a breathless moment held the aircraft straight and level. But the ordeal had been too much; the plane nosed over and dived into the ground. The last fight of the *Uncle Tom's Cabin* had lasted seven minutes during which, witnesses attested, its gunners shot nine Japanese fighters out of the sky.

The year ended with morale at low ebb. In a little more than a month, the command had lost 188 men, of whom 116 had ditched and been lost at sea. There were empty bunks in the barracks and stacks of unopened mail to be returned to sender. The B-29s had dropped 1,550 tons of high explosives in the course of seven missions against Japan's aircraft industry. But only one bomb in 50 had hit within 1,000 feet of the point of aim. And only one strike, the first against the Mitsubishi engine works at Nagoya, had produced substantial damage.

Confronted with these figures, the Superfortress crews struggled to rationalize the sacrifice. "We feel it has been worthwhile; we have to believe that," a B-29 pilot told *Time* correspondent Robert Sherrod. "But the cost has been high. We've lost a lot of good men, especially key men like group and squadron commanders."

Cost and benefit were being weighed in Washington as well. The increasing losses, particularly the ones that involved ditching the planes, brought a stern complaint from General Arnold. "Some of these airplanes naturally must be ditched," he wrote Hansell, but he felt that the loss rate had become untenable. "The B-29 cannot be treated in the same way we treat a fighter, a medium bomber or even a Flying Fortress," Arnold concluded. "We must consider the B-29 more in terms of a naval vessel, and we do not lose naval vessels in threes and fours without a very thorough analysis of the causes."

Hansell responded with a letter defending the sacrifice and disputing Arnold's logic. If the Navy committed its de-

Hunched against the searing heat, a heroic bulldozer driver on Saipan pushes dirt over a flaming B-29 following a Japanese air raid in late 1944. The men at left are trying to rig a hose to spray the bulldozer with water. Although singed, the fire fighters were able to smother the blaze before it spread to other Superfortresses parked nearby.

stroyers to battle five or six times a month as the B-29s were committed, he argued, the losses would be prohibitive.

By the end of 1944, casualties inflicted by the B-29s had not had far-reaching effect. Their bombs had killed or wounded several hundred Japanese, but they were far from terrorizing the populace or driving people from their jobs. It was even possible for some Japanese to draw poetic inspiration from the approach of the great bomber fleets.

"In the eastern sky loomed a flight, another flight and yet another of B-29s," wrote one woman. "Trailing white streamers of exhaust gas, they sailed in perfect formation through the blue-gold sky like pearly fish riding through the seas of the universe."

From the American viewpoint, matters did not improve with the beginning of the new year. On January 3, 1945, Hansell finally sent off the full-scale incendiary test that Norstad had put on his agenda in November. He sent up 97 Superfortresses, but only 57 reached the primary target area over Nagoya; their fire bombs, dropped from about 30,000 feet, ignited 75 fires and burned out a total of 140,000 square feet, an area equivalent to three football fields. As a test, the raid was inconclusive. It was certainly no holocaust—and five B-29s were lost.

One Superfortress, called *American Maid,* took a beating from the Japanese fighters. But the plane survived, and the experience of one of its crew became the stuff of legend.

Staff Sergeant James R. Krantz, the *American Maid's* left blister gunner, had a recurring premonition that someday he was going to become separated from his airplane in flight. Krantz decided to take precautions that would forestall such an event. He fashioned a stout safety harness and made it fast, at his station, to a sturdy section of the *American Maid's* frame.

Krantz's fear became fact that January day over Nagoya. A Japanese fighter shot out the plexiglass blister behind which Krantz sat. As the blister disintegrated, the explosive decompression of the cabin blew Krantz out of the plane. But his homemade safety harness arrested his fall and left him dangling spread-eagled in the wind. The 200-mph slip stream blew off his oxygen mask and his gloves and added to the difficulties of his crew mates, who were trying to haul him back in. Krantz passed out for lack of oxygen, but after

10 minutes, four tugging men had retrieved him. To the astonishment of the flight surgeons who examined him at Saipan, Krantz had suffered nothing worse than severe frostbite in the hands and one leg, and a dislocated shoulder.

Hansell had fulfilled headquarters' request for an incendiary bombing test, but his service in the Marianas was about to end. On January 6, General Norstad arrived on Guam to inform him that Major General Curtis LeMay was to replace him as commanding officer of the XXI Bomber Command. There would be a two-week hiatus before LeMay took over and Hansell decided to apply the time to the work he preferred: high-level precision bombing. On January 9 he sent a flight of 72 Superfortresses once more against the B-29s' nemesis, the Nakajima engine works at Musashino.

Their luck did not change. Once again the raging jet stream broke up the B-29 formations. Only 18 planes succeeded in dropping bombs anywhere near the target and only 24 bombs fell in the plant area, destroying one warehouse and damaging two others. The cost: two B-29s to enemy aircraft and four to other causes. On January 14 another five were lost while inflicting meager damage to the Mitsubishi aircraft assembly plant at Nagoya.

The losses were severe and they would have been worse, but for some escapes that bordered on the miraculous. Before leaving San Francisco the previous November, the crew of a Superfortress called *Lassie Come Home* had smuggled aboard two cases of good stateside whiskey and hid the bottles in the insulation lining the fuselage. In Saipan, the crew was at first too busy to off-load the forbidden liquor, and the *Lassie Come Home* went on its first mission with the whiskey still on board. When the plane returned intact, the crew decided that the contraband was a lucky charm; they took a vow not to drink any of it.

On the January 14 mission to Nagoya, half the Japanese fighters in the sky seemed to concentrate on the *Lassie.* It was the plane's 13th mission. The fighters first shot out the No. 1 engine, then No. 4. With both outboard engines dead, the *Lassie* began to lose altitude. The fighters came again. Their spraying bullets started a fire in the bomber's midsection, knocked out the radio and oxygen systems, set one of the two remaining engines afire and wounded three of the crewmen. The *Lassie* should have been done for. But the engine fire went out and the one remaining undamaged

Airmen inspect a B-29 that landed at Isley Field on only two of its three
pairs of wheels. The plane had been hit by enemy fire during the first B-29
night-bombing mission over Tokyo on November 29, 1944, and on its
return to Saipan the forward landing gear failed to lower. Both plane and
crew escaped the perilous landing almost unscathed.

engine stubbornly kept on performing. The hub of one dead engine's propeller, without lubrication and windmilling out of control, kept spinning until it grew red hot—one gunner even mistook it for the rising moon. At last the propeller broke off and spun away in the night without damaging the *Lassie* any further.

An observer on the flight, Major Hugh Mahoney, crawled through the crippled plane, inspecting the damage and giving first aid. A crewman asked whether they ought to ditch. "Don't talk about ditching," Mahoney insisted. "*Lassie's* going home." He was right, and when the B-29 dragged into Isley Field an hour behind the other planes, almost the only unbroken things on board were the bottles of whiskey.

For a strike on January 19, Hansell chose a new target, the Kawasaki Aircraft Industries plant at Akashi, near the city of Kobe. This time, he struck gold. Like other aircraft builders, the Kawasaki plant was a prime target; in 1944 it had produced 17 per cent of Japan's airframes and 12 per cent of its engines. Kawasaki's premium product was the dangerous Ki-61 fighter, called Tony by the Americans; equipped with German-designed engines, it was a fast, hard-hitting plane that American aircrews had come to respect.

In unusually good weather, 62 planes bombed Akashi visually from between 25,000 and 27,000 feet. It was a lower than usual altitude, avoided until now for fear of Japanese fighters; Hansell had decided that the increased risk was worth taking for the sake of improved accuracy. His gamble paid off. As a precision-bombing operation, the strike approached perfection. Photographs showed more than one third of the Kawasaki plant's roof area destroyed, and actual results were better than that. Though the Americans did not know it, this single raid cut the plant's production of both airframes and engines by 90 per cent. And despite flying at lower altitudes, not a single B-29 was lost.

Hansell's most satisfactory raid was also his last. The day after the Kawasaki strike he was relieved by LeMay, who had once served under him in Europe and who was now senior to him by one star. Fresh from the China experience and acutely aware of the B-29's problems, LeMay brought no illusions to the assignment. He did bring an iron determination to succeed. "Now the turkey is around my neck," he told his staff. "I've got to deliver."

For a time it appeared that the turkey—or albatross—would haunt LeMay as it had Hansell. The new commander had been briefed on the ferocity of the jet stream over Japan—something he had not encountered in Europe—and decided that the solution was to fly beneath it. Reduced altitude would also improve the B-29's accuracy, ease the strain on the engines and reduce fuel consumption. It made little sense, LeMay told his crews, to burn up 22 tons of gasoline to carry three tons of bombs to Tokyo.

LeMay let the remaining strikes on the January agenda go forward as Hansell had planned them. A repeat raid against the Mitsubishi engine works at Nagoya on January 23 inflicted some damage despite heavy cloud cover that prevented all but 28 of the 73 planes from finding the target. Another on January 27 that sent 74 bombers one more time against the Nakajima factory at Musashino was an unrelieved disappointment. Japanese fighters came up in great numbers, spoiling for a fight. The B-29 gunners claimed 60 Japanese planes destroyed, but the Japanese shot down five of the American bombers. Two more ditched at sea, one crashed on returning to base and another simply vanished. Little damage was done to the target.

A few months earlier, the loss of nine planes would have been critical. Only one of Hansell's missions in January had been able to muster more than 100 planes. But from the beginning of LeMay's tour in the Marianas he enjoyed an advantage over his predecessor in having more planes and men to work with. The 313th Bombardment Wing had been added to the 73rd Wing—the original Marianas unit—and began flying missions at the end of January from newly constructed North Field on Tinian. Thereafter, reinforcements arrived steadily. The 314th Wing, which was stationed on North Field, Guam, began combat in late February. LeMay's old 58th Wing was transferred from India and China to West Field, Tinian, and would resume operations in May; still another wing, the 315th, would join the campaign in June from Northwest Field, Guam.

On paper, each additional wing contributed 120 B-29s to the strength of the XXI Bomber Command, but entire units did not arrive at the same time, and the number of planes available for missions varied, depending on losses and maintenance problems.

LeMay opened his campaign in February by honoring a

renewed request from General Norstad for a sizable incendiary strike—at Kobe, Japan's most important shipyard city. Washington wanted more data on fire bombing and on February 4, LeMay sent out 129 B-29s carrying mixed loads of incendiaries and fragmentation bombs. Kobe was partly obscured by cloud and fog, and barely half the planes found their primary targets. Nevertheless, the results of the 159 tons of fire bombs and 13 tons of high explosives they spilled were impressive. Photographs showed 2.6 million square feet of roof surface damaged. The raiders had destroyed more than 1,000 buildings, and had severely damaged one of Kobe's two major shipyards and five other war industries. Adopting Hansell's precedent, LeMay had sent the bombers in at 24,500 to 27,000 feet—where the jet stream was less intense. Once again the Japanese had come up fighting, shooting down one B-29 and damaging 35.

Six days later, LeMay dispatched another flight of 84 Superfortresses carrying mixed loads of incendiaries and 500-pound general-purpose bombs. Their target was the Nakajima aircraft plant at Ota, whose assembly line turned out the Nakajima Ki-84, which the Americans code-named Frank and considered one of Japan's best fighter planes. Although nearly one third of the plant's 37 buildings were damaged, the B-29s' accuracy left much to be desired. Only seven incendiaries and 97 GPs (of which 43 were duds) fell in the factory area. The B-29s still seemed unable to find a sure formula for success.

In late January and early February of 1945, the U.S. Navy and Marines were finishing their preparations for the invasion of Iwo Jima—described by Marine Lieut. General Holland M. "Howlin' Mad" Smith as "the toughest place we have had to take." Capturing the five-mile-long volcanic island, Smith predicted, would cost 15,000 American casualties. Yet the B-29 crews in the Marianas considered Iwo Jima a thorn well worth removing. Japanese fighters on the island still sporadically raided the Marianas. Radar on Iwo Jima warned the Japanese home islands when the B-29s were coming, and the presence of Japanese forces on the island forced American planes en route to Japan to fly a dogleg to avoid them. The extra distance cut bomb loads and boosted fuel requirements.

For terrifying moments, a B-29 gunner dangles from his plane by a life line and is repeatedly slammed against the fuselage by the slip stream. The man, Staff Sergeant James R. Krantz, was ejected when his plexiglass blister blew out during a Japanese fighter attack. Hanging by a safety harness he had designed himself, Krantz was suspended—29,000 feet over Japan—for 10 minutes before the crew could pull him in.

Mindful of the high price that might have to be paid for Iwo Jima, Admiral Raymond A. Spruance, who would be in command of the invasion, asked LeMay to join him for a conference on board his flagship, the *Indianapolis*, at Ulithi in the Caroline Islands. Spruance, who initially had believed taking Iwo would be a fairly easy proposition, now asked LeMay whether the invasion was worthwhile.

LeMay answered a firm "Yes." In American hands, he said, the island would be invaluable as a staging area and emergency landing field for B-29s, as a home for fighter escorts to protect the bombers over Japan, and as a base for air-sea rescue efforts.

The invasion plan went forward, and on February 12, a week before D-day, B-29s and Navy planes combined to pummel the island with 84 tons of bombs. Holland Smith's forecast of high casualties turned out to be on the low side: The actual cost of taking Iwo Jima was 7,000 U.S. Marines and Navy men killed, 19,000 wounded. This was hardly the bombers' fault, or that of Navy gunners who had been shelling the island for months. The Japanese garrison simply dug in; their tenacity was abetted by the volcanic soil of the is-

land, which tended to diminish damage by absorbing the shock of high explosives. Patching the bomb craters in their two airfields, they managed to keep them in operation, and even began building a third.

To protect the ships disgorging men and supplies off the beaches of Iwo Jima from air attack, Spruance ordered a carrier task force to bomb the complex of Japanese airfields near Tokyo. He scheduled the strike for February 16 and 17 and assigned it to Task Force 58 under Vice Admiral Marc A. Mitscher. Mitscher's command included 16 carriers, eight battleships, and numerous lesser craft as escort.

Because it would have to venture close to the home islands to launch its planes, Task Force 58 expected to meet with massive resistance in the air—much of it from Kamikazes whose suicidal attacks were capable of sinking ships. As a result, each air group on the large carriers was assigned at least 73 fighters, mostly Grumman Hellcats and Vought Corsairs. The remainder of each group's strength was divided between Curtiss Helldiver dive bombers and Grumman Avenger torpedo bombers.

Launching about 125 miles southeast of Tokyo, the first

carrier planes took off into bad weather—rain and snow squalls. The planes were mainly fighters ordered to clear the skies for the bombers, which were to attack next day. The ceiling was down to 4,000 feet as they approached the Japanese coast. Opposition was spotty. About 100 Japanese fighters rose to meet one American contingent sweeping in over the Chiba Peninsula east of Tokyo, and the Americans shot down about 40 of them. Other squadrons were scarcely challenged as they strafed their assigned airfields, destroying aircraft caught on the ground.

Because of the inclement weather, Mitscher telescoped his operations schedule to get in some bombing missions on the first day, before the rain and fog forced him to shut down. And in spite of the poor visibility, some of the bombers found their targets—airframe and aircraft-engine plants northwest of Tokyo.

The weather eased long enough the following day to allow more bombing strikes, one of them an attack on the old B-29 nemesis at Musashino; the Navy planes hit the plant hard. Then the weather grew worse, and Mitscher turned his carriers back toward Iwo Jima, where a Naval bombardment had begun simultaneously with Mitscher's air strikes on Japan's home islands. For their two days' work, the carrier pilots claimed 340 Japanese aircraft shot down and 190 destroyed on the ground. The Americans lost 88 airplanes, 60 of them to enemy action.

The Navy's raids made headlines in the United States. According to The New York Times, "The carrier strike against the Japanese home islands," which had approached close enough to enemy shores to enable Navy planes "to sweep the streets of Tokyo with strafing attacks, is the most daring operation of the Pacific war to date."

The Marines were to go ashore on Iwo Jima on February 19. For that day, General LeMay scheduled a 150-plane strike of B-29s on Musashino. Chagrined by the Navy's results, he was determined to obliterate the Nakajima plant once and for all.

But Musashino remained virtually impregnable against the B-29s. A cold front met the Superfortresses on their way. Musashino lay under an unbroken mass of cloud and the raiders turned their attention to secondary objectives. They damaged a spinning mill, a railroad yard and a bridge. But the engine plant at Musashino escaped almost untouched.

LeMay was learning, as Hansell had before him, that one of his major handicaps was Japanese weather—and the difficulty of predicting it. "If we had had any weather cooperation from the Russians in Siberia, it might have helped," he wrote later, "but they gave us almost no assistance whatsoever." And though accurate forecasts were useful for planning, the weather itself was the real issue. "There is no way," the general lamented, "in which any weather personnel—however experienced, discerning, hard-working and devoted—can make good bombing weather out of bad bombing weather."

LeMay concluded that at best he could expect no more than seven days a month sufficiently clear to allow visual bombing. "And what weatherman," he asked rhetorically, "hankered after the job of determining which seven days?"

LeMay and his command were beginning to smart under Navy taunts that their ships had to haul tons of supplies to the Marianas, where the B-29s devoured most of them but hit very little; meanwhile, the Navy's carrier pilots got what was left of the supplies, and complained that they were expected to carry on the rest of the Pacific campaign.

Such criticism was perhaps less than fair, but the fact was that the Superfortresses had not produced results to justify the cost of their missions. One reason for the difference between their performance and the Navy's, it seemed, was that the Navy Hellcats, Helldivers and Avengers went in very low and fast, delivering their bombs in perilous proximity to the targets. The big bombers were not designed to operate that way.

Or were they? LeMay asked the question and set out to find the answer. One matter that concerned him, given the frequent necessity of the high-altitude Superfortresses to bomb blind through wretched weather, was the quality of his radar operators who, like most of the B-29 crew members, were severely handicapped by inadequate training. If LeMay could not influence the weather, at least he might improve the skill of his personnel.

The general called in the Guam base radar specialist, a civilian from the Massachusetts Institute of Technology, and ordered him to go to Saipan. As LeMay recalled the encounter, he told the scientist: "Go up there and pick out a couple of the stupidest radar operators they have, and Lord knows

Geysers of smoke roil up from the Kawasaki aircraft plant near Kobe on Japan's Inland Sea as American bombs effectively knock the factory out of the War on January 19, 1945. The attack was a rare textbook example of the high-altitude precision bombing by daylight for which the B-29s were originally designed. Untouched to the right of the tight bomb concentration on the factory is an airfield bordered by triangle-shaped revetments, which were used to shelter completed aircraft.

Bursts of antiaircraft fire pockmark the sky over Kure Naval base, under fierce attack by U.S. Navy bombers on March 19, 1945. Despite the murderous flak, the carrier-based planes destroyed dockyards, warehouses and barracks and damaged 17 Japanese ships, including the 72,800-ton battleship Yamato and the carrier Amagi.

that's pretty stupid. You go up and fly with them and see''—he pointed to a chart—''if they can fly over this spit of land sticking out on the northern side of the island.''

The expert returned from Saipan shaking his head at the difficulties a radar-training program there would face. But he conceded that with sufficiently intense training, most of the operators could learn to identify that point of land sticking out into the water—or one like it. LeMay nodded. He was thinking of a similar tip of land protruding into Tokyo Bay east of the city. Here was a handy guide, if men could be trained to find it unerringly.

The elements of a plan were forming in LeMay's head, but he recognized it as both radical and risky. He knew that his aircrews were going to be appalled when they learned what he had in mind. He decided to try his hand at psychology, and play a dirty trick.

LeMay sent an order to General O'Donnell, on Saipan, for a special training mission. The target was a tiny island near Saipan. A dozen B-29s were to approach in columns of three and drop their bombs, with delayed fuses, from an altitude of 50 feet.

Back from O'Donnell's headquarters came a message protesting, ''Altitude in error. Two ciphers missing.''

''No. Altitude correct,'' LeMay's office replied. ''Five zero feet.'' O'Donnell himself shot back a request for an immediate hearing. Within an hour he arrived from Saipan to declare angrily, ''I cannot fly that mission.''

LeMay, pipe in hand, calmly stared O'Donnell down. ''You will fly that mission,'' he said softly.

The mission was flown, and all the bombers returned safely. For days, wild tales circulated through the Marianas of bombs that had bounced nearly up to the bomb bays of Superfortresses following one another in column. All the exaggerations finally crystallized in a story about a bomb that bounced up level with the horizontal tail surfaces of a B-29 and flew formation with it for a while.

Eventually, the credibility of the tales diminished. But no one doubted LeMay's shrewdness in ordering the hedge-hopping mission—or underestimated its psychological effect on every B-29 crewman in the Marianas. In the future, when LeMay ordered his crews to do something really outrageous, it would not seem quite so dreadful.

RESCUE AT SEA

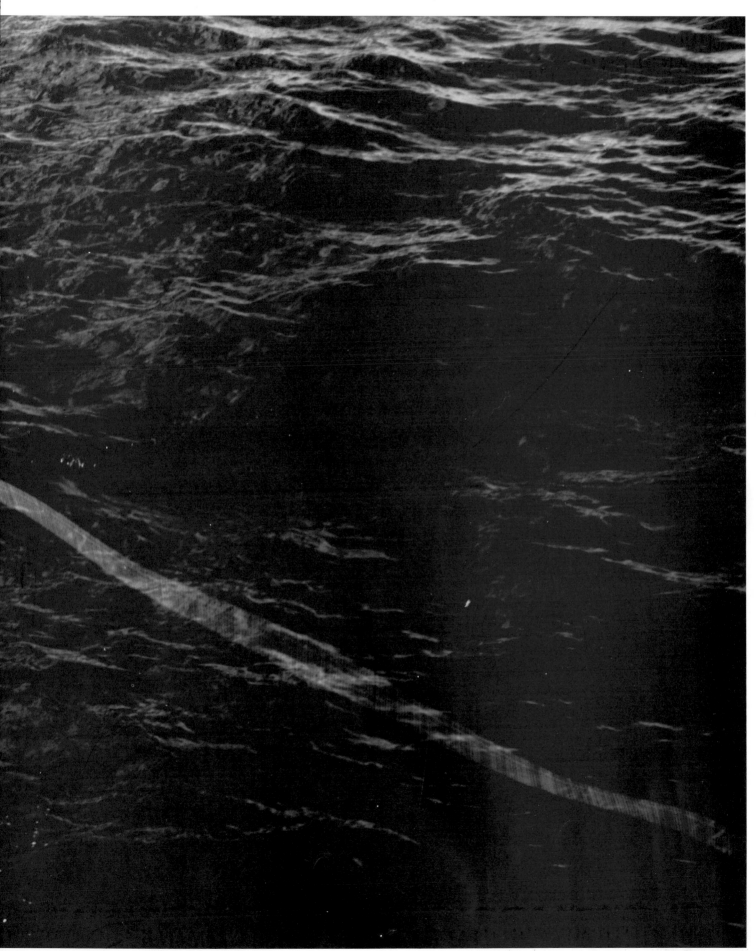

A downed B-29 crewman in a raft reaches for a life line—shown in blurred motion—thrown from a U.S. rescue ship, one of several on the bombers' route.

A SAFETY NET FOR AIRMEN IN DISTRESS

The prospect of being forced down in the vast and empty western Pacific gnawed at the morale of B-29 crewmen. "My greatest worry," one of them admitted later, "was thinking of the possibility of ditching in that dreary ocean." The fear was well founded: Of the 264 airmen killed during the first two months of bombing from the Marianas, more than half were lost at sea.

The American command's answer was to establish a line of search-and-rescue units along the B-29s' 1,500-mile route to Japan. Beginning in November 1944, whenever a raid was scheduled, destroyers and submarines were posted at intervals along the route, and long-range aircraft patrolled the areas in between. Mission briefings for combat crews now included the locations of the rescue units, and in an emergency, pilots were instructed to come down—if they could—as close as possible to these "lifesaver" vessels.

It was not easy. High winds, rain squalls and reduced visibility were commonplace in the misnamed Pacific; even a controlled landing under power—called ditching—meant smacking a 65-ton machine into rough seas, and most likely breaking up within minutes. Moreover, the rescue operation required a degree of sophisticated teamwork among separate commands that was not achieved in a day. Search planes came from both the Army Air Forces and the Navy; rescue destroyers took orders from one command, submarines from another. It was months before a common distress radio frequency was set up.

After an uneven start, however, the rescue system began to work wonders. Crewmen on search planes, squinting at the rolling sea for up to 14 hours on end, learned to identify the speck that was a life raft or part of a wrecked plane. Radio signals were funneled quickly through a central control on Saipan, and ships and submarines became accustomed to the risk of responding in enemy-infested waters—venturing even into Japan's Inland Sea. By the spring and summer of 1945, an airman who went down in the "dreary" Pacific had a 3 in 5 chance of being saved.

A motorized lifeboat that can be dropped by parachute to men in the water hangs from the underside of a B-17 that has been modified for rescue duty.

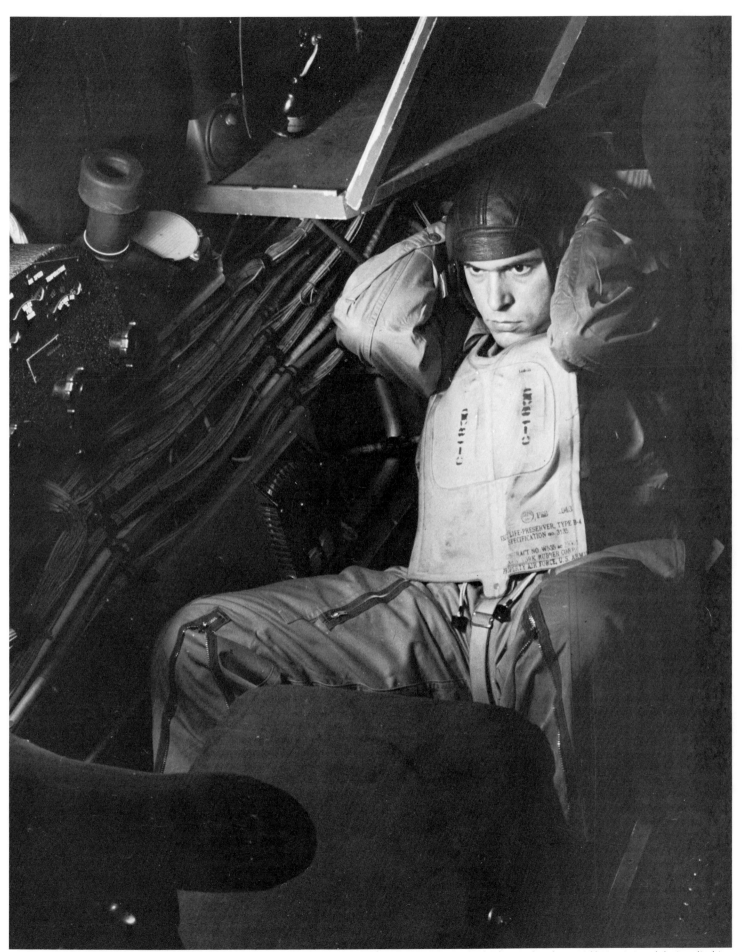

Facing the rear, his head braced and knees flexed, a navigator demonstrates the correct position for lessening the chance of being injured during ditching.

From the nose of a B-17 on air-sea rescue duty, an airman patiently scans the sea below for a reflection, a wisp of smoke or a bit of wreckage that could mark the location of a downed aircraft or its survivors.

Seen from a Navy PBY, the 11-man crew of a B-29 huddles in rafts on December 14, 1944. The smoke trailing to the right of their still-floating plane comes from a marker dropped to help a rescue ship find the site.

Swooping low, a PBM drops an emergency pack by parachute to sustain the survivors of a ditching until a submarine or destroyer can pick them up. A typical pack contained a self-inflating raft, a first-aid kit and food.

THE "DUMBOS" EVERYBODY LOVED

If a plane in trouble could ditch close to a rescue ship, its crew's chance of survival was excellent. The prospect was bleaker for those who had to come down between stations. The survivors' tiny life rafts, adrift in an area that could cover thousands of square miles, might be overlooked by the most intensive air search.

The difficulties were compounded by a shortage of aircraft suitable for search-and-rescue duty. The Navy contributed PBY Catalinas and PBM Mariners, slow but dependable flying boats equipped with life-saving gear and dubbed "Dumbos" after the heroic flying elephant of a Walt Disney movie. But the Dumbos lacked the range and armament to patrol close to Japan, where most bombers went down. The AAF assigned some B-17s to patrol duty and, as more B-29s became available, some were outfitted with droppable lifeboats and other rescue equipment. Called Super Dumbos, they had both staying power and the muscle to defend themselves; they could also drive off enemy ships and aircraft attempting to attack rescue vessels—or the helpless men in the water.

The crew of a destroyer turns out to welcome the survivors of a B-29, who have come alongside in life rafts roped together. Rescue vessels could reach any point on the B-29s' route within three hours.

A WELCOME SIGHT IN ENEMY WATERS

Dozens of American destroyers and submarines shared the tedious, risky duty of manning lifesaving stations off the coast of Japan. Aviators, for a long time, favored the surface ships as rescue vehicles over the unseen submarines, which might or might not be lurking where they were needed. Rather than ditch near a submarine's supposed station, a pilot often took his chances on getting his crippled plane home any way he could.

Lieutenant Frank Ayres was one who had no such choice. When his P-51 took an antiaircraft shell in the wing over Tokyo on June 23, 1945, he kept the plane flying just long enough to clear the Japanese coast. Ayres radioed a distress call and bailed out. He hit the water just as the submarine U.S.S. *Tigrone* eased up alongside him. Before the pilot even had time to doff his parachute harness and clamber into his life raft, he was safe on the deck of the sub.

From January to April of 1945, submarines rescued 133 airmen. As the pace of the air war quickened, the fliers learned—sometimes from repeated experience—to depend on them. In the final three months of the War, the submarines nearly doubled their rescue count to 247.

Surfacing in the East China Sea, the U.S.S. Sea Devil is a godsend to a raft full of airmen in June 1945. The Sea Devil rescued a total of 15 airmen during the final months of the War.

A submarine crew member visits an injured airman who has been given a sailor's bunk. The submarines had no doctors, but pharmacists-mates could provide basic medical treatment.

Rescued fliers, some still wearing their Mae West life vests, gather on the deck of the U.S.S. Tigrone, which picked them up in late June, 1945. In all, the Tigrone saved 31 airmen, more than any other submarine on rescue duty.

4

On the island of Cheju, off the southern tip of Korea, a Japanese radar station picked up a signal half an hour before midnight on June 15, 1944. From the evidence on their scopes, the radarmen concluded that more than 30 B-29s and B-24s were headed out of China toward Kyushu, the closest major Japanese island. The force of bombers, which actually contained no B-24s, was the first launched by the U.S. Army Air Forces' XX Bomber Command against Japan from its forward China base at Chengtu; the target of the raid was the steel-manufacturing city of Yawata.

The Korea radar station signaled a warning to Japanese Western Army headquarters at Fukuoka, the command responsible for Kyushu's air defense. The Army's Fourth Air Group at Fukuoka had 35 planes available to throw against the raid, but only eight of them qualified as night fighters. They were Kawasaki Ki-45s, a plane called the Toryu (Dragon Killer) by the Japanese and code-named Nick by the Americans. The two-seated, twin-engined craft were the only night interceptors the Army had. Some models had been designed to carry airborne radar, but radar was actually installed in only one Army aircraft. All the Dragon Killers were heavily armed with up to five machine guns and cannon; a number had twin 20mm guns mounted on top, thus enabling the pilot to fire upward at a 30-degree angle as he attacked the vulnerable underside of a bomber.

The interceptors began to scramble at 12:52 a.m. Japan time, a little less than an hour and a half after the first radar signal, and at 1:30 a.m. they encountered the first of 47 high-flying B-29s. A confused two-hour battle unfolded in a series of running fights between the Japanese defenders—mostly the Dragon Killers—and individual Superfortresses that arrived over the northern part of Kyushu every two or three minutes. Japanese ground-based searchlights occasionally picked out solitary bombers, and about 120 antiaircraft guns of various calibers blazed away at them, firing a thunderous 9,000 shells.

The first B-29s destroyed by enemy action were shot down during this engagement. The first to fall may have been the victim of an attack by Lieutenant Isamu Kashiide, whose wartime total eventually included seven B-29s. Kashiide charged the Superfortress head on over Yawata and fired his guns at close range. "The hull of the bomber seemed to enlarge before me," he wrote later. "I could see

"WE ARE EAGLES WITHOUT WINGS"

my shells hit the point where the left wing joined the fuselage. Automatically I disengaged, watching the bomber as I climbed away. The flames spread and the plane went down at an angle.''

In all, the Japanese claimed seven Superfortresses destroyed on June 15-16 (the Americans acknowledged seven losses from all causes, but none over the target). Nevertheless, Japanese authorities regarded the engagement as an embarrassing failure. The high command had established the minimum goal for planes shot down as 50 per cent of the attacking force—and by that ambitious reckoning the defenders had fallen far short.

Indeed, analysis of the June 15-16 encounter was to reveal it as a profile of the troubles that afflicted Japanese attempts to thwart American bombing from the beginning of the B-29 offensive until the end of March 1945; at that time, a pivotal decision to accept no more pilot trainees for anything but a last-ditch battle against an Allied invasion signaled the end of Japan's high-priority defense against the B-29. From March onward, planes and pilots were increasingly reserved for the climactic struggle, and by early summer of 1945, air defense was just a shrunken adjunct of the anti-invasion strategy.

Though the outcome of the investigation that began the day after the June 15-16 encounter over Kyushu flattered no one, the weight of authorities' disapproval fell most heavily on the antiaircraft artillery. Despite their prodigious expenditure of shells—averaging about 75 rounds per cannon—the flak gunners had not claimed even one B-29 shot down. As punishment for this horrendous performance, the senior staff officer of the Western Army antiaircraft command was reprimanded by his superiors, and the commander of the 131st AA Regiment, covering the Yawata area, was ignominiously transferred to Manchuria.

As for the fighter command, the investigation leveled some disturbing charges against the aircraft, their equipment and their deployment. The eight Dragon Killers that had been sent aloft were found to have insufficient speed and rate of climb to close effectively on the B-29s; lack of adequate radar was another factor in the failure of the night fighters to down more bombers. Most of those claimed, it seemed, had been spotted not by radar but by searchlights.

Still, the night fighters had borne the brunt of combat.

The other planes available to the Fourth Air Group were mostly Kawasaki Ki-61s (Hiens, or Swallows, to the Japanese, ''Tonys'' to the Americans). These aircraft were single-engined day fighters without radar or other special equipment. However, a number of their pilots were highly skilled and might have given a good account of themselves had they been allowed to fight. But few had been ordered into action, and the investigators were particularly irked that the fighter commander had not used every machine he could lay his hands on. Veterans of the encounter speculated that he may have been too inflexible to imagine that day fighters properly coordinated with radar, searchlights and night fighters could play a role at night.

There was more. The Cheju radar station, for example, had sounded a timely general alert, but had not been able to provide accurate information about the raiders' numbers or types. Communications were execrable; almost no information was passed from the ground to the pilots aloft. And some pilots were sent up to hunt for bombers without receiving even the most rudimentary briefing. Incredibly, one fighter pilot was told almost nothing of what was going on before he took off and had to work things out for himself as he gained altitude, basing his guesswork on fragments of what sounded to him like American radio transmissions. As the pilot remembered it later, ''Everything was dark below me and I had difficulty maintaining my position, but as I climbed I heard something like jazz coming over my radio and I guessed that an air raid was coming that night.''

The inquiry painted an exceedingly dismal picture—a portrait of one of the least effective air-defense systems of any World War II belligerent. The bleakness of the situation extended far beyond matters directly considered by the official June 16 post-mortem. Among the most pervasive ills was a bitter interservice rivalry between the Japanese Army and Navy. A unit of Navy fighters in Kyushu, for example, apparently never got into the battle. The reason probably lay in the needlessly obstructive competition between separate Army and Navy air forces and antiaircraft gun units, negating their effectiveness and poisoning communications.

Each service jealously guarded its independence and its separate responsibilities. By tradition, the Navy's planes and

LAST HURRAH FOR A ONE-EYED ACE

The rise and fall of Japan's air forces were epitomized in the remarkable career of its most durable ace, Saburo Sakai. Rigorously trained, supremely skilled—and flying the feared Mitsubishi Zero—Sakai early in the War personified the invincibility of the Rising Sun. By the end he was half blind, desperately flinging himself and his Zero, now sadly obsolete, against a mighty American armada.

Sakai saw it all. He enlisted in the Japanese Navy in 1933 at the age of 16 and four years later was accepted for training in the Navy's elite air service. Sent to China in 1938, as a noncommissioned pilot, he shot down a Russian-built fighter on his first combat mission. Such were the rigorous standards of the day that on landing Sakai received a reprimand for breaking formation instead of congratulations for his kill.

On Pearl Harbor day Sakai's squadron attacked Clark Field in the Philippines. He shot down a P-40, and two days later, protecting an invasion convoy, he bagged bigger game: a B-17, flown by Captain Colin P. Kelly Jr., who posthumously became a hero in the United States for his solo attack on the enemy convoy.

Sakai's unit moved steadily forward as a cutting edge of the Japanese juggernaut: to Borneo, Bali, New Britain and as far as New Guinea. Sakai enjoyed spectacular success, running his victory toll to 60 by early August of 1942. But on the day he got the 60th kill—contesting the U.S. landing on Guadalcanal—Sakai made a grievous error, mistaking rear-firing Grumman Avengers for Wildcats, whose guns could only shoot forward. "Flames spurted from two bombers," Sakai recalled. "The world burst into flaming red and I went blind."

Sakai somehow made it back to his base at Rabaul, five hours away, but he had been permanently blinded in

one eye. The Navy found a use for him as an instructor. By 1944, however, Japan was desperate for pilots and Sakai once more went to war.

He found it much changed. Most of his comrades from the glory days were dead, replaced by shockingly undertrained young pilots, flying and quickly dying in outclassed machines. The Zero Sakai now flew, except for a slightly stronger engine and better cannon, was a virtual duplicate of the plane in which he once had ruled the sky. Nevertheless, he added four more kills to his score and gained promotion at last to ensign.

In the War's last hours, the one-eyed pilot took a last bead on the hated symbol of American air power, the B-29. On August 13th, with surrender imminent, Sakai and a fellow pilot, Ensign Jiro Kawachi, made a compact to fly one more time. When the alert sounded near midnight they were waiting beside their Zeroes and took off into the moonless sky. Sakai, distrusting his one good eye, asked Kawachi to lead him off the ground.

Guided by starlight, it was Kawachi who found the Superfortress, alone over Tokyo. Sakai could not see the B-29 until tracers flashed from Kawachi's guns. Then Sakai joined the attack. "The counterfire was terrible," he wrote later. "Tracers spilled into the air from the multiple turrets on the B-29, and I felt the Zero shudder as the enemy gunners found their mark."

The bomber, apparently damaged, ran for home. The Japanese pilots had no intention of losing it now. "Kawachi cut inside the B-29's wide turn and led me down in a shallow diving attack," Sakai wrote. "We had a clear shot and both Kawachi and I kept the triggers down, watching the tracers and shells ripping into the glass along the bomber's nose. We had him!"

The stricken aircraft lost speed and went into a long dive. Saburo Sakai could make out the splash of white foam as it hit the water and disappeared. His shared 65th kill was the last B-29 shot down in World War II.

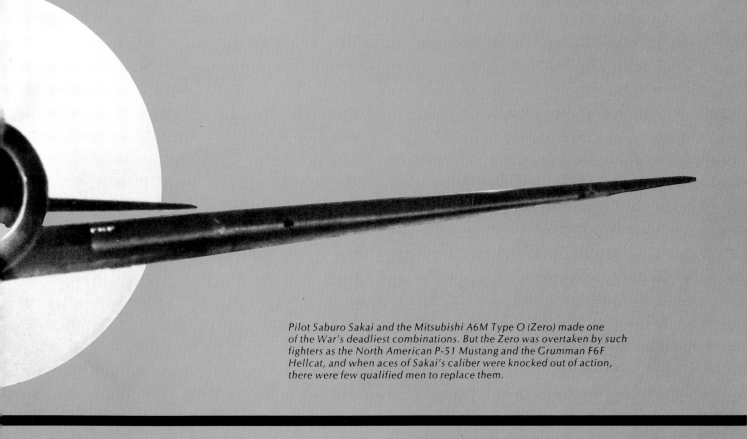

Pilot Saburo Sakai and the Mitsubishi A6M Type O (Zero) made one of the War's deadliest combinations. But the Zero was overtaken by such fighters as the North American P-51 Mustang and the Grumman F6F Hellcat, and when aces of Sakai's caliber were knocked out of action, there were few qualified men to replace them.

antiaircraft guns were supposed to defend its ships, bases and other installations, while the Army was responsible for protecting cities and industrial targets as well as its own bases. The arrangement made some sense, but there was no machinery—and little inclination—for one service to help out another in time of need.

The gulf that separated the services extended virtually to every aspect of their operations. Procurement officers specified that planes for the Army and Navy be armed with machine guns of different calibers and equipped with electrical systems of different voltages. Partly as a result of this friction and incompatibility, no overall air-defense combat command was ever set up—although desperation eventually forced some local cooperation, and a number of Navy planes were assigned to regional Army defense commands.

Most disastrous of all, for both services, was the drain of pilots that had begun within a few months after the attack on Pearl Harbor and had continued without letup. From the Battle of Midway in June 1942 through the end of 1943, no fewer than 10,000 Japanese pilots had been killed. Replacing these highly trained men was an insuperable task.

The combat in which these fliers perished had in its early phases been conducted over distant seas and shores. Japanese strategy in World War II had been always to protect Japan by keeping the foe far from the homeland and defeating him in a short war. As a matter of tradition, Japanese military thinking was permeated by the offensive spirit; in imperial war councils, the idea of defending against attack had little standing.

At the time of Pearl Harbor, Japan's air defenses had included only 210 antiaircraft guns to cover the 66 important industrial cities that later were targeted by the XXI Bomber Command. There were a mere 10 squadrons of fighters—

about 160 planes, manned by the most junior of pilots. The worst situation envisioned by Japanese planners was a suicidal one-way raid launched from somewhere in the Pacific—possibly from a carrier. But that was scarcely found credible—until it actually came to pass with the carrier-launched raid on Tokyo conducted by 16 B-25s under Lieut. Colonel James H. Doolittle in April 1942. After the Doolittle raid, the Japanese undertook the first overhaul of their air-defense system—bringing some experienced fighter units back from the combat zones and adding 60 guns to the antiaircraft artillery.

In the spring of 1944, when the Japanese military perimeter was crumbling rapidly in the central and southwest Pacific, the high command seriously began to reexamine the "best-defense-is-a-good-offense" attitude. But it went against the grain, and only a few staff officers managed to alter their thinking radically. For many others, threats on the ground and at sea loomed larger than aerial bombing—and in any case, the extent of the B-29 menace at that time was far from manifest.

Since no one had ever really envisioned a defensive role for Japanese fighters, their ability to repel a heavily armed, high-performance bomber such as the Superfortress was very much in doubt from the outset. The June 16 Western Army investigation had arraigned the Dragon Killer—a relatively advanced Japanese aircraft—for insufficient speed and climbing ability against the B-29. Carried to a logical conclusion, the investigation would have gone on to impeach the Japanese government's management of the country's entire aircraft industry. No one in authority had ever truly realized that the War would be a long, drawn-out affair with enormous attrition, and that the outcome would be decided as much in the nation's factories and workshops as on the battlefield. The aircraft industry, in particular, was crippled by poor planning—mainly a failure to consider what would happen if Japan suffered reverses—along with shortages of vital materials. Nor did anyone think of stockpiling sufficient fuel on the home islands in case the oil fields of Indonesia were denied to the Japanese.

Given the priority that Japan's leaders assigned to operations overseas, the establishment of an effective air-defense force was probably foredoomed in any case. Japanese industry simply lacked the capacity to accomplish both tasks at once. Nonetheless, the Japanese launched a massive effort. Beginning in 1943, textile plants, a centerpiece of Japan's peacetime economy, were converted with a stroke of Prime Minister Hideki Tojo's pen into aircraft plants. Thousands of women who had worked in the textile mills were trained to build airplanes. The sprawling Mitsubishi industrial empire, which built ships and refined oil as well as made planes, now concentrated on aircraft manufacture.

By the end of 1944, aircraft production had increased 69 per cent over 1943. The growing emphasis was on fighters for defense, and such planes ultimately accounted for half of Japan's total aircraft production; in 1941, the proportion of fighters had been only 21 per cent.

Striking though these figures might seem, they fell woefully short of what was needed. Japanese planners had called for 97,000 aircraft to be manufactured between January 1944 and August 1945; in the end, only 40,000 could be delivered, most of them light, obsolete fighters, such as the Mitsubishi Zero, for use primarily against an invasion. Raw-material shortages plagued the production effort—particularly a lack of steel alloys that was the major factor in holding engine production below planned levels. An aluminum shortage handcuffed the manufacture of airframes; Nakajima's engineers sought to get around the problem by building some planes partly or entirely of wood.

Despite all efforts, the fierce level of combat in the South Pacific had virtually wiped out any gain in production. The American factories were winning the battle; the balance of Japanese and American frontline aircraft strength in the Pacific Theater, roughly equal in January 1943, stood in favor of the United States in January 1945 by a margin of four to one.

When the B-29 campaign began, the Japanese were organized into four regional defense zones, each under local Army command. All but one command, designated as Central, were named for a point of the compass. The Tokyo area was covered by the Eastern Army, Kyushu and the southwestern end of Honshu by the Western command. The Central Army was responsible for the midsection of Honshu, and the island of Hokkaido was the domain of the Northern Army. Each Army controlled its own defense facilities, including radar, lookouts and other warning systems, fighters,

In the Kawasaki aircraft plant near Nagoya, workmen assemble Ki-61 Swallow fighters. The Swallow, which the Americans called the Tony, was fast, maneuverable and structurally sturdier than most other Japanese fighters. It was also the first to use cockpit armor and self-sealing fuel tanks. Production of the plane was crippled in early 1945 by a B-29 raid on another plant, where the Swallow's engines were made.

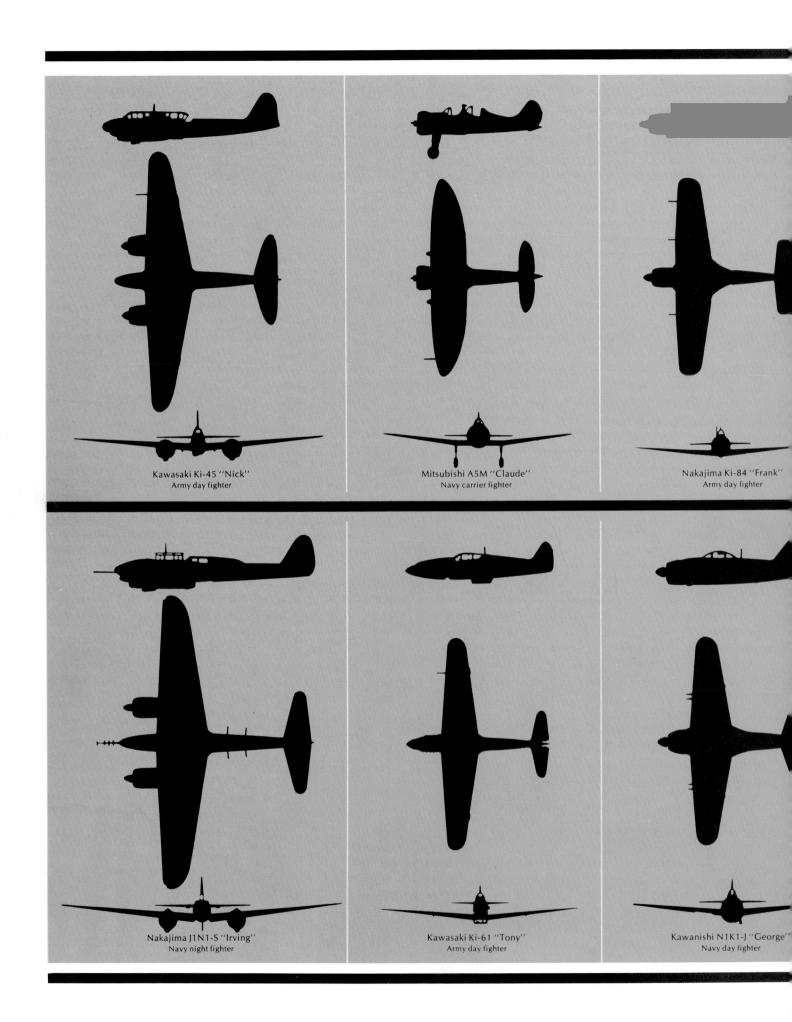

Kawasaki Ki-45 "Nick"
Army day fighter

Mitsubishi A5M "Claude"
Navy carrier fighter

Nakajima Ki-84 "Frank"
Army day fighter

Nakajima J1N1-S "Irving"
Navy night fighter

Kawasaki Ki-61 "Tony"
Army day fighter

Kawanishi N1K1-J "George"
Navy day fighter

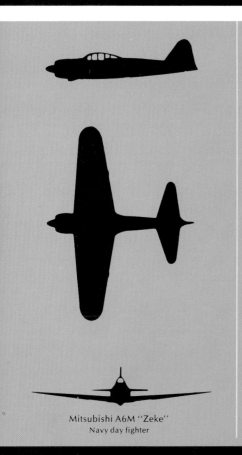

Mitsubishi A6M "Zeke"
Navy day fighter

Nakajima Ki-43 "Oscar"
Army day fighter

Nakajima Ki-44 "Tojo"
Army day fighter

Nakajima Ki-27 "Nate"
Army day fighter

Mitsubishi J2M "Jack"
Navy day fighter

SILHOUETTES FOR INSTANT RECOGNITION

Superfortresses flying over the Japanese homeland in 1944 and 1945 encountered almost a dozen different types of enemy fighter planes. In order to recognize—and deal effectively with—them, B-29 crews and their fighter-pilot escorts studied recognition charts of Japanese planes such as those shown here. The charts enabled pilots and gunners to identify an attacker in an instant by its silhouette—whether seen from the side, from above or below, or head-on. Planes with retractable landing gear were shown with their wheels up.

Intelligence officers supplied information on the characteristics of each aircraft, including its speed, maneuverability, armament, rate of climb and the highest altitude at which it could operate.

To simplify communications, the Americans coined code names for most of the Japanese planes, including the three new high-performance fighters introduced during the War's final months: the Mitsubishi J2M became Jack, the Kawanishi N1K1-J George and the Kawasaki Ki-61 Tony.

antiaircraft guns and searchlights. The total of aircraft assigned to defense came to just under 1,000, about two thirds in the more heavily industrial Eastern and Central Army areas of Kyushu and Honshu. Because of maintenance problems, only 300 to 500 were combat-ready on any given day. But despite the shortage of mechanics and parts even these numbers would have been formidable had the planes themselves been up to the task.

Far and away the greatest number were day fighters bearing such poetic names as Peregrine Falcon, Devil Queller and Violet Lightning and code-named by the prosaic Americans with the labels Oscar, Tojo and George. By and large they were too slow, too low-flying and too poorly armed to pose a serious problem for the B-29s, with their 357-mph maximum speed, 33,000-foot altitude and 10 to 12 computer-controlled .50-caliber machine guns.

Most of the Japanese fighters lacked armor for the pilot, or worse, gasoline tanks with rubber casings capable of sealing themselves if pierced by bullets. Japanese attempts to beef up the armament of their fighters often proved ineffectual. The Nakajima Ki-44 Devil Queller, or Tojo, boasted two huge 40mm cannon in addition to a pair of 12.7mm machine guns; but the cannon, with a very low muzzle velocity, had an effective range of only 150 yards compared to the 1,200-yard range of the B-29's guns.

Typical of Japanese problems were their experiences with two relatively advanced fighters, the Mitsubishi J2M Thunderbolt, code-named Jack, and the Kawanishi N1K1-J Violet Lightning, or George. The Thunderbolt was a heavy, powerful plane that was intended to take the famed Zero's place as the Navy's premier fighter. But one veteran test pilot, Navy Ensign Saburo Sakai, had reservations. He judged the Thunderbolt capable of reaching the B-29's altitude and carrying sufficient firepower, at speeds exceeding 380 mph, to knock the bomber down. But he found the plane a truck to fly compared to the Zero in which he had built his reputation (pages 128-129). It required superior skill from its pilot at a time when Japan was running very short of fliers who were even adequately trained. Many a neophyte assigned to fly the Thunderbolt before he was ready lost his life.

In the hands of a man who understood it, however, Sakai conceded that the fighter was a weapon of great power. He cited the case of a flamboyant pilot named Teimei Akamatsu. The man drank to excess, yelled, boasted and refused to attend briefings. He had his own alert system wired into a brothel, and when an alarm sounded, raced to the field in his ancient automobile, waving a bottle in one hand. For all his eccentricity, Akamatsu could handle the Thunderbolt; although he apparently never shot down a Superfortress, Sakai gave him credit for shooting down at least six of the American fighters—Army P-51 Mustangs and Navy F6F Hellcats—that began flying over Japan in February and March of 1945. But there were very few pilots of Akamatsu's caliber, and the Thunderbolt was essentially a plane without pilots.

A contemporary of the Thunderbolt, the Violet Lightning, or George, was another potentially formidable craft that was full of problems. It had armor plating and a good turn of speed at about 360 mph, and its main virtue was maneuverability to match the Zero's—along with heavy armament: up to four wing-mounted 20mm cannon. But the Lightning, with an engine subject to sudden failure, was also treacherous. "Too many men with little time behind the controls of a fighter plane," said Sakai, "never lived to fly the Lightning into combat. Their familiarization flights killed them."

The greatest overall handicap faced by the Japanese defenders was their inability to reach the altitudes where the B-29s normally cruised and fight there effectively. Designed primarily for tactical support of attacking surface forces, most of them had slow rates of climb and required 50 to 60 minutes to reach a height of 32,000 feet (compared, for example, to the British Supermarine Spitfire, designed for defense, which could climb to 34,000 feet in less than 15 minutes). Only one plane, the Nakajima Ki-84—Hayate, or Gale, to the Japanese, "Frank" to the Americans—was rated for 40,000 feet, which should have been more than enough to punish the B-29s. But the plane had severe fuel-pressure problems, which handicapped its usefulness.

Most Japanese fighters had an effective ceiling of only about 16,000 feet; this meant that at twice that height, even a slight bank resulted in a loss of altitude that might take 10 to 20 minutes to regain—by which time the B-29s were long gone. About all most Japanese fighters could do was make one pass, attacking in straight and level flight.

To accomplish even this much at night, it was first necessary to find the target. The airborne radar carried by the Navy's primary night fighter, the twin-engined Nakajima J1N1-S Gekko, or Moonlight ("Irving" to the Americans)—was primitive and unreliable. Their crews—and the pilots of the day fighters that formed the bulk of the forces—relied mainly on their unaided eyes. To compensate for inadequate technology, training for night combat stressed maintaining a precise flight pattern, within an assigned interception area, that was designed to sweep a sector of sky. Contact with a B-29 was thus almost literally a shot in the dark—little more than a chance encounter.

The only real chance the defenders got to stalk a visible quarry lay in the searchlights on the ground that were assigned to spot bombers for antiaircraft guns as well as fighters. Searchlights were generally about five feet in diameter and were effective to about 26,000 feet; above that altitude, at the B-29's level, they were only marginally useful. But in mid-1944, Japan's searchlight units suffered from so many shortcomings that they were largely useless.

Searchlight operations were a sorry contrast, for example, with those of Germany. As early as 1940, the Luftwaffe had set up its searchlights to operate with night fighters in western Europe and attack Allied bombers both coming and going. By 1941, radar-controlled master searchlights were able to spot a bomber and lock onto it until the manually controlled lights could find it.

Few such devices were available to help Japanese searchlights find their targets. Apart from the altitude of the bombers, which often exceeded the lights' range, the worst problem was basic: a shortage of lights. Typically, when the air defenses of Nagoya were reinforced in 1944, newly formed searchlight units were scheduled to receive 96 lights; only six were actually issued by mid-December. And though most of the rest were delivered in a slow trickle, 18 never arrived. Moreover, for lack of training facilities crews were mostly assigned to operational units with little or no instruction and had to teach themselves on the job. Their performance showed it; in December 1944, according to a Japanese report, searchlight defense in the Nagoya area was so poor that on any given raid, the chances of an individual B-29 being fixed by a beam was about one in a hundred.

Similar fundamental flaws afflicted the antiaircraft artillery. Until mid-1944, the standard Japanese flak weapon was a 75mm gun that was capable of hurling a shell only 20,000 feet into the air, well below a B-29 at altitude; and even by the spring of 1945 more than half of the cannon in northern Kyushu were of this obsolete type. The Japanese did produce a more powerful 88mm weapon, of the same caliber as the celebrated German gun (which was even more effective against tanks than aircraft); but the Japanese version of the 88 never earned the same reputation, and production was slow in any case. A second weapon that seemed to promise much—a giant 150mm gun weighing more than 100,000 pounds, with a barrel nearly 30 feet long—was rushed into production during the last months of the War. In the spring of 1945, two of the first models were emplaced in the Tokyo area, where they may have accounted for some of the seven Superfortresses lost to enemy action on May 23 and 25, in the last two incendiary raids on the capital.

Ammunition for guns of all calibers was a standard artillery high-explosive shell, fitted in some cases with spring-activated fuses that could be set to detonate at a predetermined height. Other shells had so-called powder-train fuses, which combined a preset timer with a slow-burning train of powder that acted as a delayed detonator. Shells with such time fuses depended on accurate calculation of a target's height and speed for their effect. Beginning in 1944, antiaircraft units received instantaneous fuses designed to explode on impact; these were somewhat more effective than spring-activated or powder-train time-delay devices, which had a tendency to explode too soon or even pass through a target and explode harmlessly in the air.

The shells themselves were soon in grievously short supply. The scarcity grew worse as industrial production plummeted due to the American bombing; in May 1945, for example, the production of flak shells fell 53 per cent from the April figure. As for radar sighting mechanisms, a few devices were available to units near Nagoya beginning in the fall of 1944. Though such equipment was fully installed by the following March, the gunners continually complained about the inaccuracy of their radar computations—particularly for the altitude of hostile aircraft.

Between the start of B-29 raids in June 1944 and the summer of 1945, records of Japanese claims for their antiaircraft gunners against B-29s do not contain a cumulative total. American records, however, list more than 2,000 B-29s as damaged, but credit antiaircraft with taking part in the actual downing of only 29 bombers. These statistics confirm that in military terms, the effectiveness of antiaircraft was relatively minor—though there was probably some benefit to morale. As one Japanese put it after the War, "Apparently the brass felt better when AA guns could be heard firing during an air raid. The sound conveyed the feeling that something effective was being done."

In the litany of Japanese failure, no greater example of inadequacy could be found than the performance of the early-warning systems designed to pinpoint Superfortresses approaching from China or the Mariana Islands. The Japanese early-warning system, like those of Britain and Germany, comprised not only long-range radar but ground observers and intelligence units assigned to monitor American radio transmissions.

Unlike the British radar, which could detect planes approaching either very high (up to 30,000 feet) or as low as wave height, the types of radar employed by Japan could pick up little above 26,000 feet or below 9,000 feet. When Japanese radar did find a target, it could determine distance within a range of about 155 miles, but until late 1944 it could not determine altitude. It could not detect single planes or small groups, and it could not distinguish a B-29 from any other type of plane, although that distinction was not important until North American P-51 Mustangs began escorting the Superfortresses in the spring of 1945.

Patrolling about 600 miles offshore, 50 Navy picket boats were assigned to report enemy naval activity as well as inbound aircraft. The vessels were strung out at wide intervals on a line running east to west through the Bonin Islands so as to cover the approaches to Japan from the Marianas. The boats were in excellent position to spot the B-29s, but their effectiveness was soon reduced as aggressive American naval operations drove them farther and farther back toward the home islands. Another of the boats' handicaps was their lack of radar; only one picket was equipped with a set, and in March 1945 that boat was sunk.

In predicting and providing warning of air raids, radio intelligence was relatively more successful than any other

SELLING THE SOUNDS OF DOOM

The sounds made by B-29 engines, recorded through "do-or-die efforts under an air raid," were sold in Japan for civil defense. The May 1945 newspaper advertisement below promised the purchasers of a pair of 10-inch records, endorsed by the government, that they would learn to recognize the distant roar of approaching planes before the bombs fell—and thus improve their chances of taking shelter in time.

An advertisement offers the sound of a single B-29, or many.

method. The basic tools of this operation were a receiver and a radio direction finder. They were used to pick up patterns of American radio traffic, and to figure out roughly where they were coming from. American security procedures protected codes and other high secrets, but among the Superfortress crews radio discipline was poor. By studying which frequencies the Americans favored and monitoring their careless chatter and repeated use of the same call signals, the Japanese could identify B-29 squadrons as they assembled for a strike. The intelligence units became very adept at their work, and by early 1945 they were able to give the defenders four or five hours' warning of an impending raid.

Unfortunately for the Japanese, even this margin was not of much help—partly because the information, though timely, was too general. Unless the target of a raid could be pinpointed, fighter commanders were reluctant to send their planes aloft; for one thing, fuel was in such short supply that every drop was precious. Confirmation from radar and other elements of the system was necessary to complete the warning cycle and justify scrambling planes. As the B-29 raiders bore down on the islands, however, the limitations of Japanese communications facilities combined with geography to put the defense seriously behind schedule. Communications were old-fashioned and centralized to a degree guaranteed to create major tangles and bottlenecks. To reach combat contingents, warnings from radio intelligence had to be funneled through the telephone switchboard at the War Ministry in Tokyo—which, naturally, took too much time.

As the B-29 attacks grew ever more devastating, strenuous efforts were made to unsnarl such problems, and some improvements were made. Direct telephone lines were hooked up to link intelligence groups and combat-control centers. But there was little that could be done about the physical makeup of Japan itself, which posed a fatal problem for efficient air defense.

In Germany, raiding Allied bombers could be tracked and attacked for many miles as they approached their inland targets, with ground-based radar and aerial observers announcing their every move. However, the topography of Japan, with its long, thin string of islands, made for a constricted aerial battleground. Most of its vulnerable areas —the Superfortresses' targets—were bunched along the east coast, facing the Pacific; the American bombers could set course out over the ocean and appear above their target with very little notice.

Under the best of circumstances late in the War, solid confirmation of a raid on Tokyo could come from island radar stations when the bombers were still about 325 miles from the capital. But the fighter units had to wait for the uncertain communications system to transmit news of the sighting. This took at least three minutes. Then the fighters had to wait for the actual orders to scramble, which might take another seven minutes. Takeoff time just for the lead planes of the units assigned to intercept might add up to 15 minutes—and then it took between 50 minutes and an hour to reach the Superfortresses' lofty height. Total: between 75 and 80 minutes from confirmed alarm to any possible contact.

It all took too long. The B-29s, which could fly from the maximum-defense radar range to Tokyo in an hour, could often roar in, drop their bombs and beat a swift retreat almost before their adversaries were able to fire a shot. Yet for all the obstacles in their way, the fighter pilots, the gunners and the other defenders gave the struggle all the effort they could muster.

The Japanese use of suicidal Kamikaze attacks on American ships, beginning in October 1944 during the Battle of the Philippines, inflicted awesome damage. The practice may have had its origin in a similarly desperate tactic used by fighter pilots against the B-29s. The first recorded instance of a ramming attack against B-29s might have been an accident; it came during the second Yawata raid on August 20, 1944—a day that produced one of the most successful all-around efforts by the Japanese air defense, which brought down 14 B-29s.

Two of the Superfortresses were destroyed by a Japanese sergeant pilot named Shigeo Nobe, flying a twin-engined Dragon Killer. Swooping in on the B-29s, Nobe fired a burst at a bomber but missed his target. Then, as fellow fliers recalled hearing it on their radios, Nobe exclaimed, "I'm going in after him!" Whether he meant to or not, Nobe slammed his fighter into the huge American craft. There was an instantaneous explosion that disintegrated both planes—and a large piece of the Superfortress, apparently an engine, hurtled back and slammed into the bomber to its right rear. Fatally damaged, the second plane lost a wing and spun to the ground.

In the months to come, the ramming tactic became a recognized, if unofficial, part of Japanese air-defense doctrine, justified as an admittedly desperate means of compensating for the lack of experienced pilots. It took little skill to steer a fighter into a B-29, at least in theory. Army pilots experimented briefly—and generally unsuccessfully—with a technique that called for jumping out of a fighter just before it hit the target. Ramming was later officially sanctioned in a January 18, 1945, directive from the Japanese high command arguing that the tactic was economically profitable. Since the Japanese would be sacrificing only one plane and one pilot to wipe out a huge, expensive B-29 and all 11 men of its highly trained crew, the directive stated, "It would be a great mistake to hold the view that this method does not pay."

In truth, the suicide tactic was not particularly fruitful. The maneuver was more complicated than it seemed: A stern or beam approach put the attacker at the mercy of the B-29's many guns, while a head-on or front-quarter attack, at a closure rate of better than 500 mph, demanded an experienced pilot—which contradicted a major purpose in using the tactic.

What little success Japan enjoyed against the B-29 often came through the agency of its night fighters, the Army Dragon Killer and the Navy Moonlight, both twin-engined and cannon-equipped, some with obliquely mounted guns. The Navy planes first went into action defending against the Yawata raid on August 20, 1944. The engagement introduced one of the few aces in Japan's home-defense force: Lieutenant Sachio Endo, a veteran of the battles against American B-17s and B-24s in the Solomons and at Rabaul. Flying a Moonlight, Endo slipped underneath a Superfortress and destroyed it by firing upward with the fighter's obliquely mounted 20mm cannon; the victory was the Navy's first over a B-29.

Endo's name appears again on the record of a November 21 engagement, when he chased a bomber returning to China as far as Cheju Island and sent it flaming into the sea. By now, Endo was becoming known for his technique in at-

Curious Japanese crowd Tokyo's Hibiya Park to peer at a full-scale model of a B-29 along with the Kawasaki Swallow that brought down the original aircraft on December 3, 1944. The fighter pilot managed to crash-land his damaged plane in a rice paddy. The B-29 was demolished, but the Japanese made a reasonably accurate guess at the arrangement of crew stations in its nose. Beneath the painted cutaway are remnants of the bomber: tires, machine-gun parts and, at far right, a fuel tank.

tacking B-29s, firing from behind and beneath with his angled guns. In December, after Marianas-based Superfortresses began pounding the Tokyo and Nagoya areas heavily, Endo was named to command a squadron stationed near the capital. The unit fought with great valor in battles on January 9 and 14, 1945, claiming four bombers downed and 14 damaged. Endo's heroic path through the sky came to an end on the 14th. He was shot down in combat with B-29s of a 40-plane bomb run over Nagoya. He had been accorded six B-29 victories, and he was given a double promotion, from lieutenant to commander, an honor almost never granted in the tradition-bound Japanese Navy—except posthumously.

At this point in its travail, Japan's hard-pressed air defense was forced to face an entirely new enemy. On February 16, the carriers of Vice Admiral Marc A. Mitscher's Task Force 58 launched seven waves of fighters, assigned to clear the way for later bombing missions against airfields in the area around Tokyo. The Navy aircraft, flying in at low altitude, had eluded the radar warning system and were first spotted by a Japanese lookout post when they were only about 75 miles south of Tokyo.

The day's action did not go well for the defense forces. When it was over, the Japanese Army acknowledged 37 planes lost in the air and two on the ground (the Americans made a total claim for that day and the next, undoubtedly exaggerated, of 341 Japanese planes shot down and 190 destroyed on the ground). The defenders had great trouble determining their own bag of American planes because pilots and ground observers, accustomed to seeing four-engined bombers and unused to the smaller American carrier aircraft, got Japanese and enemy planes mixed up (U.S. combat losses were actually 60). A bold plan to go after the American carriers with bombers on February 17 was canceled on account of bad weather. But the carrier planes managed to fly and returned to the attack. After the brief period of combat over Japan before the weather caused both sides to break off, the Japanese admitted losing an additional 14 planes.

The United States Navy would return to Japanese home waters twice during the course of the next four weeks, and then not again until July. But these engagements, although they were less successful, further decimated Japan's dwindling reserves of fighters and the airmen to fly them.

By March 1945, only 500 serviceable fighters were available to Japan's air-defense force. Many aircraft factories were damaged and unable to replace losses, let alone raise Japan's air strength to a level capable of recapturing the initiative. The shortage of pilots was beyond recall, and training facilities lacked instructors, planes and fuel to conduct a cohesive program. Fuel, in fact, was becoming the most critical of the many shortages for the air-defense forces. Even in late 1944, high-octane gasoline was so scarce that there were three or four student-pilots to each training plane for which fuel could be found. The authorities abandoned all thought of the meticulous training once characteristic of the Japanese air forces. Now, the high command decided to opt for the largest number of pilots they could train in the shortest time.

Among the instructors was the veteran fighter pilot Saburo Sakai. Grievously wounded in action, he had been assigned to provide advanced training for recent graduates of flight school. His pupils were discouragingly green, and Sakai's heart sank, as he wrote later, when he saw them arrive at his training wing. "They were eager and serious young men, unquestionably brave. But determination and courage were no substitute for pilot skill."

Instructors like Sakai had to hector their pupils: "That's a control stick you're holding there, not a broom handle," Sakai remembered saying to a pupil sitting in the cockpit of a training aircraft. In gunnery drills, he had to prod students: "Squeeze your trigger for short bursts; don't burn out your guns."

Whatever the level of training, scarcity of fuel inevitably curtailed it to a degree guaranteed to frustrate an eager student. One such learner, Ryuji Nagatsuka, had soloed in 1944 after some months of instruction; he felt he was progressing toward his goal of challenging the Superfortresses when the fuel allotment for his training unit ran out. Grounded, the students read textbooks and—smarting at the ignominy of it all—were kept busy at bayonet drill like ordinary infantrymen.

After a 10-day fuel drought, a new supply arrived. It was not standard aviation gasoline, however, but a substance called A-Go—a mixture of gasoline and alcohol that was

Cliffside entrances in a rock quarry (top left) lead to an aircraft factory that was moved underground at Oya, Japan, in 1945 to escape the B-29s. The 537,000-square-foot plant was set up to manufacture engines, fuselages and wings for a fighter plane, the Nakajima Gale. A shortage of materials and skilled labor created a bottleneck in the engine section, shown at left, and in three months only 70 of the engines were completed.

hazardously unreliable. Engines began quitting in flight; four student pilots were killed. Nagatsuka himself had a narrow escape when his engine quit and he had to land in a plowed field; his plane flipped over, but he suffered only a sprained ankle.

Toward the end of November 1944, Nagatsuka's school ran out of fuel again; this time the authorities said there would be no more. With navigation and gunnery still unlearned, the students were told that they would be shipped off to combat units. Whatever advanced training they might receive from now on would be sandwiched between combat missions. Nagatsuka was assigned to a unit on Kyushu, where he qualified to fly against B-29s in a Nakajima Ki-27, a prewar monoplane with fixed landing gear and two light machine guns.

Nagatsuka went out on December 20 in a flight of 15 Ki-27s with seven other cadets and seven veteran noncommissioned pilots. At 16,000 feet they saw a B-29 below them, its wings gleaming in the winter sun. Nagatsuka dived through a cloud, followed closely by his wingman, an NCO named Tanizaki. The B-29's upper turrets began firing at them. Tanizaki moved in to take out the B-29's tail gun while Nagatsuka tried to strafe the cockpit, believing that the only way to bring down a Superfortress with a Ki-27's light guns was to kill the pilot. Nagatsuka missed. The bomber's bullets began to tear up his own cockpit and he sideslipped away. "Our Ki-27s were like gadflies on the back of a large, impassive cow," Nagatsuka reflected. "One flick of her tail, and the gadflies scattered." In impotent rage, he thought perhaps he ought to ram. But he thought better of it, and flew home.

As far as the records show, no Superfortresses were lost to the heroic but hapless trainees that day. Nor do the postwar accountings indicate how many students and noncoms went to their doom. After March of 1945, with certain exceptions—men who were selected to form the cadre of a future, postwar air force—most pilots in training were destined to be assigned to the so-called Special Attack, or

A decoy fighter constructed of bamboo and draped in camouflage netting is set up on a Japanese airfield to draw American bombing and strafing attacks. Such dummies were easy to build and could fool a pilot flying at high speed. Meanwhile, the real planes were dispersed to hiding places a safe distance from the airfield.

Kamikaze, units. Many members of these units went to their deaths in suicide attacks on American ships during the invasion of Okinawa; the remainder awaited the climactic battle for the homeland. Their planes were hidden well away from airfields, shrouded under camouflage nets, concealed beneath groves of trees or kept in underground caves or dugouts.

Even as they struggled to organize the remnants of their air forces for a final apocalyptic struggle, the Japanese were by no means entirely deflected from the immediate task of fighting the Superfortresses. Though outgunned by the B-29's armament and outclassed by its speed and its ability to fly at great heights, the defenders devised a number of expedients designed to penetrate the bomber's guard from a safe distance.

Some of these devices were ingenious, although most of them—like the ramming tactic—were generally futile. There were a number of variations, for example, on a bomb intended to be dropped into a formation of Superfortresses from above; in one configuration, the bomb's casing was designed to split open and spray smaller containers of explosives among the B-29s. Another approach involved several small bombs connected by a length of chain; the chain would, it was hoped, wind itself around one or more aircraft and pull the bombs in close to the planes' fragile skins. As far as anyone knows, no such contraption ever destroyed or even damaged a B-29.

These special weapons were consistent with the overall futility of the Japanese air defense, as reflected in its results. From the start of the B-29 raids to the end of the War, the total number of Superfortresses lost to Japanese action amounted to a mere 87 in the course of 31,387 combat sorties. That worked out to a bit more than one quarter of 1 per cent, or one plane in approximately 360 sorties. By striking contrast, American Air Forces in Europe lost 5,514 bombers of all types to German air defenses for a loss-sortie rate of 1.18 per cent. In fact, nearly five times as many B-29s were

lost to accidents in the Pacific theater as to enemy action.

However weak their defense of home airspace, the Japanese maintained to the bitter end a highly positive approach based on their nation's hallowed military tradition. A highly placed civilian official such as the Home Defense chief, Prince Higashikuni, could utter doubts about the eventual outcome of the War following the occupation of the Marianas by American forces. But few Japanese in uniform would admit such thoughts. Told that they would have ample ammunition soon, antiaircraft troops in the Nagoya district trained fervently through the awful summer of 1945. They believed that they would soon annihilate the American bombers by the dozens, firing 10,000 shells every time the B-29s appeared overhead.

Along with a faith that they would win, the Japanese had a strong instinct for sacrifice, as shown by the willingness of pilots to ram B-29s. Such sacrifices were a matter of obedience to the Emperor and, to many, of personal military honor. Indeed, some pilots who returned from suicide missions were imprisoned.

The conformity induced by such beliefs forbade criticism. When the chief of the government's aeronautical research bureau rebuked the armed forces for risking the lives of crew members in badly maintained aircraft, he was set upon and beaten by a special army unit established to deal with defeatists.

Under these circumstances, it was easy for commanders to keep all news—and even suggestions—of the plight of Japan from their subordinates. Only at the very end, when the B-29s, escorted by swarms of long-range American fighters, roamed Japanese skies without challenge did the truth penetrate. Starved of planes, scarcely trained, barely supported, parched for fuel, the Japanese air-defense forces for all practical purposes ceased to exist. The raw emotions of defeat were summed up after the War by an air-defense officer who said, "Our pilots' spirit was squelched and the brilliant feats of our fighters almost vanished. We became eagles without wings."

JAPAN'S AERIAL WARRIORS

Japanese ace Teruhiko Kobayashi (center) and his Ki-61 fighter are surrounded by admirers—two of whom wear masks to avoid spreading their colds.

KAMIKAZE TACTICS TO STOP THE BOMBERS

In late 1944 Captain Teruhiko Kobayashi, 24 years old, became the youngest commander of a fighter unit in the Japanese Army's air force. One of a dwindling number of pilots lucky and skillful enough to have survived the American onslaught, he was credited in the War's final months with downing 10 B-29s. Kobayashi was also very brave: One of his kills resulted from a desperately risky tactic—ramming.

Such desperation was a new experience for the proud airmen of Japan. Before Pearl Harbor, Japanese pilots had been among the world's most highly trained: The best fliers went into battle with about 800 hours of flying time, far more than most pilots of other nations. But by 1944, the attrition brought about by defeat after defeat had wrought major change. The demand for replacements was so great that pilots with only 60 hours of flight training were being sent up against Americans with many times their experience.

To rebuild the air forces, the Japanese launched a program in 1943 to produce 30,000 pilots annually by 1945. Flying schools sprang up around the country, and to fill them the authorities recruited the country's educated young elite—drafting even boys of high-school age. A propaganda campaign lauded the trainee pilots while they lived as "flying eagles," and when they died as "gods of the air."

The preponderance of green pilots and the might of the American B-29s—combined with the ingrained Japanese desire to find an honorable death in battle—led to suicidal tactics. While most pilots continued to use conventional methods of attack, special units were formed to carry out ramming missions. A pilot intent on ramming was a fearsome opponent, and yet the tactic was not as successful as the Japanese had hoped—ironically, because colliding at high speeds with another plane called for a degree of skill that not all pilots had. Since night fighting also required relatively adept fliers, some night-fighter pilots began to double as rammers, and at this point the value of experience was acknowledged: Veterans like Teruhiko Kobayashi were encouraged to survive if they could, to ram again.

Before a mission in twin-engined Ki-45 Dragon Killers, night-fighter crews salute their flight commander (left foreground) at Ozuki airfield in Honshu.

Pilots in training at Chofu air base outside of Tokyo use a tripod-mounted model of a four-engined bomber to practice sighting and estimating range.

FINDING THE VULNERABLE POINTS OF ATTACK

One of the most effective conventional methods of attack for Japanese fighter pilots required the use of specially mounted guns. Some Japanese planes were fitted with two small cannon tilted to fire upward; the pilot would try to slip under a B-29 and rake its belly from below. It was a tactic most likely to succeed at night.

For daylight attacks, the preferred Japanese tactic was a shallow head-on dive at the nose of a B-29, firing straight ahead at the cockpit. The frontal approach—out of the field of most of the B-29's defensive fire—was calculated to cripple the bomber by killing its pilot and copilot. Failing that, the fighter pilot hoped at least to prevent accurate bombing by hitting the bombardier, stationed in the B-29's nose.

A veteran Japanese fighter pilot uses a model to illustrate the technique of head-on attack for an attentive group of young pilots at Matsudo airfield on the outskirts of Tokyo.

A close-up of a Ki-45 Dragon Killer night fighter at Matsudo air base shows its twin 20mm cannon mounted aft of the forward cockpit to fire upward at an angle.

In a photograph taken from another plane in the formation, a Japanese fighter is seen swooping beneath the B-29 at top after a frontal attack on its cockpit.

One of two off-duty Army airmen wears a pair of sunglasses to keep his eyes accustomed to darkness. Most of the night-fighter pilots, whose planes did not have radar or even searchlights, depended entirely on their night vision to spot enemy bombers.

Back from night fighting in the skies over
Nagoya in December of 1944, Captain Junichi
Ogata recapitulates the encounter for his
commander (near left). Eight of the pilots shown
here were later killed in action.

A trio of camouflaged Ki-45 Dragon Killers flies
in attack formation. The Japanese Army built
1,700 of the heavy fighters, capable of a top
speed of 340 mph, and even though they
had no radar they became the Army's primary
defense against the night raids of the B-29s.

ELITE SQUADRONS OF RAMMERS

Beginning in November 1944, Japanese Army headquarters for the defense of Tokyo ordered its fighter units to provide pilots for ramming missions. The Navy issued a similar call. The new ramming squadrons, some of them equipped with night fighters, generally were manned by the most experienced available pilots.

At first, the rammers flew planes that had been stripped of guns and armor to enable them to climb above the high-flying B-29s. Later, unwilling to accept suicide as inevitable, they alternated conventional head-on attacks using guns with a stunt man's approach to ramming. After setting his plane on a collision course, the pilot would try to jump out an instant before the crash; but most of the men, incapable of managing the necessary split-second timing, were killed.

At an airman's altar dedicated to Japan's Shinto religion, a section of propeller from a rammed Superfortress is presented as a solemn offering.

An arrow with open jaws painted in red and white on the fuselage identifies these Ki-45 Dragon Killer night fighters as part of the 53rd Air Regiment's specia

Survivors of ramming, Lieutenant Tohru Shinomiya (left) landed with a wing tip torn away, and Sergeant Masao Itagaki parachuted from his plane.

attack, or ramming, unit. The solid red circle behind the arrow is Japan's national symbol, and on the vertical stabilizer are the flamboyant numerals of the 53rd.

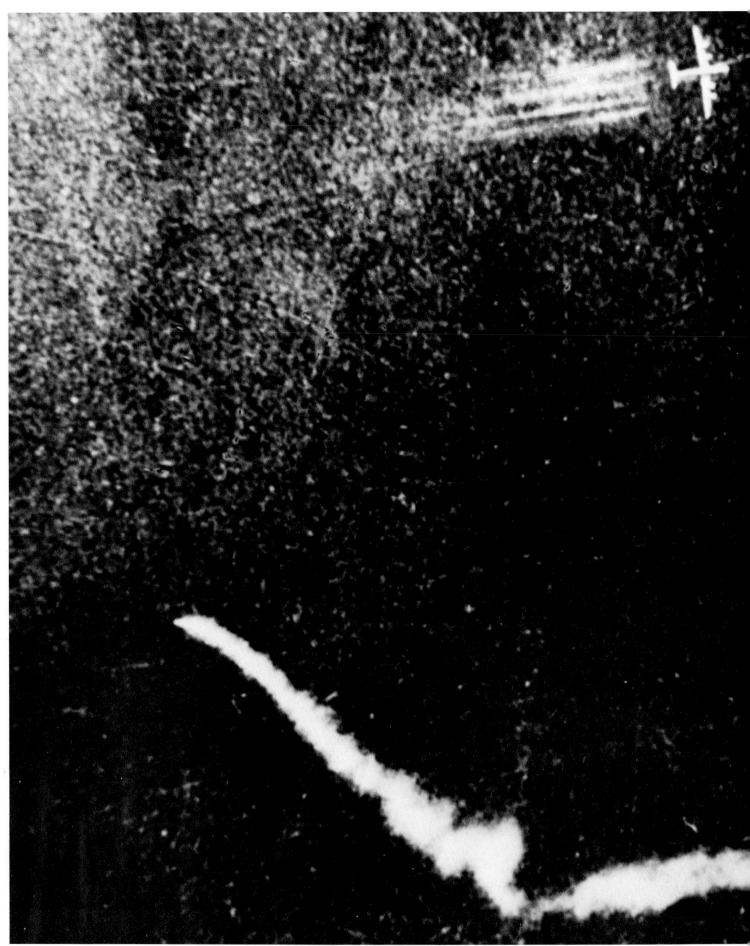

The results of a ramming attack over Tokyo unfold in a photograph taken from the ground on January 9, 1945. Trailing smoke from an engine, a B-29 holds

place in the bomb-run formation after being rammed by a Japanese fighter, which leaves a similar trail (left) as it hurtles earthward from the point of impact.

THE THUNDER OF MUSTANGS

Formed into four-plane Vs, a squadron of Iwo Jima-based Mustangs is shepherded toward Japan by a Superfortress equipped for long-range navigation.

THE SUNSETTERS' SPECIAL MISSION

Brigadier General Ernest M. Moore (center), commander of the VII Fighter Command, hears an account of the Sunsetters' first mission to Tokyo.

Equipped with new P-51D Mustangs, arguably the best fighter planes in the world, the U.S. Army Air Forces' VII Fighter Command arrived on Iwo Jima in March of 1945. Their mission—to fly escort for B-29s raiding Japan—had a climactic ring. Iwo Jima was the last stop in a campaign of vindication for the fighters that had begun more than three years earlier, during the surprise Japanese attack on Pearl Harbor; one fighter group now part of the VII had been caught on the ground at Wheeler Field that December 7. The fighters' new base, a cone-shaped slip of land barely eight square miles in area, was within range of Japan, 750 miles away, and from there the men of the VII meant to help finish off the Rising Sun; they called themselves Sunsetters.

The Mustang, built by the North American Aviation Company, was admirably suited to its assignment. Well-armed, fast and agile, it had a ceiling of nearly 42,000 feet and a top speed at 25,000 feet of 437 mph. With a pair of 108-gallon drop tanks under its wings, the P-51D had a range of 2,000 miles, twice that of its nearest rival, Republic's P-47 Thunderbolt. Despite a lack of navigational equipment, the P-51 was fully capable of reaching Japan and fighting for up to an hour before turning for home.

The Sunsetters' first mission was auspicious. On April 7, more than 100 Mustangs joined a like number of B-29s from the Marianas and escorted them on a daylight raid to Tokyo. Japanese fighters rose to intercept and the result was a one-sided brawl. "I'll never forget it," said an American airman. "For a while there were Japanese parachuting all around us." The Sunsetters shot down 21 Japanese planes while losing two Mustangs and three B-29s.

A switch in B-29 tactics to more raids at night, when all but a few Japanese fighters were grounded, soon freed the Sunsetters to carry out strikes on their own. In mid-April, strafing P-51s swept over an airfield on Kyushu, the first of 33 such raids. The independent attacks, however, required an ironic reversal of roles. Now the P-51s needed one or more B-29s, with their superior navigational gear, to escort them to and from Japan.

A pair of Mustangs are framed in the gunner's blister of a B-29 they are escorting. An expendable fuel tank, for extra range, is visible under the P-51 at top.

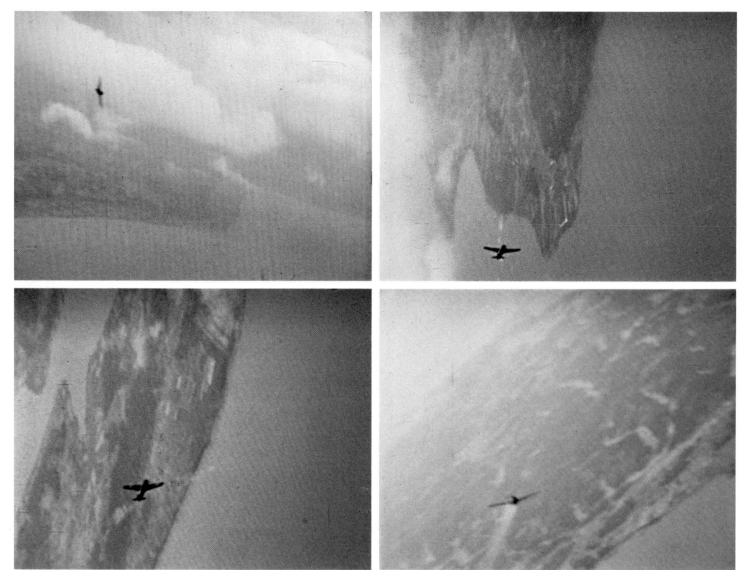

In the sequence above, taken by a P-51's wing camera, a Japanese fighter (top left) tries desperately to evade pursuit. The horizon rotates 90 degrees (top right) as the pilot of the faster Mustang maneuvers to catch up, and a few additional degrees (bottom left) as he approaches his quarry. At bottom right, the Japanese plane has been hit and trails smoke. The camera was triggered when the Mustang fired its guns; these frames represent bursts squeezed off about two seconds apart.

In time-honored fashion, Lieutenant Frank Garcia (standing at right) uses his hands to describe to debriefers how he made his first kill, then peeled away.

TACTICS OF HIGH-SPEED PURSUIT

Flying escort, the Sunsetters usually encountered Japanese planes as they crossed the coast and spent the next 30 to 60 minutes in a more-or-less-continuous running fight. Enemy bullets were not all the P-51s had to worry about: In the confusion of battle, there was always the risk of being hit by the defensive fire of the bombers they were escorting.

Combat under such conditions demanded a calculated daring. One tactic, considered a "turkey shoot" by the pilots, called for slipping up on the last enemy interceptor in a four-plane formation. On the first Tokyo mission, Captain Robert W. Moore employed the maneuver to perfection. He shot down the trailing fighter, undetected by the others—then attacked the third in line. When the second and first Japanese pilots caught on and turned to attack him, Moore dived straight down—catching a glimpse of the third fighter in flames. He then sped away to safety—having scored two kills in 45 seconds.

LOW-LEVEL STRIKES AT TARGETS OF OPPORTUNITY

When they were not needed as escorts, the Sunsetters operated under the broadest of orders: Attack enemy airfields, shipping, railroads, factories and "targets of opportunity"—meaning just about anything.

By the summer of 1945, Japanese air opposition had almost disappeared: Japan was saving what was left of its air force to stave off an imminent invasion. Nevertheless, the Mustangs—flying low to strafe and bomb—made enticing targets for Japanese antiaircraft guns and for those fighters that did appear. Even during the final month of the War, the Sunsetters lost 36 planes and 20 pilots.

Armorers load ammunition for one of a Mustang's six .50-caliber machine guns. For use in missions against surface targets, the plane was also capable of carrying two 1,000-pound bombs or six 5-inch rockets.

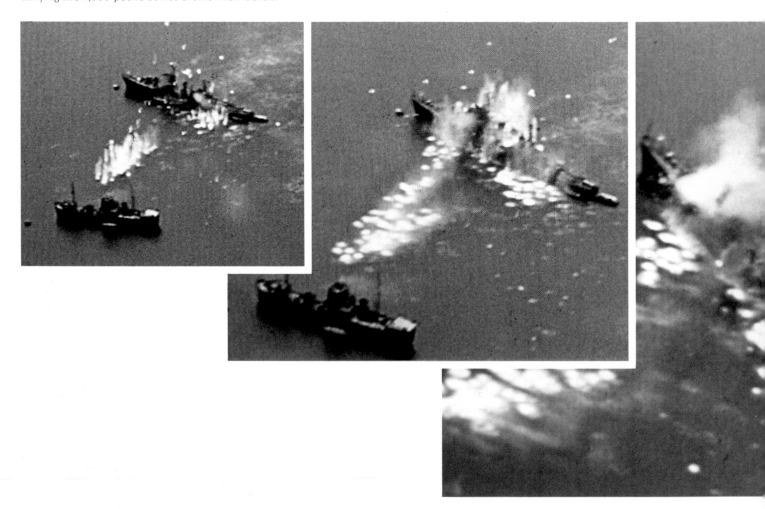

The destruction of a Japanese destroyer in a raid on Nagoya harbor in July 1945 is vividly documented by a series of photographs from the wing camera of an attacking P-51. The pilot of the Mustang, 21-year-old Lieutenant Leon Sher, later described the action: "As we approached Nagoya, I noticed heavy ack-ack fire coming from a cove on the shore. I dropped down and spotted two Jap destroyers and seven cargo vessels. I singled out one destroyer, made a run for it, and strafed the area just ahead of the forward turret. I must have made a lucky hit, probably on an oil line or powder magazine, because the whole ship just lifted right out of the water amid a big explosion, and then settled to the bottom."

At an airfield near Nagoya, a Japanese fighter disintegrates after being hit by a P-51's bullets. By this stage of the War, most of the planes the American raiders found on the ground were either disabled or dummies.

A train in a Japanese railroad depot takes strafing hits (center) from the plane that made this photograph. Another Mustang—seen at upper left—trails smoke from a rocket launcher after firing a missile.

A long day's mission behind them, a formation of Sunsetters heads through open skies toward Iwo Jima. A Marine guard (left inset) watches a P-51 with a sho

up horizontal stabilizer making its approach; at right, a Mustang is doused with foam after being hit on the ground by another plane making a crash landing.

5

Among those who served closest to him, General LeMay was renowned for his stolid, seemingly immobile style. A subordinate, trying to explain LeMay's approach to his duties, once observed that the general "doesn't appear to work much, but he *thinks* more than any man I have ever known." In early 1945, the frustrations of the B-29 campaign had LeMay thinking overtime, and the ideas churning beneath his impassive, heavy-jowled demeanor left him uneasy. A pipe smoker by preference, he took to chewing a cigar to help himself concentrate—the humid climate of Guam having spotted his pipe tobacco with mildew.

The chief of the XXI Bomber Command grappled with an unpalatable fact: Conventional high-altitude bombing was not producing results to match the expectations so passionately nurtured by General Arnold. LeMay had been brought to the Marianas to get such results. Now, as he pondered the likeliest way to achieve them, he found himself weighing the risks of a dramatic change in tactics: bringing his B-29s down from the relatively safe substratosphere and sending them in at low altitudes to sweep Japan with fire.

The idea did not originate with LeMay. As early as 1943, American bombing experts, using wood, paper and straw matting, had simulated Japanese buildings at a test site for incendiary bombs in the Utah desert. They had not succeeded in burning down this "village" until early 1944, when a group of manufacturers that included Standard Oil and E. I. Du Pont, the chemical company, came up with a compound of jellied gasoline called napalm; the material stuck to anything it hit and set ferociously hot fires.

At Arnold's insistence, both LeMay and his predecessor, General Hansell, had run experimental incendiary raids to test a theory that Japan's closely packed cities would burn. Nothing much had been proved. The best results LeMay had seen were from his own raid the previous December on Hankow, Japan's major supply facility in China. The B-29s had taken off from the bases at Chengtu and their bombs started fires that burned out more than 40 per cent of the target area.

As LeMay chewed on his problem, Brigadier General Thomas S. Power, newly installed commander of the 314th Bombardment Wing, the third wing to join the XXI Bomber Command, carried out another fire-raid test over Tokyo. On February 25, Power's planes had flown through very bad

A SCOURGE OF FIRE

weather that forced them to approach the target at an extremely low altitude, and they had been able to climb to only 25,000 feet before dropping their bombs. The strike had burned out a full square mile of the Japanese capital. Surprised, Power wondered whether this relatively low bombing altitude had provided greater-than-usual accuracy. He studied the strike photographs, and his report to LeMay included a provocative question: If the planes had gone in much lower—and with a bigger bomb load—would the result have been even greater destruction?

The answer, and the risks it involved, were becoming clear to LeMay. He saw that for maximum accuracy he must send in his B-29s, not at the relative safety of 30,000 feet, but at 10,000 feet, or even lower. Lower altitudes, of course, implied greater dangers from the enemy's defense; staging the raids at night would offer some protection, but the pressures on his aircrews would be tremendous. In a vividly personal memoir written after the War, LeMay recounted the dilemma: "A lot of people will tell me that flesh and blood can't stand it. Maybe they'll be right."

There were few ways to find out. In early March, LeMay had tested Brigadier General Rosey O'Donnell on a hedge-hopping mission near Saipan to gauge how well a B-29 and its crew could perform, flying very low in a giant aircraft designed for the substratosphere. That mission had gone well enough; still, Tokyo, bristling with defenses, was a very different target from the tiny island O'Donnell had bombed.

One major problem that would be solved by low altitude was weather. The unpredictable cross winds that hampered bombing from high altitudes were much less severe below 10,000 feet. And the crews knew how to operate at very low levels; LeMay had taken care of that when he sent an MIT expert to teach his radar operators how to identify a spit of land—like the one in Tokyo Bay east of the city—from low altitudes in any weather conditions.

Some perils of low-altitude bombing were still to be measured, however. Even at night, there would be flak and fighters. "I sat up nights," LeMay remembered, "fine-tooth-combing all the pictures we had of every target which we had attacked or scouted." From the photographs, it appeared that the Japanese did not have the best kind of antiaircraft guns—rapid-fire 20mm and 40mm weapons—to use against bombers coming in at low or medium altitudes.

The pictures were less helpful when it came to estimating Japanese fighter capabilities. LeMay could only thrash the question over and over: "We don't think that their night fighters amount to anything," he concluded. "And we could be wrong as hell."

LeMay knew that the tactics he was considering were radical enough to intimidate any sensible aircrew. It would have frightened his men even more to know how he was planning to lighten his planes in order to add payload tonnage. "No bomb-bay tanks," he decided. "Nothing but bombs in those bomb bays. We won't need all that extra gas if we're not going to altitude." And defensive armaments would also be removed: "Every gun goes out, all the ammunition goes out," he concluded. "At least our folks won't be shooting at each other. Take out all the gunners, too. Less weight, and fewer people jeopardized. But I think we'd better leave the tail gunners in, for observation purposes."

Disposing of fuel, guns, ammunition and three crewmen, LeMay figured, would enable each of his B-29s to load six tons of bombs instead of the three tons they had been carrying. And there was one other positive factor to consider: the sheer unexpectedness of the approach. "If we go in low—at night, singly, not in formation—I think we'll surprise the Japs," LeMay said. "At least for a short period. If this first attack is successful, we'll run another right quick."

LeMay was well aware that his career was on the line. He decided not to say anything to Arnold in advance about the first low-altitude raid. "If it's a failure, and I don't produce any results," LeMay concluded, "then he can fire me."

Considering the risks, LeMay needed to be very sure of his goals. What did he expect to hit? How would success be measured? The answers he worked out were grim: Japan's industrial targets were surrounded by civilian residences. In his postwar memoir, LeMay recalled arguing with himself over the fate of the people who lived beneath the bombs, knowing that their casualties would multiply. "No matter how you slice it," he told himself, "you're going to kill an awful lot of civilians. Thousands and thousands. But if you don't destroy Japanese industry, we're going to have to invade Japan. And how many Americans will be killed in an invasion? Five hundred thousand seems to be the lowest estimate. We're at war with Japan. Would you rather have Americans killed?"

LeMay ended his private debate by acknowledging to himself that he was taking a huge gamble. "I hope you're right, Curt," he said. Then he committed his command to the new course: "Crank her up. Let's go."

The general at first informed only a few staff members of his decision—those essential to the planning that must now be done. All of them were stunned, and some openly appalled. "We'll get the holy hell shot out of us," muttered one officer. "It's nothing but a suicide mission." Behind LeMay's back, some of those serving under him for the first time called him crazy, and a butcher. Veterans of the air war in Europe said bluntly: "If we tried this over Germany, we'd lose 80 per cent of our planes."

General LeMay's rebuttal was simple: "If this raid works the way I think it will, we can shorten this war," he told his staff. But privately, he admitted, "I was very nervous about the mission."

On March 9, the B-29 crews assembled on wooden benches in their units' Quonset-hut war rooms. Their target was Tokyo, and the initial briefing scared them badly. Then they settled down to study the details of their orders, information ranging from radio frequencies to map coordinates.

Takeoffs began at Guam at 5:35 p.m. and 40 minutes later at Saipan and Tinian, which were nearer the target. By a quarter past eight, 334 B-29s were in the air, strung out in three parallel streams 400 miles long, heading north.

The planes soon ran into heavy clouds and turbulence, but the sky cleared as they neared Japan. When the lead planes turned over Tokyo Bay, only scattered clouds lay between the city below and the altitudes at which the B-29s were stacked up—from 4,900 to 9,200 feet. Pathfinder planes—each carrying a load of 180 napalm-filled, 70-pound canisters—flew over Tokyo on crossing courses. They seeded one napalm bomb every 100 feet, searing a flaming X across the heart of the city.

Guiding on the X, the main body of B-29s flew over in groups of three, about one minute apart. They carried loads of incendiaries that automatically fell from the bomb bays at regular intervals; a timing mechanism called an interval-ometer, coordinated with each bomber's ground speed, was set to plant one 500-pound cluster of fire bombs every 50 feet. The target area, about three by five miles in size, in-cluded a considerable portion of Tokyo's industrial and commercial districts and a densely packed residential area that held an average of 103,000 people per square mile.

Plane followed plane over the targets. Flames sprang to life and soon ran together, driven by a 28-mile-per-hour March wind that was accelerated to 40 miles per hour by the fire. Within 30 minutes the blaze was beyond control. The Tokyo fire department tried valiantly to guide people to safety, but the task was hopeless and the department soon lost many of its own men and machines to the blaze.

Hit with string after string of incendiaries, central Tokyo became a holocaust. In the heart of the fire storm, temperatures rose to 1,800° F. Water boiled in the canals crisscrossing the city. The fire fed upon itself, creating thermal updrafts that tossed the bombers like errant leaves.

For nearly three hours the B-29s kept coming. Soot blackened the silver fuselages of the late arrivals, which were forced to bomb around the fringes of the target area to avoid the turbulence and the blinding smoke that filled cockpits with the stench of burning wood, flesh and hair.

One pilot, keeping a hand on the wheel, crossed himself with the other and was heard to say, "This blaze will haunt me forever. It's the most terrifying sight in the world, and, God forgive me, it's the best."

Some flak came up but it was much lighter than LeMay and his apprehensive crews had expected. One Superfortress took a direct hit over the heart of the city. It "exploded before our eyes like a magnesium tracer bullet," wrote a Japanese journalist watching from the ground. A few Japanese fighters appeared, but they inflicted little damage—far less than the B-29 crews had anticipated. Altogether, 42 of the bombers were damaged for one reason or another, and 14 were lost. Of these, five ditched at sea and their crews were picked up by air-sea rescue units.

As they unloaded, the B-29s turned and started home. General Power, who led the raid, had climbed from 5,000 feet to 10,000 and then to 20,000 feet for a better view. Finally, he too headed for the Marianas, his jubilant tail gunner staring back at the incandescence until, when they were 150 miles at sea, it dipped below the curve of the earth. Power landed at Guam at 8:30 a.m. after 15 hours in the air. "It was a hell of a good mission," he told LeMay.

The toll in enemy lives and property had been enormous.

Major General Curtis E. LeMay (center), commander of Marianas-based B-29s, reads a report of the first low-altitude fire bombing of Tokyo in March 1945. Brigadier General Lauris Norstad (left), representing Army Air Forces headquarters in Washington, looks over LeMay's shoulder; at right is Brigadier General Thomas S. Power, who led the mission.

mander in charge of the Okinawa operation, was haunted by the memory of Japanese Kamikazes—suicide pilots diving into his ships during the invasion of the Philippines the previous October. Nimitz was determined to use every means available to guard his fleet off Okinawa.

Under the Joint Chiefs' rules for the operation of B-29s, Nimitz had no operational control over the XXI Bomber Command, but he was empowered to call for the Superfortresses in an emergency. Sounding the alarm as Okinawa's D-day approached, Nimitz exercised his option and ordered LeMay to neutralize the Kamikazes. B-29s were to destroy as many planes on the ground as possible, and render Japanese airfields on the islands of Kyushu and Shikoku unusable until the Okinawa invasion force was safe ashore and solidly enough established to allow the fleet to retire out of the Kamikazes' reach. To LeMay, sending a force as formidable as his B-29s to pockmark enemy airfields with bomb craters seemed the equivalent of killing gnats with baseball bats. But he prepared to comply.

Five days before the invasion, the B-29s began their work, pummeling 17 airfields that were within easy Kamikaze range—a one-way flight—of Okinawa. After a week, with

the landings well under way, LeMay thought his Superfortresses should be released. "We've got everything flat on Kyushu," he told Nimitz. "All we can do now is put more holes in the fields, and we can't stop an occasional airplane from taking off. We've done all we can."

But Nimitz was not so sure. After discussing the issue with his operations officer, Rear Admiral Forrest Sherman, the theater commander told LeMay to stick with the job a while longer. Angrily, LeMay went back to bombing what he called "Target Nothing." Despite LeMay's claim to have finished off the Kamikaze fields, it was soon apparent that the Japanese could make something out of "Nothing." On April 6, Kamikazes sortied from Kyushu in force and began to tear pieces out of the invasion fleet.

The B-29s redoubled their efforts to wreck the Kyushu airfields, despite LeMay's contention that the strikes were doing little harm. "Whenever we beat up a field enough," he commented later, "they'd take whatever airplanes were not destroyed—or those that they'd put together, wired up, ready to go—and take them down the road half a mile or a mile, and hide them in the bushes. Then the Japs would bring out one or two airplanes a day and, with a bunch of coolies working with baskets, they'd fill up enough of our cratered holes to take off on the grass."

In the middle of April, LeMay tried again to break loose from the assignment by appealing directly to General Arnold. Arnold, in turn, went to Admiral Ernest J. King, Chief of Naval Operations. He was told bluntly that if the Army Air Forces did not want to help the Navy now, the day might come when the Navy would not want to help the Army. LeMay was ordered to get back on the job.

Kamikazes continued to harass the American fleet off Okinawa—a fact that fed LeMay's resentment, since he felt that bombing Japan's aircraft industry would have been more effective against suicide planes than hitting airfields. "We kept it up for a month, and destroyed or damaged about 400 Japanese airplanes," he later wrote. "During the period that we were tied down to strikes against airfields, we could have knocked out every engine plant in Japan."

Actually, the XXI Bomber Command was never as restricted to fleet support as LeMay's complaints made it seem. In April his old China command, the 58th Bombardment Wing, arrived on Tinian. The addition of its planes

NOSE ART: A GREAT NEW FORM

In their Marianas outposts, the Superfortress crews were half a world away from the girls they had left behind, so it was not surprising that many of them named their airplanes in the jaunty, glamor-girl fashion of the day. And certainly planes that had evocative nicknames, like *Joltin' Josie* or *Coral Queen,* had to have equally evocative ornamentation. The resulting demand for cheesecake pictures—painted on the forward fuselage—spawned a specialty known as "nose art."

The paintings, life-sized and even larger, were the work of moonlighting military sign painters or other GIs talented with a brush, who charged up to $175 per illustration. At first the nose artists enjoyed al-most unlimited freedom, and nudity flourished in their work. Later, second thoughts among chaplains or commanding officers led to increasing censorship.

The downfall of nose art began when several fulsomely decorated B-29s were retired from combat and returned to the United States. When religious groups protested to AAF headquarters, a board was appointed to suggest "proper limitations" for the 73rd Wing, whose planes on Saipan had sported some of the most daring paintings. Ultimately, a Washington directive banned nose art altogether, prompting one American correspondent to mourn "the loss of one of the last personal touches in an already impersonal war."

A nose artist (inset) paints panties on a blonde adorning Joker's Wild. Air Forces censors approved Tanaka Termite's art (above), but not the nude a

...rely beaded female decorates the fuselage of Geisha Gertie, a B-29 that ditched at sea in January 1945—before censors required modesty in nose art.

...n' Josie won pioneer status as the first B-29 to arrive in the Marianas.

Texas Doll, piloted by Captain E. W. Cutler, survived three dozen missions.

brought the total number of Superfortresses on hand to more than 700. LeMay was able to keep hammering the Kamikaze bases and at the same time turn a substantial force against strategic targets in Japan. Missions were to be flown not only by night, at low altitudes, but also by day, at higher altitudes—escorted now by fighters.

One such strike, on April 12, was the 73rd Wing's 11th attack on its old nemesis, the Nakajima engine works at Musashino. The daylight raiders succeeded at last in dropping most of their high-explosive bombs on target, and the damage they inflicted—combined with what the Navy's carrier planes had done back in February—effectively eliminated the vital factory.

On that same day, the 314th Wing attacked a chemical plant at Koriyama. Their mission produced an extraordinary act of heroism and resulted in the only Medal of Honor conferred on a B-29 crew member during the War. A Superfortress named the *City of Los Angeles,* flown by Captain George Simeral, was the lead plane of one formation. As the plane neared the assembly point 175 miles—about 45 minutes—short of the target, Staff Sergeant Henry Eugene "Red" Erwin stood near the flare-release chute in the deck of the plane's cockpit, waiting for Simeral's signal to drop first a colored flare and then a phosphorous smoke bomb as signals for the other planes to close in tight on the leader.

When Simeral raised his hand, Erwin dropped the flare. When Simeral's hand went up again, Erwin pulled the pin that armed the smoke bomb and dropped it into the tube. The smoke bomb stuck, went off and backfired up into the plane. It seared Erwin's eyes and burned his nose before it fell on the deck, filling the cockpit with smoke and the glare of phosphorus burning at 1,300° F.

Erwin struggled erect. Scarcely able to see, he grabbed the blazing bomb in his bare right hand, intending to throw it out of the aircraft. He staggered forward, his clothing and flesh afire. He stumbled against the machinery of the upper gun turret, fumbled his way around it, and encountered a new obstacle, the navigator's folding table, which was locked in a down position. In order to free his hands to unlatch the table and swing it up, Erwin grabbed the bomb with his left hand and tucked it like a football between his right arm and his chest.

Once past the table, Erwin groped forward into the pilot's compartment, screaming for somebody to open a window. Erwin half fell into the lap of Lieut. Colonel Eugene Strouse, the copilot, who was trying to tell him that the window was already open. When he understood, Erwin reached across Strouse, felt for the opening and flung his deadly burden out into space. Then he collapsed on the flight deck.

With pilot Simeral blinded by the smoke, the B-29 had fallen to within 300 feet of the ocean during Erwin's battle with the bomb. Now Simeral climbed and headed for Iwo Jima with full power settings. Someone grabbed a fire extinguisher and drenched Erwin's flaming Mae West.

Five weeks later, in a hospital on Guam, a general pinned the Medal of Honor to the bandages that covered most of Sergeant Erwin's body and head.

That Erwin lived to receive his medal was due largely to the availability of a landing strip for the B-29s on Iwo Jima. Although Marines were still rooting Japanese from the sulfurous bedrock of the island in late March, Navy Seabees had repaired and extended Iwo Jima's airfields, and disabled B-29s began using the little island 750 miles from Tokyo as an emergency roost. Moreover, squadrons of P-51 Mustang fighters were arriving on Iwo Jima; in April, for the first time, flights of 100 or more of the Mustang "little brothers" joined the B-29s as they came by from the Marianas to escort them to Japan—at least during daylight raids.

The B-29s liked the company. Praising the first Mustang escort on April 7, a B-29 commander reported that "30 Mustangs swept the area ahead of us, and only two Jap fighters got in to us. Both of them went down smoking."

In mid-April, his stockpile of incendiaries growing, General LeMay turned his attention once more to Tokyo. On the 13th of April, 327 Superfortresses stacked from 6,750 to 11,000 feet swept over Tokyo at night, unloading 2,139 tons of fire bombs as well as 82 tons of GPs. The primary target was an arsenal area northwest of the Imperial Palace—a center for the manufacture and storage of small arms, machine guns, artillery, bombs and gunpowder. The bombardiers were accurate, and the arsenal and the surrounding neighborhood erupted. Before the fires subsided, another 11 square miles of Tokyo had been reduced to smoking ash and twisted steel.

Two nights later, 303 Superfortresses were back over the

An aerial photograph of Hakodate, a port on the island of Hokkaido, shows a harbor crowded with small vessels and a vulnerable waterfront area of docks and warehouses. The ragged light-colored strips near the bottom of the picture are firebreaks—areas cleared of houses and anything flammable to keep fires from spreading after an incendiary raid.

capital, carrying 1,930 tons of incendiaries. They burned out six square miles in the dock area on the western shore of Tokyo Bay. They also burned three and a half square miles of the factory town of Kawasaki just south of Tokyo and a square mile and a half of the adjacent city of Yokohama, hit by bombs that overshot the primary targets.

As much as LeMay wanted to devote his entire air fleet to bombing cities, other duties continued to claim many of his planes. The Kamikaze fields on Kyushu required almost daily attention. And Admiral Nimitz, looking ahead to the Okinawa landings, had found another unorthodox chore for the B-29s. He wanted them to mine the Shimonoseki Strait between Honshu and Kyushu to block any Japanese attempt to reinforce Okinawa with troops and supplies.

For months, Nimitz had sought a commitment for the Twentieth Air Force to undertake such mining operations in Japan's strategic waterways. General Arnold was reluctant; he considered the planting of mines strictly the Navy's affair; he also remembered, as did other senior officers and men of the AAF, that strategic targets in Germany had escaped attack while the bombers were diverted to support operations in North Africa and Normandy.

Nimitz carried the day, and LeMay was confronted with the mining assignment just before the invasion of Okinawa. He decided that if the B-29s had to do the job, they would do it right. He assigned the entire 313th Wing to the task, dubbed Operation *Starvation,* and ordered the wing to plant at least 2,000 mines during April.

LeMay soon had reason to congratulate himself on Operation *Starvation,* for it virtually shut down Japan's dwindling lines of supply. The six-million-ton merchant fleet with which Japan had begun the War had shrunk to two million tons, attrition that was largely the work of American submarines. This destruction had forced Japan to abandon all but 12 of its 47 convoy routes, including all of those in the Pacific. The remaining traffic, carrying vital cargo to Japan from the Asian mainland, was confined almost entirely to the shallow East China and Yellow Seas and the Sea of Japan. Most of it reached ports on the Inland Sea through the narrow western gate of the Shimonoseki Strait.

Guided by Navy experts in the handling and placement of underwater explosives, the 313th Wing began its work

on the night of March 27, releasing almost 1,000 heavy magnetic and acoustic mines, which were attached to six-foot-wide parachutes. The minelayers concentrated first on the Shimonoseki Strait, then expanded their work to Japan's harbors and their approaches. Beginning with Kobe and Osaka on the Inland Sea, they mined the harbors of Kure, Hiroshima, Sasebo, Tokuyama, Nagoya and Tokyo itself. Eventually, ports on the western shores of Kyushu and Honshu and even the coastal waters of Korea were planted.

Operation *Starvation* was dull night work, enlivened only by flak from harbor defenses and from anchored ships. But it began to pay dividends almost at once. During April, 18 Japanese ships were sunk. In May the count rose to 85 ships, for a total of 213,000 tons sunk or put out of action. The toll became a source of exuberant pride for the men of the 313th Wing; they were sinking enemy ships even faster than American submariners were. June brought another harvest: 83 ships, 163,000 tons.

For the Japanese, the mine laying brought chaos and desperation. "The result of the mining by B-29s was so effective that it eventually starved the country," the commander of Japan's mine-sweeping force told an American interrogator after the War. "I think you probably could have shortened the War by beginning earlier."

The Japanese had committed a ragtag collection of 349 vessels and 20,000 men to mine sweeping, but whenever they succeeded in clearing a channel, the Superfortresses returned to seed it again. Ports were paralyzed for five to 10 days at a time. During May, an average of 80 ships per day were immobilized because their captains dared not venture out. Altogether, in 1,528 single-plane sorties, the B-29s planted 12,053 mines. It was the largest aerial mining operation ever undertaken, and by early August, traffic through the crucial Shimonoseki Strait had been cut to less than one tenth of its March level.

The 313th's success won LeMay warm praise from Nimitz, who called the results "phenomenal." It was a moment of rare good feeling between the services. LeMay was usually prone to refer to his Navy colleagues as "webfooted boys," and during his first months on Guam he had complained that they expended more effort building recreation halls, tennis courts and hilltop dwellings for admirals than they did in constructing base facilities for his B-29s.

UNSWEEPABLE MINES TO STIFLE SHIPPING

In Operation *Starvation*, the B-29s mined the key stretches of the Japanese coast shown on the map below. The campaign had three objectives: to cut off imports of food and raw materials from Japanese-occupied Asia, to prevent the supply and deployment of Japanese military forces, and to cripple the coastal shipping that accounted for 75 per cent of the island nation's domestic transport.

Flying at low altitudes and navigating by radar, the bombers relied on cloud cover and darkness as protection against enemy defenses. The mines they dropped were of three types: magnetic, triggered by the presence of metal; acoustic, activated by the sound of a ship's engines and propel-lers; and a relatively new mine detonated by increases in pressure from water displaced by the hulls of passing ships. Explosives and metal sweeps were familiar devices for clearing acoustic and magnetic mines, but the only defense the Japanese were able to develop against the pressure mines was to slow water traffic to a crawl. The Americans thwarted even this defense by mixing the types of mines they laid.

Operation *Starvation* strangled sea traffic so effectively that after March 27, 1945, no large ships dared to navigate Shimonoseki Strait, the vital western gateway to Japan's Inland Sea. By midsummer, Japan was importing only a fraction of the food it needed, and no raw materials at all.

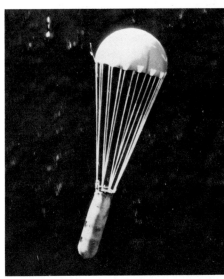

A parachute slows the fall of a magnetic aerial mine, supplied to the B-29s by the U.S. Navy.

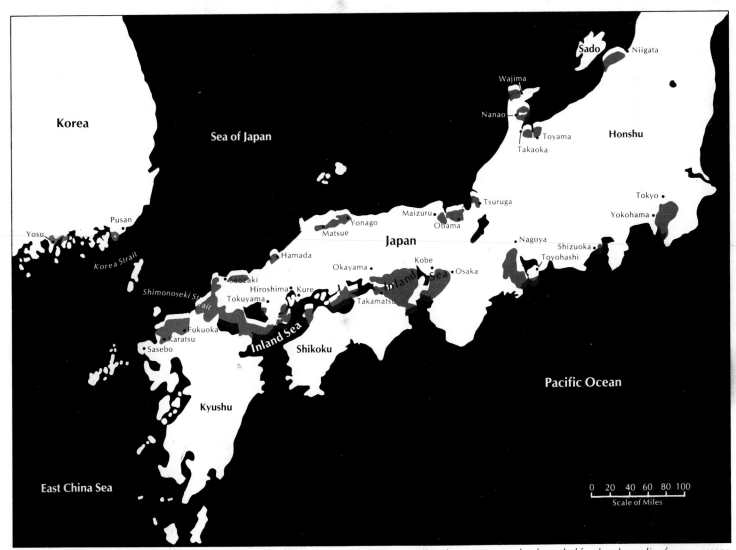

B-29 mining targets (red areas) included coastal routes used by domestic shipping as well as the ocean ports that funneled food and supplies from overseas.

The Navy's role in resupplying the XXI Bomber Command with fire bombs, however, evoked even LeMay's admiration. "Actually, when the Navy got to stirring their stumps they did an excellent job of getting that stuff out there to us," he wrote afterward. "What we did was take the bombs right from the ships to the airplanes. Those Seabees were terrific. They worked like supermen. They'd get up at 4 o'clock in the morning and dig in for two or three hours, helping us with the bombs."

LeMay also praised the officers who led the work parties of sailors and Marines: "They worked like dogs. Majors and lieutenant commanders were handling those crates if they were big enough and strong enough, able-bodied seamen and lieutenant colonels and privates from the rear rank, all rolling out of bed in the middle of the night when they learned that another shipload of stuff had just come in."

On May 11, Admiral Nimitz, satisfied that enough land-based fighters were on Okinawa to protect the fleet, released the Superfortresses from their obligation to raid the Kamikaze airfields. In six weeks the B-29s had flown more than 2,000 sorties to Kyushu and Shikoku, and claimed 218 aircraft destroyed in the air and 483 on the ground.

With plenty of munitions on hand and Kyushu's Kamikazes off his duty list, LeMay turned the XXI Bomber Command back to fire bombing. His highest priority was Nagoya, the city that had refused to burn despite two mass raids in March, and the still-considerable remains of Tokyo.

On May 14, four wings of 472 Superfortresses loaded with 2,515 tons of incendiaries flew over the northern section of Nagoya and burned out a little more than three square miles. It was not enough. Nagoya seemed as stubbornly indestructible as had the Nakajima plant at Musashino. Two nights later, 457 planes hit Nagoya again with a record load of 3,609 tons of fire bombs, and the city at last succumbed. The nearly four square miles of fire-swept devastation included the Mitsubishi aircraft-assembly plant, the largest in Japan. Nagoya's name was struck from LeMay's list of cities remaining to be destroyed.

Tokyo, more than a third obliterated in four previous fire raids, was not yet punished to LeMay's satisfaction. On the night of May 23, a force of 520 Superfortresses dropped 3,646 tons of incendiaries on a mixed industrial and residential area west of Tokyo's harbor and south of the Imperial Palace. The weather was poor, and the target area was almost entirely obscured by low clouds, probing searchlights, blinding smoke and heavy flak. Night fighters drove in from every quarter, frequently hidden from the B-29 gunners by the glare of the searchlights.

The bombers also had a new antagonist. The Japanese were now sending manned, winged and rocket-propelled bombs called *Bakas* into the air battle. Originally designed for suicide attacks on ships, the *Bakas* were launched from mother planes. They streaked toward the B-29s at up to 600 miles per hour, nearly the speed of sound. But despite their great speed, they were not very effective; the raiders lost 17 planes, but only one was definitely attributed to the *Bakas*. And another five square miles of Tokyo was in ruins.

Two nights later, 502 planes returned. Their targets were the capital's financial, commercial and governmental districts as well as the famed Ginza shopping area. The weather was better, with only slight cloud cover, but the defense, fanatically intense, inflicted the severest losses yet suffered by the XXI Bomber Command. Searchlights swept the sky, illuminating individual Superfortresses and holding them pinned for the fire of the defenders' guns. Twenty-six B-29s were lost and 100 damaged. But on the ground, devastation was enormous; another 17 square miles had burned. Tokyo by now was more than half destroyed, with 56 square miles of the city reduced to ashes. The capital was removed from the list of important targets.

Inadvertently, the May 25 raid came close to including Japan's Royal Family among its casualties. As a matter of policy, American bomber crews had been instructed to avoid Emperor Hirohito's palace. The order defining this policy read in part: "The Emperor of Japan is not at present a liability and may later become an asset." Though not hit directly during the May 25 raid, the Imperial Palace caught fire and was severely damaged. After earlier raids, however, Hirohito had moved his family and entourage into the Imperial Library, a building separated from the main palace, with an underground shelter. There they escaped the fires unharmed, and there they lived for the remainder of the War.

Yokohama, the great port city just southwest of Tokyo, had not yet been chosen as a primary target although it had suffered considerable damage from bombs intended for Kawa-

Photographed from a sister plane high above, a formation of B-29s makes its bomb run over the Navy arsenal at Kure, which is already smoking from earlier hits. In this two-pronged operation to obliterate the Japanese Navy, B-29s bombed land bases from high altitude, while carrier-based U.S. Navy planes swept in low to sink individual ships.

saki and Tokyo. Yokohama's turn came on May 29. Shaken by heavy losses to his planes in the two most recent night assaults on Tokyo, LeMay decided to send the B-29s to Yokohama in daylight, formidably escorted by P-51 Mustangs from Iwo Jima. Under unusually clear skies, bombers and fighters swept toward the target, the Mustangs flying about 2,000 feet above the bombers. The fighter protection was timely; about 150 Mitsubishi A6M "Zekes" rose to challenge the raiders. In the ensuing mass dogfight, the Mustang pilots claimed 26 Japanese planes shot down, nine damaged and 23 probables. Three American fighters were lost.

Despite the muscular escort, the B-29s suffered. Five were shot down and another 175 damaged. But Yokohama was crippled: 2,600 tons of bombs had wiped out nine square miles of the city's commercial and industrial heart.

The Yokohama raid eliminated the last worthwhile targets in the dense metropolitan region on the western shores of Tokyo Bay. The XXI Bomber Command now turned westward to concentrate on Japan's remaining industrial com-

plex, on the Inland Sea. On June 1, LeMay targeted Osaka, Japan's second-largest city. Once again, he ordered his fire bombers to attack at medium-high altitude in daylight. Again, he summoned the Mustangs as escorts—a decision that this time had tragic consequences.

From their base on Iwo Jima, 148 Mustangs rose to join the northbound bombers, but they soon ran into a weather front towering to 23,000 feet. On the advice of a B-29 weather plane ahead of them, the flight leader elected to fly on. But the fighter pilots, lacking the navigational instruments of the bombers, were soon blinded and trapped in surging turbulence. Planes collided in the murk and 27 of them crashed into the sea. Only three of the pilots were found alive by rescue planes and ships.

A mere 27 Mustangs succeeded in joining 458 Superfortresses over Osaka. They were not enough to repel a fierce assault by Japanese fighters, which shot down five B-29s. Nevertheless, the raiders burned out more than three square miles, destroyed 136,107 houses and 4,222 factories of

"Attention, Japanese people! Read this carefully as it may save your life or the life of a relative or friend." So began the message on the back side of an American propaganda leaflet that showed B-29s filling the sky with incendiary bombs and indicated the cities (circled) scheduled for raids in the next few days. *"We are determined to destroy all of the tools of the military clique, which they are using to prolong this useless war,"* the message warned. *"But unfortunately, bombs have no eyes. So, in accordance with America's well-known humanitarian policies, the American Air Forces, which do not wish to injure innocent people, give you warning to evacuate these cities and save your lives."*

ANNOUNCING THE APOCALYPSE

The payload delivered by some B-29s was aimed at destroying not Japan's cities but its morale. In the last weeks of the War, the planes dropped blizzards of Japanese-language flyers that, like the Apocalypse, warned of devastation to come, and singled out the cities that could expect to be raided.

A message that was printed on the flyers urged people to flee the target cities. Americans hoped they would have the double effect of further disrupting the Japanese war effort and reducing civilian casualties in the raids that were about to begin.

The campaign was a psychological

success, contributing to the civilian population's feeling of impotence and impending doom. "The leaflets had a great effect on the morale of the people," conceded one Japanese factory manager. "They figured that if the enemy could announce a raid beforehand, the enemy was superior."

various types, and left 3,960 Japanese dead or missing.

Kobe, across the bay from Osaka, also ranked as an important piece of unfinished business despite the damage inflicted by the heavy raid in March. Without escort this time, 473 B-29s attacked Kobe by daylight on June 5. The planes were stacked up from 13,650 to 18,800 feet, flying unusually low for a daytime raid because of heavy cloud cover higher up. Their 3,077 tons of incendiaries burned out more than four square miles of factories, transportation facilities, businesses and homes. By now, 56 per cent of the city had been destroyed, and Kobe was eliminated as a target.

The raid was not without cost to the B-29s. Flak and fighters hammered at them as they came over Kobe; nine planes were shot down and 176 damaged, many so seriously that they had to take refuge at Iwo Jima instead of trying to reach their home bases in the Marianas. One plane crashed at sea attempting to approach the runway at Iwo Jima. Another, piloted by Lieut. Colonel Thomas Vaucher, landed safely on the island, but his crew counted more than 400 flak and bullet holes in their plane.

One casualty of the Kobe raid was especially poignant. LeMay had been considering the advisability of rotating his aircrews home after 35 missions; men who had completed that many were taken off flight duty while the general made up his mind. Like others, Major Shorty Hull found waiting for LeMay's decision irksome, and his edginess increased when he received word that his wife had given birth. More than half convinced that LeMay would order him on more missions anyhow, Major Hull demanded and won reluctant permission to fly the Kobe mission. Hull's aircraft was shot down over the target, and he and members of his crew parachuted to earth near a Japanese military compound. They were seized and taken before the commander, who ordered a summary court-martial. The American aviators were tried for committing war crimes, convicted and beheaded the same day.

Two more mass fire raids pounded Osaka on June 7 and 15. The planes, carrying both incendiaries and 1,000-pound explosives, burned out another four square miles. By the end of June, Osaka had found a place on the roster of Japan's dead cities. Except for a few precision attacks to mop up isolated industrial targets, the final Osaka strikes closed out the XXI Bomber Command's wholesale incineration of metropolitan Japan.

By any measure, the results were impressive; in comparison with the frustrating first nine months of B-29 operations, they were astounding. In 17 mass fire raids, administered over a period of 14 weeks, the B-29s had wiped out 105.6 square miles—almost half the land area—of Japan's six most important cities. At the cost of 136 bombers, 6,690 sorties had dumped 41,592 tons of fire bombs, destroying hundreds of major war industries and thousands of small feeder plants. Japanese casualties ran well into six figures; millions of people were left homeless, and such industry as remained was severely crippled by the flight of terrified workers away from the cities. Civilian morale was near the breaking point, and the people's confidence in their political and military leaders was evaporating. After the War, Motoki Abe, Minister of Home Affairs, said that following the Tokyo raids of late May, "Civilian defense measures in that city, as well as other parts of Japan, were considered a futile effort."

A highly optimistic LeMay had already advised the Twentieth Air Force Chief of Staff, Brigadier General Lauris Norstad, that his B-29s could soon win the War by themselves. "I feel that the destruction of Japan's ability to wage war lies within the capability of this command, provided its maximum capacity is exerted unstintingly during the next six months," he wrote. Characteristically, LeMay did not mention the past, present or potential contributions of other American arms, including the Army, Navy and Marines.

"Most of us in the Army Air Forces," he observed later, "had been convinced for a long time that it would be possible to defeat the Japanese without invading their home islands. We could bomb and burn them until they quit. The ground-gripping Army and the Navy didn't agree. They discounted the whole idea."

LeMay's scathing comment about the Air Forces' sister services was only partially accurate. To be sure, in mid-June an Allied invasion of Kyushu, designated Operation *Olympic,* had been ordered for November. Planning was well under way for Operation *Coronet,* a second-stage assault on Honshu. Yet the Navy, contrary to LeMay's assertion, did not believe that the invasion was inevitable. Admiral King thought it could be avoided, and Admiral Nimitz—who had been pressing his submarines and carrier task forces across the Pacific for three and a half years, and whose Marine and Army assault forces had bought with blood the islands from which LeMay's B-29s now flew—was firmly convinced that invasion would be unnecessary.

Nimitz believed that, no matter how numerous Japan's home army or how fierce its will to fight, the island nation could not long survive the squeeze of steel being applied by the U.S. Navy's submarines, battleships and aircraft carriers. Nimitz did not discount the effect of strategic bombing. While inspecting new navigation equipment in a B-29 named for him, Nimitz applauded LeMay's assembled fliers on Guam for their "tremendous success in bringing Japan closer to surrender." But he demanded for the Navy a primary role in making that surrender complete.

The Navy had to wait for its opportunity. Until mid-1945, apart from the fast-carrier strikes on Tokyo in February under Admirals Spruance and Mitscher, the planes and guns of the Pacific Fleet were occupied with the task of safeguarding the invasions of the Philippines, Iwo Jima and Okinawa.

At this stage of the War, the risks of such duty came largely from Kamikazes. But for Admiral Halsey's Third Fleet, the Navy's principal combat arm in the central Pacific, another enemy appeared on the winds of June: a typhoon. The storm seemed to single out the carriers *Hornet* and *Bennington:* Each lost an aircraft catapult and suffered major damage to its flight deck. In all, Halsey's carriers lost 76 aircraft, 6 per cent of their total complement—33 were swept overboard and 43 were battered beyond repair and jettisoned. Six men were killed or lost overboard and four were seriously injured.

Other ships in Admiral Halsey's fleet suffered as well. The cruiser *Baltimore* was so twisted by the churning seas that she had to be sent to dry dock. The cruiser *Pittsburgh* broke

One of the 16-inch guns on the battleship Massachusetts fires on the Kamaishi ironworks in northern Honshu on August 9, 1945. In its final campaign, the U.S. Third Fleet steamed within sight of Japan's coast to augment carrier-plane attacks with broadsides from the ships' big guns.

apart and lost 104 feet of her forward section, but both halves remained afloat. The *Pittsburgh* was able to reach port at Guam under her own power, and her bow arrived the next day, under tow.

While the cripples limped away for repairs, Halsey took the remains of his fleet to the waters off Okinawa for another stretch of guard duty, and detached one carrier task group for further assaults on the airfields of Kyushu. Then, as ground-based Marine fighters became available in mid-June to replace the carriers as guardians at Okinawa, the fleet was released. Halsey took his ships to San Pedro Bay in the Philippines for two weeks of repair and replenishment.

The fleet sailed from Leyte on July 1 under a directive from Admiral Nimitz that was as broad as Halsey could have wished. His orders were "to attack Japanese naval and air forces, shipping, shipyards and coastal objectives." Halsey had the franchise he had long coveted, to go for the heart of the Empire.

Halsey intended to venture close enough to the home islands to use the guns of his battleships, cruisers and destroyers as well as the carrier planes. He planned to strike the whole arc of Japanese islands from Hokkaido and northern Honshu—still out of range of the B-29s—southward to Tokyo and the cities on the Inland Sea. The scope of the operation called for special preparations: Photoreconnaissance planes went ahead to identify targets; submarines prowled Japanese waters to destroy picket boats and to rescue fliers shot down or forced to ditch.

The first carrier strike was scheduled to hit the Tokyo area on July 10. The weather report was good; clouds covered most of the distance to the launch point, 170 miles southeast of Tokyo, then broke up into clear skies over the target. At 4 a.m. the fleet began launching its fighters and by daybreak all units were in the air.

To the astonishment of the fliers, aerial opposition was nonexistent. Two reconnaissance planes ventured out to investigate the fleet, but they were shot down by the carriers' combat air patrol. Over the targets, antiaircraft fire was light. All day, waves of American fighters, dive bombers and torpedo planes roamed over the Tokyo plain, strafing and bombing its numerous airfields. They returned to their carriers to refuel and rearm, then sortied again.

Despite the lack of opposition, however, the hunting was thin, and the results hard to evaluate. "Tokyo was a poor target," Halsey recalled later. The few planes his pilots found on the ground were empty of fuel, protected by revetments and widely dispersed.

"A plane with empty tanks does not always burn under strafing," Halsey complained, "so damage appraisal becomes difficult. Still, we could count 109 definitely destroyed and 231 damaged. We also damaged hangars and other installations."

The true count probably was much smaller than the fleet pilots claimed. Not until after the War did Americans learn—though LeMay suspected it—that the Japanese were leaving few operable aircraft on or near their airfields. Many of those found on the fields were junk, or dummies cleverly crafted from rattan frames and camouflage netting.

On July 14, after a pause for refueling and a day of blinding fog, Halsey ran in on Kamaishi, on the Honshu coast 275 miles northeast of Tokyo. There the fleet added a new and humiliating dimension to the punishment it inflicted. Three battleships—the *South Dakota*, the *Indiana* and the *Massachusetts*—two cruisers and an escort of nine destroyers closed to a range of less than 15 miles. "The force was clearly visible from the beach," Halsey remembered. "However much propaganda a Japanese civilian will swallow, it must have been hard for him to digest the news that certain American warships had been sunk when he had just watched them blast his job from under him."

The admiral was referring to the fact that his fleet's heavy guns were aimed at factories. Fire commenced at 12:10 p.m. Deep in the main battery plot, the fire-control center aboard the *South Dakota,* Seaman First Class Glenn Durnold held a pistol-gripped trigger in each hand. At the order to begin firing he pulled the left-hand trigger, which broadcast a *dit-dit-dah* salvo warning to exposed personnel. With the *dah* he squeezed the right-hand trigger and the *South Dakota* shuddered as her nine 16-inch guns fired a monstrous broadside. The first naval salvo of the campaign against Fortress Japan was on its way toward the Imperial Iron and Steel Works. It was the first time that a Japanese city had been shelled from the sea since a flotilla of American, British, French and Dutch ships had bombarded Shimonoseki in 1864, to avenge attacks on foreign merchants in Japan. The steel plant disintegrated, and the big shells' concussion started serious fires in the surrounding neighborhoods when cooking braziers were knocked over and their coals scattered.

As the guns pounded Honshu, the carrier air groups struck Hokkaido, the northernmost home island, for the first time. Opposition was negligible. In the harbors of Hakodate and Muroran, the American planes sank a destroyer, two destroyer escorts and eight auxiliaries, damaged a number of other ships and sank 20 merchantmen. Most significantly, the strikes almost completely cut sea communication between Hokkaido and Honshu. Among the vessels sunk or put out of commission were 10 of the dozen large ferries that regularly carried railroad cars filled with Hokkaido's vital coal to Honshu.

On the second day, Halsey joined the one-sided scrap. His flagship, the *Missouri,* led two sister battleships, the *Wisconsin* and the *Iowa,* along with two cruisers and eight destroyers, into a deep bay at the head of which lay Muroran, a steel-manufacturing city. There, with land on three sides, the flotilla bombarded the Nihon Steel Company, the Wanishi Iron and Steel Company and a synthetic-oil refinery. Although Halsey had nervously expected an air attack during his force's approach and withdrawal—three hours each way—the only opposition that developed was sporadic and ineffective artillery fire.

Following the Hokkaido strikes, Halsey withdrew to refuel and to make a rendezvous that he was not looking forward to. During the fueling interval, the Third Fleet was to be joined for the first time by Task Force 37 of the British Pacific Fleet. Halsey was worried about making the combined operation work. He knew that Admiral King had been profoundly opposed to accepting a British force in the Pacific to

share in Japan's final defeat, and had agreed only at President Roosevelt's insistence.

The British, under the command of Vice Admiral Sir Bernard Rawlings, had recently played a modest role in the Pacific. They had been stationed about 100 miles east of Formosa, to keep Japanese Kamikaze air forces in the nearby Sakishima Islands from threatening the Okinawa invasion. On this screening mission, His Majesty's ships had operated independently of the American fleet.

Now the Royal Navy was to take a hand in the naval pummelling of Japan. At 6:45 a.m. on July 16, the British ships hove in sight: the battleship *King George V* flying Rawlings' flag; three carriers, the *Formidable*, the *Victorious* and the *Implacable,* carrying 255 aircraft; six light cruisers and 18 destroyers. A fourth carrier, the *Indefatigable,* lagged behind with mechanical problems.

Admiral Rawlings and his air commander, Vice Admiral Sir Philip L. Vian, came alongside the *Missouri* in destroyers and boarded the American flagship.

"I knew both these gentlemen by their splendid reputations," Halsey recalled in his memoirs, "but we had never met, and I am afraid that my appearance did little to recommend me. They were wearing smart blues; I was wearing a Marine woolen jacket, a blue flannel shirt, green flying trousers, and a long-billed cap like a sword fisherman's."

Halsey's apprehension stemmed in part from his orders. "When I was informed at Pearl Harbor that the British Pacific Fleet would report to me," he wrote, "I naturally assumed that I would have full operational control, but when I reread the plan at Leyte, I discovered that tactical control had been reserved"—meaning that the British were to retain a measure of independence.

The British were almost as nervous as Halsey about the new partnership. Their experiences with the Americans so far had been mixed. From the start—first at the Quebec Conference in 1943, and then while working out the details in Washington—the Americans had seemed stiffly unaccommodating, an attitude that probably reflected Admiral King's open dislike of having the British in the Pacific.

Once on the scene, however, the British were finding interfleet relations more cordial than they had expected. Admiral Sir Bruce Fraser, Nimitz' opposite number in Sydney, found this out when he tried to borrow three Avenger torpedo planes for one of his carriers. He filed a formal request through Nimitz to Washington, and was turned down. But a little later, on a visit to the American supply base at Manus, an island north of New Guinea, Fraser called on the admiral in charge and repeated his request for the three planes. "Well, actually we don't issue them in less than six at a time," the American replied. "And if you've got a bottle of whiskey you can have a dozen."

On the *Missouri* that July 16, the question before the admirals was more delicate, and complicated by shadings of protocol and seniority. How was the operation to be run and who was going to run it? Halsey was in no mood to tolerate a divided command; on the other hand, he could not afford to snub the British openly. He offered three alternatives. In the first, the British fleet, nominally commanded by Rawlings and receiving Halsey's orders as "suggestions," would operate on the American flank. Or the British could operate semi-independently some 60 or 70 miles distant. If Rawlings elected that course, Halsey wanted his decision in writing so that the record would show the separation of fleets as a British choice, not an American stiff arm. As a third option, Halsey offered the British complete independence, restricted only in their choice of objectives—the "soft" or secondary targets that Halsey's staff would identify for them; he wanted, at all costs, the significant strategic targets for the American fleet. To the relief of those present, Rawlings chose the first alternative. It preserved the appearance of his independent tactical command, while giving Halsey the reality of control over the combined force.

The Anglo-American fleet went to work the next day, hitting airfields and shipping around Tokyo. But it was a bad day for fliers—spoiled by rain, fog and a low and blinding overcast. Only two strikes got off the carriers before air operations were halted. That night, with the weather still bad, a force of six battleships, including—at Halsey's suggestion—the *King George V,* steamed up to the coast 80 miles northeast of Tokyo. Their target was the city of Hitachi, an important industrial center that produced copper, steel, electrical appliances and arms.

The battleships had their own air contingent in the night-fighter carrier *Bon Homme Richard.* Despite the soupy weather, the carrier succeeded in launching 11 planes to spot targets for the big ships. But the overcast was so low

A smiling Admiral William F. Halsey (right) welcomes Vice Admiral Sir Bernard Rawlings (left), commander of the Royal Navy's Task Force 37, aboard the U.S.S. Missouri in August of 1945 to discuss joint fleet operations against Japan. Both men had been apprehensive about the relationship between British and American forces, but they were soon working together on a first-name basis.

and thick that the observers were useless. Two of the planes crashed; the rest fumbled their way home through the fog. In classic fashion, the battleships formed a line and fired salvo after salvo of heavy shells into Hitachi. The results of the bombardment were later assessed in combination with other raids on the city: Hitachi's industrial production was reduced almost to zero, and rail service, electrical and water supplies were interrupted.

Halsey's prime target for July 18 was Yokosuka's Navy yard south of Tokyo—particularly the battleship *Nagato* berthed there. Earlier in the month, Admiral Nimitz had ordered that "the remaining heavy enemy ships must be eliminated. This is the responsibility of the Pacific fleet."

Ever since Pearl Harbor, the U.S. Navy had looked upon the Japanese Navy as its sole concern; even now with nearly all Japanese warships already on the bottom, the Americans were in no mood to invite a third party to share their preoccupation. While the U.S. carrier air groups concentrated on the Navy yard and the *Nagato*, Halsey suggested that the British put in another useful day working over the airfields and other installations on the Tokyo plain.

The *Nagato* was a tough nut to crack. The Japanese had her camouflaged, encircled with antiaircraft batteries and moored so that she was protected from aerial torpedoes by a pier on one side, and on the other by a channel too narrow for a plane to make a torpedo run. Submarines were excluded by nets and constant patrols. The Avengers arrived first with fragmentation bombs to silence the ship's antiaircraft guns; they were followed by F6F Hellcats carrying 1,000-pound armor-piercing bombs. The *Nagato* survived, much damaged topside but still afloat. Other ships in the Navy yard were less fortunate: One destroyer was blown apart, the stern was blown off another, a submarine was sunk and other small vessels were sunk or damaged. The Americans lost 12 planes and 22 men. The British mission lost two planes, but both pilots were rescued at sea.

Most of the remaining Japanese fleet, largely immobilized for want of fuel, was concentrated in the waters around Kobe and Kure on the Inland Sea. Like the *Nagato*, most of the ships were moored alongside docks or close to shore in coves, where it was difficult to get at them with torpedoes. On July 24 Halsey set out to destroy them, again excluding the British with a suggestion that they bomb the airfields in

Shikoku and attack shipping in the Inland Sea and at Osaka.

The weather was good and the carriers of Vice Admiral John S. McCain launched 1,747 sorties. Three ships on the target list were veterans of other slugging matches in the South Pacific. They were the battleship *Haruna* and the so-called hermaphrodites, or combined battleship-carriers, the *Hyuga* and the *Ise*. The *Hyuga* was the first to succumb, as a dozen bomb hits and twice as many near misses opened her seams and left her sinking; the crew drove their ship aground. Five direct hits sent the *Ise* down by the bow. The *Haruna*, a survivor of the Battle of the Philippine Sea in June 1944 and the Battle for Leyte Gulf the following October, took only one hit and survived once more. Of three carriers, the *Katsuragi*, the *Ryuho* and the new *Amagi*, that came under attack, only the *Amagi* was hit, and she stayed afloat. The heavy cruisers *Tone* and *Aoba* were hit several times— the *Tone* driven onto the beach and the *Aoba* settling to the bottom. The light cruiser *Oyodo* was hit and disabled.

Bad weather enforced a pause in what had become a "turkey shoot." But on July 28 the carrier planes returned to put an end to the matter. By day's end the *Haruna* had at last been finished, beached and on fire with a gaping hole in her stern. The carrier *Amagi* had rolled over and lay on her side in the mud. The *Katsuragi's* flight deck was shredded and buckled but she still floated. The *Ryuho* was sunk. Three old cruisers, the *Iwate*, the *Izumo* and the *Settsu*, were on the bottom. Japan no longer had a fleet.

Privately, the British resented their pointed exclusion from the main event. One Englishman called it a "churlish way to treat an ally who had actually declared war on Japan only a few hours after the attack on Pearl Harbor." Publicly, they took the snubs with grace and went to work hacking at the secondary targets. But they happily accepted a shot at the Japanese warships. The day's second "ramrod"—the British code word for a bombing strike—turned up an enemy escort carrier and two frigates steaming near the coast of Shikoku. All four British carriers dispatched ramrods to the scene and left the Japanese ships battered and sinking.

Japanese resistance had evaporated, in large part because of the relentless work of the B-29s. Though LeMay's contention that they could have won the War by themselves remains in dispute, his view never wavered. When Arnold flew to Guam in June for what would be his last visit of the War, LeMay impressed the AAF commander with his arguments for the capacity of the B-29 to bring about victory.

At Arnold's urging, LeMay flew to Washington to try to convince the Joint Chiefs that Japan could be burned into surrender. The Chiefs did not seem very interested. Operations *Olympic* and *Coronet* remained firmly on the agenda. LeMay flew back to the Pacific grimly bent on making his point with deeds.

Over the summer, the XXI Bomber Command's strength steadily increased. The assembling of the 315th Wing at the end of June brought the number of battle-ready B-29s in the Marianas to 1,000. The 315th was a specialized outfit, highly trained and equipped with an improved radar called the Eagle that boasted 10 times the effectiveness of previous models. It was intended to provide bombardiers with a nearly perfect bombing picture at high altitude, day or night, in any weather.

With such reinforcements at hand, and with the approval of General Tooey Spaatz, who would shortly take command of all Army Air Forces in the Pacific, LeMay gave the 315th Wing the task of demolishing Japan's remaining oil refining and storage capacity. The newcomers did a thorough job of it. In 15 strikes around Japan's coastal perimeter, where the oil centers were located, they smashed six million barrels of storage capacity and reduced the country's potential refining capacity from 90,000 barrels per day to about 17,000. As it developed, knocking out refining capacity was superfluous. Japan's oil imports had already been reduced to a trickle. Most of the storage tanks were empty, and the refineries were operating at about 4 per cent of their capacity.

The June reinforcements had also brought to the Marianas an outfit named the 509th Composite Group. The 509th and its 15 B-29s were assigned to a compound at North Field on Tinian that was somewhat isolated from other areas, and from the first day their presence was a mystery. The aircrews did not talk about what they were doing or were expected to do; in fact, few of them except their commander, Colonel Paul W. Tibbets Jr., knew exactly why they were there.

Clearly, the men of the 509th enjoyed a protected status. They flew relatively tame trainer missions to Truk and to low-priority targets in Japan, upon which they dropped orange bombs of an odd, bulbous shape, called "pumpkins." Among the rest of the B-29 crews, envy and resentment of such easy duty became mixed with a rising curiosity.

Even as the XXI Bomber Command's strength swelled, the list of worthwhile objectives shrank drastically. Kyoto, Japan's fourth-largest city and its capital until the 19th Century, was still untouched, but it had been ruled off limits by Secretary of War Henry Stimson because it was the country's religious and cultural center.

LeMay ordered his planning staff to draw up a list of minor objectives. Precedence went to towns devoted to any sort of known or suspected war production. But an absence of military-industrial activity was not always enough to ensure a community's safety. "We advocated destruction of Japan's military goods—or just goods," said the chief target planner, Brigadier General John Samford. "We believed, and meant to prove, that by destroying Japan's materials—burning down her cities—and then by tremendously heavy attacks against transport we could paralyze the country and make defense against invasion impossible. Another six months would have done it."

The new program began on June 17 when a B-29 wing was assigned to bomb each of four cities—Omuta, Hamamatsu, Yokkaichi and Kagoshima. Thereafter, the Superfortress fleets took off on an average of twice a week, burning three or four cities and towns on each expedition. Opposition generally proved so light that LeMay began warning the potential victims by dropping leaflets in advance, both to save lives and to frighten people away from their jobs. In the end, the campaign devastated some 60 urban centers; the smallest was Tsuruga, with a population of only 31,000. Damage to these secondary targets averaged nearly 50 per cent, although at least one of them, Toyama, with a population of 128,000, suffered almost total destruction. Altogether, the missions against small cities added another 65 square miles to the ruins of urban Japan.

Surveying the devastation, LeMay advised General Arnold that by October he would have nothing left either to bomb or to burn—outside of four cities, in addition to Kyoto, that remained virtually unscarred. But those four—Hiroshima, Nagasaki, Niigata and Kokura—were barred to routine B-29 missions. By August, LeMay—and the men of the 509th Composite Group—knew why.

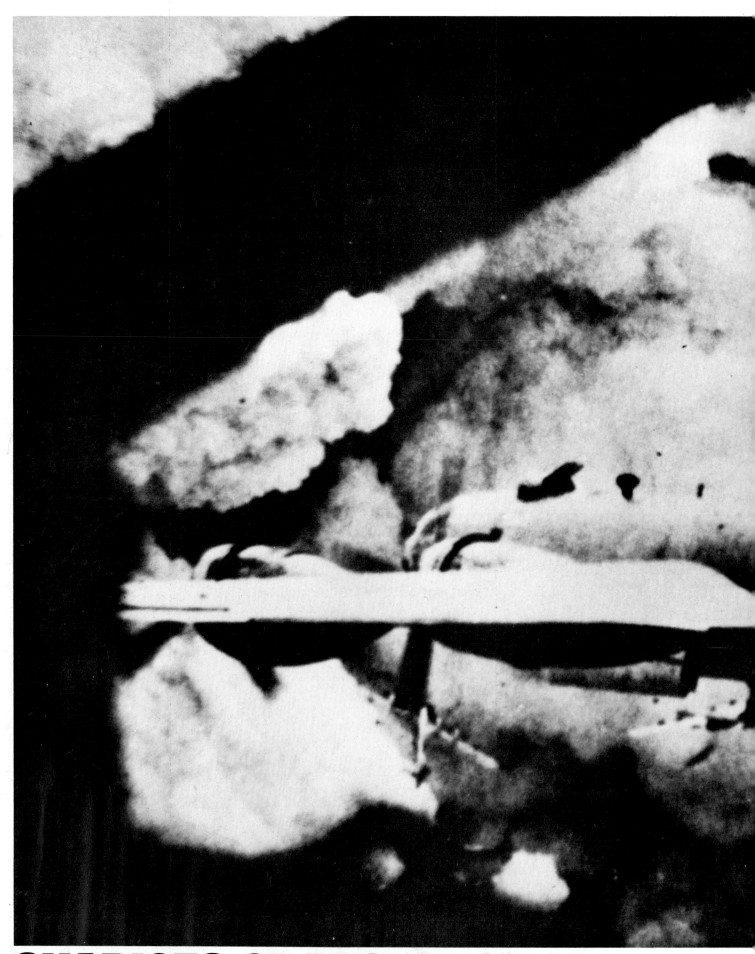

CHARIOTS OF DESTRUCTION

Framed in a cockpit window, a formation of B-29s flies into smoke billowing up from the target; one bomber, hit by flak (lower left), begins a fatal spin to earth.

THE "TERRIBLE VIRTUES" OF STRATEGIC BOMBING

When they met in China in 1944, General LeMay and General Joseph W. "Vinegar Joe" Stilwell, the commander of U.S. forces in the China-Burma-India Theater, stayed up all night arguing about the value of strategic bombing. Nothing LeMay said would convince the old infantryman that strategic bombers could make much difference in the course of the War. But soon after the War ended, Stilwell made a special trip to Guam to acknowledge his error. "You have done what you set out to do," he told LeMay. "I recognize now the terrible military virtues of strategic bombardment."

Without doubt, the B-29 campaign against Japan marked a turning point in the conduct of warfare. Because of the wholesale devastation the big bombers inflicted from long range, the importance of air power would never again be challenged. Indeed, the successful bombing of Japan—as well as Germany—contributed in 1947 to the creation of the U.S. Air Force, coequal with the Army and the Navy.

In LeMay, a fervent believer in air power, General Arnold had found a near-perfect instrument for bringing forth an independent air force. LeMay had commanded a heavy-bomber group in the campaign against Germany. He also relied on military intuition, which told him the decisive way to destroy Japan's ability to fight was a rain of fire. After the first fire bombings, Brigadier General Haywood S. Hansell Jr., who had preceded him as commander of the Marianas-based B-29s, conceded that, given the circumstances, LeMay's methods were infinitely more effective than standard high-explosive bombing. "The tactical method selected by LeMay," said Hansell, "was a superb decision."

That decision caused immense loss of life and suffering among Japan's civilian population. But LeMay admitted no regret. He later wrote, "I think it's more immoral to use less force than it is to use more." To underscore the point, he cited the story of "a stupid man who was not basically cruel—just well-meaning." The man cut off his dog's tail an inch at a time "so that it wouldn't hurt so much."

Flanked by maps of Japan and mainland Asia, an American staff officer briefs XXI Bomber Command planners in a headquarters situation room on Guam.

In the XXI Bomber Command operations room on Guam, mission controllers monitor a strike on a floor map of Japan and on a status board at rear.

Preparing for a strike on the 13th of April, 1945, that would destroy almost 11 square miles of Tokyo, an armorer checks the .50-caliber machine guns in the upper turret of a Superfortress; on the ground, ordnance men assemble clusters of incendiary bombs.

Planes from the 58th Bombardment Wing, which had flown under LeMay's command in China and India, file along a taxiway in June 1945 at their new base on West Field, Tinian.

TURNING SKEPTICS INTO BELIEVERS

In a moment of envy, a senior Air Forces officer once remarked, "LeMay is an operator; the rest of us are just planners." LeMay did have an operator's knack for getting things done—and in the most direct way. In Europe, in 1942, he ordered his pilots to fly straight into enemy flak rather than zigzag; evasive action, he argued, simply took extra time, increasing exposure to antiaircraft fire while making it harder for his bombardiers to hit the target.

LeMay admitted that some of his ideas struck colleagues as bizarre. He nevertheless drove them to put his schemes to the test; when they worked, as usually happened, the skeptics became believers.

Beyond persuading his B-29 aircrews to attack at low altitude and at night, LeMay's conduct of the initial fire-bombing missions over Japan in March 1945 demonstrated that he knew how to run an efficient command. The number of B-29s that bombed their primary targets rose dramatically from 36 to 91 per cent; partly this was due to the low altitude and the carpet-bombing nature of the attacks, but it was also a tribute to LeMay's attention to navigation and radar target identification. In the meantime, maintenance crews kept an average of 83 per cent of the B-29s operational, compared to an earlier level of 59 per cent.

Among both the air and ground crews, success begat confidence—and more success. The XXI was at last living up to Arnold's expectations and he cabled: CONGRATULATIONS, YOUR CREWS HAVE GOT THE GUTS FOR ANYTHING.

A BELLY FULL OF INCENDIARIES

The ordnance loaded aboard a B-29 for an incendiary raid contained one of three combustibles: The bombers in the leading formations generally carried napalm, or jellied-gasoline bombs, which ignited small fires. A second wave of bombers usually dropped clusters of oil containers, which sprayed their contents over the napalm fires in showers, and the mixture ran through the streets in fiery streams. Magnesium thermite bombs, mixed with the oil and napalm, set fires of fierce intensity.

The load varied with the mission, depending on the need for extra fuel or defensive ammunition. Generally, one B-29, fully loaded with six tons of incendiaries, could destroy up to 16 acres of the target.

Incendiary bombs hang in the bomb bay of a B-29. Racked in clusters of six, the cylinders were set to detonate 100 feet above the target, each releasing dozens of containers of napalm that burst into flame on contact.

Incendiary bombs shower down on the port of Osaka during a raid by 509 Superfortresses on June 1, 1945; the dock area at upper left is already smothered in smoke from fires set by an earlier wave of bombers.

Before a raid on June 5, photoreconnaissance shows the port of Kobe still worth fire bombing. Previous attacks had destroyed only one fourth of the c

After the June 5 raid, a strike photograph shows another four square miles, or 28 per cent, destroyed (light areas). On this basis, Kobe was written off as a targ

Preparing priority lists for staff planners, an operations corporal on Guam pores over some evaluations of Japanese targets still worthy of air attack.

A ROSTER OF TARGETS OBLITERATED

The toll extracted by the B-29s was mind-numbing. By August 14, a total of 602 major Japanese war industries and military installations had been destroyed or severely damaged; inland shipping had been virtually eliminated; and nearly half of the aggregate area of 66 cities—178 square miles—had been razed.

Of the sectors within those cities that had been designated as targets, the Superfortresses leveled an astonishing 92 per cent. And in one city, the chemical and textile manufacturing center of Toyama *(pages 200-201),* the devastation was total.

The aerial photographs on these and the following pages are representative entries in the B-29s' ledger of destruction. In each instance, the percentage given indicates the portion of the targeted area within each city or industrial complex destroyed by the War's end.

Sakai: 57 per cent destroyed.

Tokyo: 86 per cent destroyed.

Nagoya: 77 per cent destroyed.

Oita: 40 per cent destroyed.

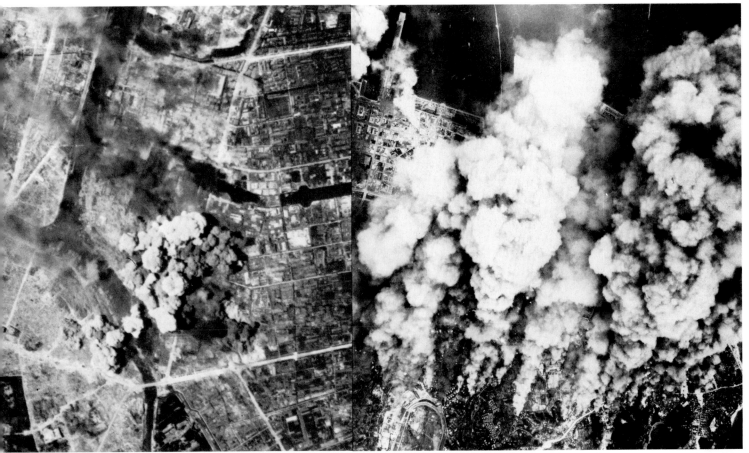

Atsuta aircraft plant: 65 per cent destroyed.

Yokohama naval installation: 100 per cent destroyed.

Otaki oil refinery: 45 per cent destroyed.

Kochi: 51 per cent destroyed.

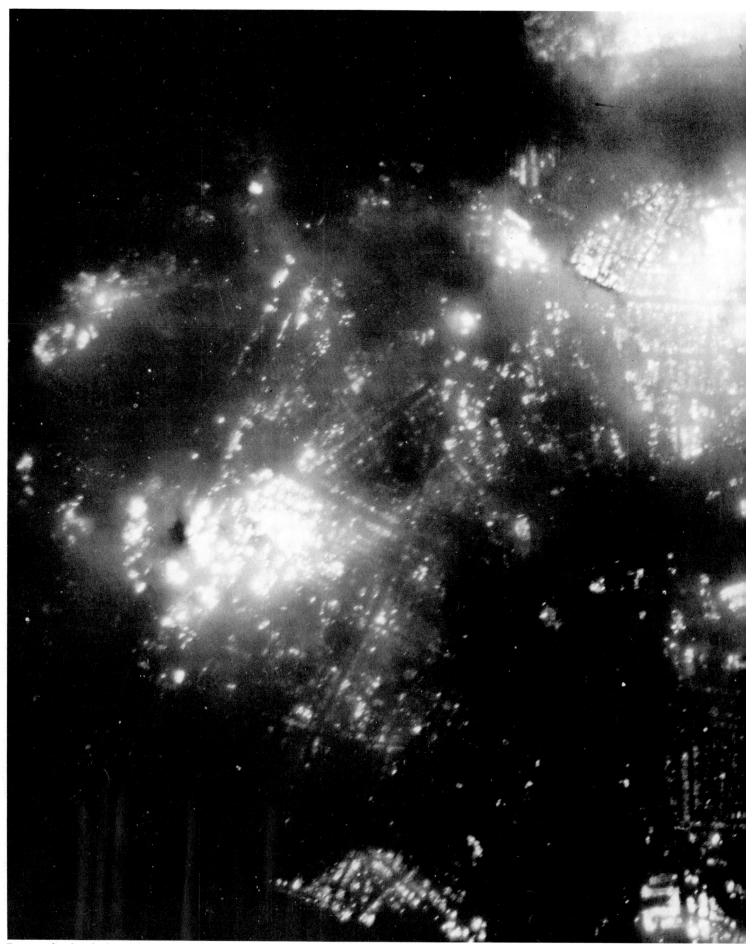

Toyama, fire-bombed once by 173 Superfortresses on the night of August 1, was assessed as 99.5 per cent destroyed. Fires in the city burned so brightly, eve

while the raid was in progress, that they set off cameras aboard the B-29s—flying more than 12,000 feet above—that ordinarily were triggered by flash units.

BIBLIOGRAPHY

Anderton, David A., *B-29 Superfortress at War*. Charles Scribner's Sons, 1978.

Army Air Forces Statistical Digest, World War II. Office of Statistical Control, U.S. Army Air Forces, 1945.

B-29: Pilots' and Flight Engineers' Training Manual for the Superfortress. AAF Manual 51-126-6, U.S. Army Air Forces, March 1, 1946.

Benedict, Ruth, *The Chrysanthemum and the Sword*. Houghton Mifflin, 1946.

Berger, Carl, *B-29: The Superfortress*. Ballantine, 1974.

Birdsall, Steve, *Saga of the Superfortress: The Dramatic Story of the B-29 and the Twentieth Air Force*. Doubleday, 1980.

Boyle, James F., "How the Superfortress Paced the Attack on Japan." *Air Force Magazine*, December 1964.

Bozung, Jack, ed., *The 20th over Japan*. AAF Publications Company, 1947.

Bridgman, Leonard, ed., *Jane's All the World's Aircraft, 1945-1946*. London: David and Charles Ltd., 1970.

Bueschel, Richard M., *Kawasaki Ki-61/Ki-100 Hien in Japanese Army Air Force Service*. Arco-Aircam Aviation Series, Arco, 1971.

Building the Navy's Bases in World War II: History of the Bureau of Yards and Docks and the Civil Engineer Corps 1940-1946, Vol. 2. U.S. Government Printing Office, 1946.

Burkett, Prentiss, *The Unofficial History of the 499th Bomb Group (VH)*. Historical Aviation Album, 1981.

Caidin, Martin:
    A Torch to the Enemy: The Fire Raid on Tokyo. Ballantine, 1960.
    Zero Fighter. Ballantine, 1969.

Calvocoressi, Peter, and Guy Wint, *Total War: Causes and Courses of the Second World War*. Penguin Books, 1972.

Central Pacific Area-Intelligence Summary. Headquarters, Seventh Air Force, June 14, 1944.

Chief Information Officer, "Weekly Intelligence Summary." Microfilm Serial No. 74. Air Command, Southeast Asia, April 15, 1945.

Clark, J. J., with Clark G. Reynolds, *Carrier Admiral*. David McKay, 1967.

Collison, Thomas, *The Superfortress Is Born: The Story of the Boeing B-29*. Duell, Sloan & Pearce, 1945.

Considine, Bob, *It's All News to Me: A Reporter's Deposition*. Meredith, 1967.

Coox, Alvin D., *The B-29 Campaign against Japan: The Japanese Dimension*. Privately printed, 1982.

Craven, Wesley Frank, and James Lea Cate, eds.,*The Army Air Forces in World War II*, Vol. 5, *The Pacific: Matterhorn to Nagasaki, June 1944 to August 1945*. University of Chicago Press, 1953.

Erection and Maintenance Instructions, B-29 and B-29A Aircraft, USAF Series. U.S. Air Force, Bureau of Aeronautics, 1951.

Eustis, Lawrence B., ed., *40th Bombardment Group*. Newsfoto Publishing Co., no date.

Francillon, René J., *Japanese Aircraft of the Pacific War*. London: Putnam & Company, 1970.

Freeman, Roger, *The U.S. Strategic Bomber*. London: Macdonald and Jane's, 1975.

Goralski, Robert, *World War II Almanac, 1931-1945: A Political and Military Record*. G. P. Putnam's Sons, 1981.

Green, William, *Famous Bombers of the Second World War*, Vol. 1. Doubleday, 1969.

Green, William, and Gordon Swanborough, *Japanese Army Fighters: Part One*. Arco, 1977.

Guillain, Robert, *I Saw Tokyo Burning: An Eyewitness Narrative from Pearl Harbor to Hiroshima*. Transl. by William Byron. Doubleday, 1981.

Gurney, Gene, *Journey of the Giants*. Coward-McCann, 1961.

Halsey, William F., and Joseph Bryan III, *Admiral Halsey's Story*. Da Capo Press, 1976.

Hansell, Haywood S., Jr., to H. H. Arnold, personal correspondence. November 1944 to January 1945. Unpublished.
    Strategic Air War against Japan. Airpower Research Institute, Air War College, Maxwell Air Force Base, 1980.

Haugland, Vern, *The AAF against Japan*. Harper & Brothers, 1948.

Heiferman, Ron, *Flying Tigers: Chennault in China*. London: Pan/Ballantine, 1972.

Hess, William, *P-51: Bomber Escort*. Ballantine, 1971.

Howard, Clive, and Joe Whitley, *One Damned Island after Another*. University of North Carolina Press, 1946.

Impact: The Army Air Forces' Confidential Picture History of World War II, Books 4-8, 1944 to 1945. James Parton and Company, 1980.

Inoguchi, Rikihei, and Tadashi Nakajima, with Roger Pineau, *The Divine Wind: Japan's Kamikaze Force in World War II*. U.S. Naval Institute, 1958.

The Japanese Air Forces in World War II: The Organization of the Japanese Army & Naval Air Forces, 1945. Hippocrene Books, 1979.

Jarrell, Howard R., "The Man Who Gave Ivan the Bird." *Air Force Magazine*, February 1957.

Johnson, Ellis A., and David A. Katcher, *Mines against Japan*. Naval Ordnance Laboratory, no date.

Jones, Lloyd S., *U.S. Bombers: B-1—B-70*. Aero Publishers, 1962.

Karig, Walter, Russell L. Harris and Frank A. Manson, *Battle Report: Victory in the Pacific*. Rinehart, 1949.

Kase, Toshikazu, *Journey to the Missouri*. Archon Books, 1969.

Kato, Masuo, *The Lost War: A Japanese Reporter's Inside Story*. Alfred A. Knopf, 1946.

Lambert, John, "Chief of the Sunsetters." *Aerospace Historian*, September 1981.

LeMay, General Curtis E., with MacKinlay Kantor, *Mission with LeMay: My Story*. Doubleday, 1965.

Liddell Hart, B. H., *History of the Second World War*. G. P. Putnam's Sons, 1971.

Lindley, John M., *Carrier Victory: The Air War in the Pacific*. Talisman-Parrish Books, 1978.

MacIsaac, David, *Strategic Bombing in World War II: The Story of the U.S. Strategic Bombing Survey*. Garland, 1976.

McKelway, Claude, "A Reporter with the B-29s." *The New Yorker*, June 9, 16 and 23, 1945.

Millot, Bernard, *Divine Thunder: The Life and Death of the Kamikazes*. McCall Publishing Company, 1970.

Mission Accomplished: Interrogations of Japanese Industrial, Military and Civil Leaders of World War II. U.S. Government Printing Office, 1946.

Morison, Samuel Eliot, *Victory in the Pacific, 1945*. Little, Brown, 1975.

Morrison, Wilbur H., *Point of No Return: The Story of the Twentieth Air Force*. Times Books/Quadrangle, 1979.

Nagatsuka, Ryuji, *I Was a Kamikaze*. Macmillan, 1972.

"Oakland Flier Sank Destroyer." *Oakland Tribune*, September 16, 1945.

Okumiya, Masatake, and Jiro Horikoshi, with Martin Caidin, *Zero!* E. P. Dutton, 1956.

Overy, R. J., *The Air War, 1939-1945*. Stein and Day, 1980.

Pimlott, John, *B-29 Superfortress*. London: Bison Books, 1980.

Potter, E. B., *Nimitz*. Naval Institute Press, 1976.

"Radar: Another of the War's Great Secret Weapons Revealed." *Life*, August 20, 1945.

Reynolds, Clark G., *The Fast Carriers: The Forging of an Air Navy*. McGraw-Hill, 1968.

Roscoe, Theodore, *Submarine Operations in World War II*. U.S. Naval Institute, 1949.

Rust, Kenn C., *Twentieth Air Force Story . . . in World War II*. Historical Aviation Album, 1979.

Sakai, Saburo, with Martin Caidin and Fred Saito, *Samurai!* Bantam Books, 1957.

Saunders, Hilary St. George, *Royal Air Force, 1939-1945*, Vol. 3, *The Fight Is Won*. London: Her Majesty's Stationery Office, 1954.

Sherrod, Robert, *On to Westward: War in the Central Pacific*. Duell, Sloan & Pearce, 1945.

Sill, Van Rensselaer, *American Miracle: The Story of War Construction around the World*. Odyssey Press, 1947.

Sunderman, James F., *World War II in the Air: The Pacific*. Van Nostrand, 1963.

Taylor, Theodore, *The Magnificent Mitscher*. W. W. Norton, 1954.

"They Slept under Our Roof." *Quonset Scout*, May 20, 1950.

Toland, John, *The Rising Sun: The Decline and Fall of the Japanese Empire, 1936-1945*. Random House, 1970.

U.S. Army Historical Division, *Japanese Studies in World War II*:
    Monograph 23, *Account of Preparations in the Event of an Invasion of Japan*. No date.
    Monograph 157, *Homeland Air-Defense Operations Record*. No date.
    Monograph 168, *Homeland Antiaircraft Records*. No date.
    Monograph 170, *Antiaircraft Defenses*. No date.

U.S. Strategic Bombing Survey:
    The Effects of Stategic Bombing on Japan's War Economy. Overall Economic Effects Division, December 1946.
    Final Report Covering Air-Raid Protection and Allied Subjects in Japan. Civilian Defense Division, February 1947.
    Interrogations of Japanese Officials, Vol. 2. Naval Analysis Division, 1946.
    The Strategic Air Operation of Very Heavy Bombardment in the War against Japan (Twentieth Air Force). Final Report. Military Analysis Division, Army and Army Air Section, September 1, 1946.

Watanabe, Yohji, *Pictorial History of Air War over Japan*. Tokyo: Japanese Army Air Force/Hara Shobo Co., 1980.

Winton, John, *The Forgotten Fleet: The British Navy in the Pacific—1944-1945*. Coward-McCann, 1969.

Wolk, Herman S., "The B-29, the A-Bomb and the Japanese Surrender." *Air Force Magazine*, February 1975.

"World Battlefronts." *Time*, August 13, 1945.

PICTURE CREDITS

Credits from left to right are separated by semicolons, from top to bottom by dashes.

COVER and page 1: U.S. Air Force. 2, 3: Maps by Leonard Vigliarolo.

FORGING A NEW AIR WEAPON—8-16: The Boeing Co. 17: bottom, The Boeing Co. 18, 19: The Boeing Co.

THE "$3-BILLION GAMBLE"—23: U.S. Air Force. 25: Consolidated Aircraft Corp. 26: The Boeing Co., courtesy David A. Anderton. 28: The Boeing Co., courtesy Alwyn T. Lloyd. 29: *The Seattle Times.* 30-33: Illustrations by John Batchelor, London. 36: The Boeing Co. 38: U.S. Air Force.

A PERILOUS LEAP INTO COMBAT—40-43: Courtesy Neil W. Wemple. 44: Courtesy Harry M. Changnon, 40th Bomb Group Assn.—courtesy Lawrence B. Eustis. 45: Courtesy Lawrence B. Eustis—courtesy Harry M. Changnon, 40th Bomb Group Assn. 46: Courtesy Neil W. Wemple—U.S. Air Force. 47: Courtesy Neil W. Wemple—courtesy Harry M. Changnon, 40th Bomb Group Assn. 48, 49: Courtesy Harry M. Changnon, 40th Bomb Group Assn.; U.S. Air Force—courtesy William A. Rooney. 50, 51: Courtesy Neil W. Wemple (2); courtesy Lawrence B. Eustis. 55: U.S. Air Force. 58: Bernard Hoffman for *Life.* 61: Courtesy Alwyn T. Lloyd. 62, 63: U.S. Air Force. 65: Courtesy Lawrence B. Eustis. 66, 67: National Archives (No. RG208-38880-FN). 69: Francis B. Morgan Collection, courtesy David A. Anderton.

AN ISLAND TRANSFORMED—72-76: J. R. Eyerman for *Life.* 77: U.S. Air Force—J. R. Eyerman for *Life.* 78: U.S. Air Force. 79, 80: J. R. Eyerman for *Life.* 81: J. R. Eyerman for *Life;* U.S. Air Force—National Archives (No. 80-G-309174). 82, 83: J. R. Eyerman for *Life.*

PROFILE OF A MISSION—84, 85: U.S. Air Force. 86: Paul Friend from Astro Photographers. 87: U.S. Air Force. 88, 89: U.S. Air Force except top left, Bernard Hoffman for *Life.* 90: The Boeing Co., courtesy David A. Anderton—Bernard Hoffman for *Life.* 91: The Boeing Co.—courtesy Lawrence B. Eustis. 92, 93: William C. Shrout for *Life* (2); 313th Bomb Wing Assn., courtesy David A. Anderton; U.S. Air Force. 94-97: U.S. Air Force.

A ROOST IN THE MARIANAS—100: National Archives (No. 208-AA-247A-15). 102: U.S. Air Force. 103: National Archives (No. 80G-267975); Anthony Migliaccio, courtesy David A. Anderton. 104-112: U.S. Air Force. 114, 115: National Archives (No. 208-N-39443).

RESCUE AT SEA—116, 117: U.S. Navy. 118, 119: U.S. Air Force. 120, 121: National Archives (Nos. 80G-293968, 80G-49753) except top left, U.S. Air Force. 122-125: National Archives (Nos. 80G-293968, 80G-490064, 80G-49450, 80G-334769).

"WE ARE EAGLES WITHOUT WINGS"—128, 129: National Archives (No. 100-490)—Wolff Archives. 130: *Mainichi Shimbun,* Tokyo. 132, 133: Henry Beville, courtesy Smithsonian Institution. 136: *Asahi Graph,* Tokyo. 138, 139: Shunkichi Kikuchi, Tokyo. 140, 142: National Archives (Nos. 243-GA-4I-5, 243-GA-5A-1, 32572-FMC).

JAPAN'S AERIAL WARRIORS—144, 145: Courtesy Chieko Kobayashi, Tokyo. 146: Masaji Kobayashi, courtesy Aireview, Tokyo. 147: Shunkichi Kikuchi, Tokyo. 148, 149: Shunkichi Kikuchi, Tokyo; U.S. Air Force; Shunkichi Kikuchi, Tokyo. 150, 151: Nobuji Negishi, courtesy Aireview, Tokyo; Jiro Furukawa, courtesy Aireview, Tokyo—courtesy Shelley Mydans Collection. 152, 153: Courtesy Chieko Kobayashi, Tokyo (2)—Shunkichi Kikuchi, Tokyo. 154, 155: *Asahi Shimbun,* courtesy Aireview, Tokyo.

THE THUNDER OF MUSTANGS—156-159: U.S. Air Force. 160: Robert S. Scamara. 161: George Silk for *Life.* 162, 163: Leon P. Sher except top left, U.S. Air Force. 164, 165: U.S. Air Force.

A SCOURGE OF FIRE—169: Wide World. 170, 171: U.S. Air Force. 172: U.S. Marine Corps, courtesy Steve Birdsall; Edward P. Donnelly Jr.; Eric T. Weber Collection. 173: Edward P. Donnelly Jr. 175: National Archives (No. 80G-490176). 177: U.S. Air Force—map by Leonard Vigliarolo. 179: U.S. Air Force. 180: Courtesy Prentiss Burkett. 182, 184: National Archives (Nos. 80G-339336, 80G-337551).

CHARIOTS OF DESTRUCTION—188, 189: Courtesy Prentiss Burkett. 190, 191: J. R. Eyerman for *Life.* 192, 193: U.S. Air Force; J. R. Eyerman for *Life.* 194, 195: U.S. Air Force. 196, 197: U.S. Air Force (2); J. R. Eyerman for *Life.* 198-201: U.S. Air Force.

ACKNOWLEDGMENTS

For help given in the preparation of this book, the editors wish to express their gratitude to David A. Anderton, Ridgewood, New Jersey; Susan F. Berman, Reference Librarian, North Kingston Free Library, North Kingston, Rhode Island; Peter Bowers, Editor, *Airline Magazine,* and Marilyn Phipps, Archivist, Boeing Company, Seattle, Washington; Walter Boyne, Assistant Director, Don Lopez, Chairman, Aeronautics Department, and Dana Bell, Museum Specialist, National Air and Space Museum, Smithsonian Institution, Washington, D.C.; Barbara Burger, James Delaney and James H. Trimble, National Archives, Washington, D.C.; Prentiss Burkett, Phoenix, Arizona; Martin Caidin, Gainesville, Florida; Paul Coggan, Norfolk, England; Ferd J. Curtis, San Bernardino, California; Colonel Edward W. Cutler, USAF (Ret.), Pebble Beach, California; Edward P. Donnelly Jr., Edmonds, Washington; Lawrence B. Eustis, 40th Bomb Group, New Orleans, Louisiana; Harry R. Fletcher, Historian, and First Lieutenant John L. Poole, Research Division, Albert F. Simpson Historical Research Center, Maxwell Air Force Base, Alabama; Manly H. Fouts Jr., Orlando, Florida; Frances Glennon, Washington, D.C.; Captain Rita Gomez and Master Sergeant Alden R. Hargett, U.S. Air Force History Center, Bolling Air Force Base, Washington, D.C.; Robert Hall, Wilmette, Illinois; Robert Hilton, Irving, Texas; Japan Information Center, New York; Victor Kanefsky, New York; Richard M. Keenan, Twentieth Air Force Association, Washington, D.C.; Dr. Brooks Kleber, Deputy Chief Historian, U.S. Army Center of Military History, Washington, D.C.; John W. Lambert, Mendota Heights, Minnesota; Claude Logan Jr., Tampa, Florida; Roy McCarter, Chief, Aviation Weather Branch, Washington, D.C.; Glenn Mc-Clure, Chairman, 73rd Bomb Wing Association, Universal City, Texas; Jayne Mac-Lean, Librarian, National Agricultural Library, Beltsville, Maryland; Colonel Ira V. Matthews, USAF (Ret.), 40th Bomb Group Association, Mobile, Alabama; Anthony Migliaccio, Groton, Connecticut; Colonel Francis B. Morgan, USAF (Ret.), Lehigh Acres, Florida; Wilbur H. Morrison, Fallbrook, California; Mike Pavone, Seattle, Washington; Richard Renz, South Bend, Indiana; Mark Sawtelle, Alexandria, Virginia; Robert S. Scamara, Atascadero, California; Leon P. Sher, Citrus Heights, California; Lieut. Colonel Eric M. Solander, Lieutenant George Jamison and Janice King, U.S. Air Force Office of Public Affairs, Magazines and Books, Arlington, Virginia; Jean Sonnhalter, Public Relations Department, Firestone Co., Akron, Ohio; William Summerville, General Curator, Staten Island Zoo, New York; Dr. Nathaniel B. Thayer, School of Advanced International Studies, Johns Hopkins University, Washington, D.C.; Dr. Vincent A. Transano, Senior Historian, U.S. Naval Facilities Engineering Command, Naval Construction Battalion Center, Port Hueneme, California; Mike Walker, Archivist, U.S. Naval History Center, Operational Archives Branch, Washington, D.C.; Denis Warner, Victoria, Australia; Colonel Neil W. Wemple, USAF (Ret.), Tucson, Arizona; Ann White, Historical Services, Pan American Airlines, New York; Ron Witt, Las Vegas, Nevada; Charles G. Worman, Chief of Research, and Ruth Hurt, Curator, Research Division, U.S. Air Force Museum, Wright-Patterson Air Force Base, Ohio.

The index for this book was prepared by Nicholas J. Anthony.

INDEX

Numerals in italics indicate an illustration of the subject mentioned.